On the
Divine
Things
and Their
Revelation

McGill-Queen's Philosophy of Religion Series
Series editors: Garth Green and George Di Giovanni

The McGill-Queen's Philosophy of Religion Series is dedicated to studies at the interface of philosophy and religion, primarily but not exclusively in the context of the Western traditions of philosophy and theology – whether the studies are historical or systematic in character, whether their motivating interests originate on the side of philosophy or of religion, and whatever their philosophical idioms or religious commitments. The goal is to clarify the nature of a philosophy of religion, and at the same time to promote it as a discipline by illustrating its relevance to philosophy, religious studies, and theology. These are the fields of study from which the series draws its main audience, among professionals as well as students. The series publishes in English and also invites translations of primary texts or important secondary sources. These publications are usually single-authored, without excluding the possibility of significant edited volumes.

1 Fichte in Berlin
The 1804 Wissenschaftslehre
Matthew Nini

2 On the Divine Things and Their Revelation
Friedrich Heinrich Jacobi
Translated and with an introduction by Paolo Livieri

On the Divine Things and Their Revelation

FRIEDRICH HEINRICH JACOBI

Translated and with an introduction by
Paolo Livieri

McGill-Queen's University Press
Montreal & Kingston • London • Chicago

© McGill-Queen's University Press 2024

ISBN 978-0-2280-2277-0 (cloth)
ISBN 978-0-2280-2278-7 (paper)
ISBN 978-0-2280-2316-6 (ePDF)
ISBN 978-0-2280-2317-3 (ePUB)

Legal deposit fourth quarter 2024
Bibliothèque nationale du Québec

Printed in Canada on acid-free paper that is 100% ancient forest free
(100% post-consumer recycled), processed chlorine free

McGill-Queen's University Press in Montreal is on land which long served
as a site of meeting and exchange amongst Indigenous Peoples, including
the Haudenosaunee and Anishinabeg nations. In Kingston it is situated on
the territory of the Haudenosaunee and Anishinaabek. We acknowledge
and thank the diverse Indigenous Peoples whose footsteps have marked
these territories on which peoples of the world now gather.

Library and Archives Canada Cataloguing in Publication

Title: On the divine things and their revelation / Friedrich Heinrich Jacobi ;
   translation and introductory study by Paolo Livieri.
Other titles: Von den Göttlichen Dingen und ihrer Offenbarung. English
Names: Jacobi, Friedrich Heinrich, 1743-1819, author. | Livieri, Paolo, trans-
   lator, writer of introduction.
Description: Series statement: McGill-Queen's philosophy of religion series ;
   2 | Includes bibliographical references and index.
Identifiers: Canadiana (print) 20240391837 | Canadiana (ebook) 2024039190X
   | ISBN 9780228022770 (cloth) | ISBN 9780228022787 (paper) | ISBN
   9780228023173 (ePUB) | ISBN 9780228023166 (ePDF)
Subjects: LCSH: God—Proof, Ontological.
Classification: LCC B3056.V662 E5 2024 | DDC 193—dc23

This book was designed and typeset by studio oneonone in Minion 11/14.
Copyediting by Kathryn Simpson.

Contents

Acknowledgments vii

A Study of F.H. Jacobi's *On the Divine Things and Their Revelation* 3
Note to the Translation 95

On the Divine Things And Their Revelation 99
    Foreword to the Present New Edition 101
    Necessary Foreword 104
    On Lichtenberg's Prophecy 107
    On the Divine Things and Their Revelation 127
    Supplement A 198
    Supplement B 206
    Supplement C 208

Glossary 213
Bibliography 217
Index 231

Acknowledgments

When I approached Prof. Garth W. Green with the project of translating into English F.H. Jacobi's *Von den göttlichen Dingen und ihrer Offenbarung*, he seemed not entirely convinced that I was doing the right thing: although Jacobi's philosophy was a fitting choice for a doctoral thesis in philosophy of religion, embarking on a project of translating a text from a foreign language (German) to a language that was not my mother tongue (English) seemed too risky. He needed to consult with Prof. George di Giovanni first. In truth, my idea was quite simple. I believed that to have a better understanding of the theoretical foundations of the philosophy of religion, I needed to delve into Jacobi's philosophy. The translation plan merely disclosed my underlying strategy: I was convinced of the necessity to route Jacobi's elaborate, complex, and sometimes intricate German toward the straightforwardness of the English phrasing. My research in the philosophy of religion would have benefitted from this operation, and the international community would have gained a further point of reference of an underappreciated philosopher. Finally, I was also sure that there was no better place in North America than McGill University to undertake this enterprise, for George di Giovanni is the authority to go to when studying Jacobi's philosophy in English. After George di Giovanni agreed to become my co-supervisor, we could not see any real obstacles to the project. The present translation and study result from a profound revision of my doctoral thesis in philosophy of religion defended in 2019 at the School of Religious Studies, McGill University.

viii ACKNOWLEDGMENTS

A project as difficult as this one would not have been possible without the help of a group of scholars, friends, and institutions. Garth W. Green is the first scholar and friend that I want to thank; he provided invaluable support when I moved to Montreal. He has endorsed all initiatives I took to deepen my understanding of the classical German philosophy of religion. When at a loss with a clear theoretical lead, he had the ability to unearth what I strove to define but did not fully grasp; our conversations often ended with a sense of clarity and relief.

In 2016 I was fortunate enough to have few private conversations with Prof. Birgit Sandkaulen. She is justly recognized as the best expert on Jacobi's work. Thanks to those meetings, I had the opportunity to shape and consolidate the grounding principles for the present study. I owe much of what I have written in my analyses to those conversations.

The translation has been made several times. Each time I approached a different colleague with the Herculean task of reviewing my efforts. Naznin Patel and Dr Hadi Fakhoury helped achieve a first good draft of the translation.

The analytical remarks of Dr Amanda Rosini are responsible for the readability of the introductory study; she made me realize how much I had to work to achieve a good control over the English mindset when elaborating an idea.

Several institutions made this project possible: the School of Religious Studies funded several travels to European libraries and centres, FRQSC (Fonds de Recherche du Québec – Société et Culture) supported my PhD project, the Institut für Katholische Theologie (RWTH – Aachen Universität) provided a friendly environment during my first post-doctoral research term, and finally HIF (Hosei International Fund) and JSPS (Japan Society for the Promotion of Science) financed my research-stay at Hosei University, first as visiting PhD student and then as postdoc fellow under the supervision of Prof. Seiichi Yamaguchi. Prof. Yamaguchi helped me find the resources to bring this work to an end while living in Japan, where Jacobi's philosophy is not yet widely studied. I also want to thank Prof. Kioei Takiguchi, Prof. Hideto Akashi, Prof. Taiju Okochi, Dr Yusuke Iizumi, and Dr Shunsuke Kudomi for their friendly support during my research time in Tokyo.

I would like to conclude by extending my warmest gratitude to George di Giovanni. I believe that much of what is right in the translation comes from him. His clear mind and mastery over both the German and the English language, his tireless spirit, have guided each and every day I spent studying Jacobi's philosophy. Without him, the last five years would have been fruitless.

On the
Divine
Things
and Their
Revelation

A Study of F.H. Jacobi's
On the Divine Things and Their Revelation

I INTRODUCTION

Friedrich Heinrich Jacobi (1743–1819) was a pivotal figure in the second half of the eighteenth century. He was a vocal critic of the German Enlightenment, Immanuel Kant's transcendental idealism, Johann Gottlieb Fichte's doctrine of knowledge, and of Friedrich Schelling's early philosophy. Jacobi could not engage with or review G.W.F. Hegel's system of philosophy; he surely would have examined Hegel's interpretation of thinking critically as well. In fact, Jacobi's notion of immediate certainty would not only have challenged Hegel's philosophy; it would also have been challenged by Hegel's notion of dialectic. Alas, this debate never really took place.[1]

Upon studying his work and reviewing the nature of his publications, one may be left with the sense that the importance of Jacobi's philosophy derives more from the far-reaching and critical questions and issues that he raised, both within and against modern philosophical debates, than from the original insight and depth he opposed to them.[2] However, this assessment does little justice to Jacobi's efforts.

Indeed, Jacobi both introduced and epitomized the main philosophical controversies of his age: the Pantheism Controversy (*Pantheismusstreit*, 1785), the Atheism Controversy (*Atheismusstreit*, 1798–99), and the Theism Controversy (*Theismusstreit*, 1799/1811–12).[3] Nonetheless, he also introduced a new series of topics that went beyond those controversies. If we examine his evolution as a thinker, Jacobi's journey begins when he identifies that Baruch Spinoza's philosophy plays a crucial role in defining the power of thinking. During an era in which Kant's philosophy and the German Enlightenment represented the main philosophical pillars, Jacobi recognized that the dialectic of Spinoza's ethics was the fundament of the intellectual enterprise of modernity, including Kant's philosophy and the German Enlightenment. In Jacobi's view, transcendental philosophy and German Enlightenment were not entirely different, although seemingly divergent, because of the intrinsic Spinozian nature of all modern philosophy. One might remember Hegel's famous equation of philosophy and Spinozism: Spinoza would be a testing point in the very notion of philosophy in view of the implementation of mathematical/demonstrative method to philosophical notions. In this sense, Jacobi's critical view of Spinoza becomes instrumental in understanding Hegel's assessment and decisive to decipher the modern debate concerning the nature of philosophy. All started, one may dare summarize, as Jacobi tried to show that the systems that modern philosophy produced lead to a complete annihilation of the "true" in exchange for sophisticated fallacies.

It is of little surprise that his distinct stance, in this rich philosophical context, drew unyielding critique. On 25 March 1802, Jacobi lamented in a letter to F. Perthes that he suffered violent reactions from professional philosophers. Their common "wrath" was aroused on different fronts, but their main point of contention was with Jacobi's "aversion" to any example of systematic philosophy. However, he does admit that his criticism did not address "their distinct system, rather it [was] generally grounded on the philosophical *Systematismus*," which he contends was "the whole spirit of the century."[4] In an era when the notion of "system" identified the cultural momentum that intended to surpass the limits of Enlightenment toward a pure and superior form of scientific thinking, Jacobi deemed the very notion of system as the source of misconceptions. Controversies and debates repeatedly surrounded almost every text that Jacobi published because, as he notes, he did not dispute with any single philosopher, rather he addressed and challenged the very spirit of his age.

What follows is a study of Jacobi's last published book: *On the Divine Things and Their Revelation* (henceforth, *Divine Things*). It does not intend to introduce the reader to Jacobi's philosophy in general; my purpose is much more limited and defined. In a sense, this study presents Jacobi's final word against the abstract illusions of systematic philosophy while it offers an analysis of a distinct philosophical understanding of human existence. The *Divine Things* is Jacobi's last effort to overthrow those illusions in favour of a speculative liberation which – one might argue – includes a doctrine of concrete existence.[5] This specific focus notwithstanding, this study is intended to introduce the reader to the greater panorama of issues that the *Divine Things* addresses. Therefore, it takes into consideration different sources from Jacobi's body of work, which will help contextualize those topics that the *Divine Things* includes. Yet each textual reference to Jacobi's texts is introduced with the sole purpose of bringing to light some of the core ideas included in the *Divine Things*, a text that until now had only been available in German, French, and Italian, and which I have translated into English.

In the first part of this study, I offer details concerning the historical context and intellectual background of Jacobi's final publication. This historical contextualization will provide a concrete support to the analysis that will follow. The analytic component will focus on the ideas that Jacobi chose to attentively elaborate upon in this final work. The present study will reveal that the *Divine Things* is thematically rooted in one of Jacobi's most famous works, the *Jacobi to Fichte* (1799).[6] However, it will also become apparent that the topics and arguments elaborated in the *Divine Things* are congruent with two of Jacobi's other philosophical treatises: *Über die Lehre des Spinoza in Briefen an den Herrn Moses Mendelssohn* (1785) and *David Hume über den Glauben, oder Idealismus und Realismus. Ein Gespräch* (1787). These textual references will provide the framework needed to give depth to the pages of the *Divine Things* and allow the reader to witness its theoretical underpinnings.

One may contend that the *Divine Things* is a unique text; it offers a great comprehension of Jacobi's philosophy as such because the writing of this work coincides with a moment in which Jacobi himself begins to reflect upon his own lifelong enterprise under the perspective of an explicit theism. In fact, the *Divine Things* was composed while Jacobi was tending to the complete edition of his works. Thus this final text bears witness to Jacobi's mature self-understanding, which crystallizes around his intent of making theism his strongest philosophical tenet. I believe that his theism, however ex post facto, introduces Jacobi's understanding of reason, God, and the order of reality in a quasi-systematic fashion. I could even argue that Jacobi's theism encompasses and connects all three these topics consistently, while at the same time disputing systematicity in philosophy.

What I call Jacobi's quasi-systematic reasoning mirrors solely his unity of vision; it does not qualify the nature of his philosophy. One could contend that Jacobi was a non-systematic intellectual because he was reacting against the systematic nature of the philosophical outputs of the day; nevertheless, he was not deficient in method, coherence, and uniformity of conception. Hence my approach presents Jacobi's theism as his ultimate philosophical achievement, which proves consistent with his main theses and provides a point of balance in which such a vision and those theses are consciously deepened. This view, I shall argue further, develops out of an intrinsic *metaphysical* background that Jacobi's theism requires.

I conclude that the *Divine Things* is an effort to define concrete existence according to a distinct metaphysical conceptualization of theism, a conceptualization that I will closely examine by investigating the features and limits of such a theism. I hope that this distinct scope will allow this work to make a valuable contribution toward defining Jacobi's general accomplishment.

II THE HISTORY OF THE BOOK

Jacobi's *Von den göttlichen Dingen und ihrer Offenbarung* was published in 1811. The work has an intricate composition history that spans over more than ten years.[7] It includes three texts: *Ueber eine Weissagung Lichtenbergs* originally published in 1802[8]; *Claudius-Rezension*, which was scheduled for publication on the Michaelis-Messe in 1798,[9] and a final long essay on "idealism and realism" in relation to matters of religion. Unfortunately, the critical edition does not help us regarding any precise date for the inception of Jacobi's *Divine Things*. However, Jacobi does give us a clue as to when the whole project of the *Divine Things* started to take shape. In a letter to Jean Paul Friedrich Richter from 13 September 1809, Jacobi indicates that he was busy at that moment bringing to completion a work on "revelation" (*Offenbarung*) that he had begun *thirteen* years before while living in Hamburg.[10] We can assume that the exactitude of the information gives credit to its reliability. We thus can assume that Jacobi started thinking about his volume on revelation as early as 1796.

In 1794, only two years earlier, Jacobi fled Pempelfort, when French troops began occupying the north-west territories of Germany. He moved to Hamburg where he bonded with Reimarus, Klopstock, Claudius, and others. In this context, Jacobi began his work on what he will later call – in a letter to Fries – an investigation into *"innere und äussere Offenbarung,"* provisionally entitled *"Philosophie und Christenthum."*[11]

I would like to clarify that these initial remarks regarding the content of Jacobi's *Divine Things* should be treated with caution. They may falsely give

A STUDY   7

the reader the impression that the volume addresses topics of philosophical theology. Instead, it would be better to rely upon the *Preface* to the third volume of the *Werke* (1816), which was published including the second edition of the *Divine Things*. In this preface, Jacobi discloses the kinship of this work with both *Jacobi to Fichte* (1799) and *Ueber das Unternehmen des Kritizismus die Vernunft zu Verstand zu bringen, und der Philosophie überhaupt eine neue Absicht zu geben* (1802).[12] The relationship of the *Divine Things* to these two important essays shows that the volume on revelation neither deals with the connection between philosophy and Christian theology, nor addresses the nature of revelation in Christianity; rather, Jacobi seems to suggest that it chiefly aims to bring attention to the necessity of a specific kind of revelation, a revelation of true being.

Published when Jacobi was 68 years old, this volume represents a "*testament philosophique*" as it brings to conclusion his lifelong endeavor to demonstrate the necessity of apprehending the object of thinking as outside the subject. This volume represents his unique perspective on the matter. In 1809, Jacobi wrote to the French translator of the *Woldemar* that he is as certain of the needfulness of his endeavor as he is of his solitude in this effort: "all my ideas together with their foundation will be expounded. I primarily try to show how I could keep them in the midst of the revolutions that philosophy has experienced in Germany in the last thirty years, notwithstanding the progress that a doctrine contrary to mine has made in all Europe. The whole world is *naturalist*. I am not. And I want to confess it once more loudly and vigorously before I die."[13] Most of his writing career had been aimed at unearthing the flaws of the idealistic soul of naturalism. This project is then here taken up in order to be able to suggest his theism as the only remedy against this European intellectual plague. Jacobi's critical analysis has always portrayed idealism (i.e., transcendental philosophy in its ultimate form) as a backward stepping that yields no progress, as it stumbles toward the *reductio ad absurdum* of its principles.[14] According to Jacobi, the key misconception that lies at the foundation of this failure consists in the assumption that the whole of reality is but the activity of an immanent principle, as if thinking on the one side and nature on the other were just echoes of a formal self-generating whole. The composition of physical reality would therefore mirror the simple activity of a principle that generates itself, making the multitude of existence only a universe of *systematic* relations. In the same vein, the theoretical realm would be a composite whole resulting from the activity of the single principle of thinking. The difference between the theoretical and the real would then be dismissed by the accomplishment of transcendental philosophy, which would prove that the reality outside the subject is just a mirror of the subject's mind. The result would be a self-sufficient, closed system; this is *idealism*, which also takes on the name of *naturalism*. As it is often advertised, but never repeated enough, for Jacobi this articulate monism refutes the existence, the conceivability, the freedom of singular entities.

Contrary to the ambitions of idealism, Jacobi maintains that both thinking and physical reality are not expressions of the activity of a self-sufficient principle; such self-sufficiency is rather a delusion that turns thinking into absurdity and reality into nothing. Instead, beyond the misconception of self-sufficiency rises the need and the power of revelation. The chief faculty of our intellectual nature, reason (*Vernunft*), wins back its original mission (the *ver-nehmen*) to apprehend from outside itself the source of any claim. Truth is thus apprehended, and not justified. In fact, the search for justification – if given free rein – would lead to an infinite regress or to an indefinite whole. Instead, the apprehension of truth (more precisely, according to Jacobi's terminology, "the true," *das Wahre*) is immediate and justification must only follow this prime instance of reality; hence, the content of such an apprehension cannot but be *revealed*, not justified. From this step, Jacobi re-establishes the necessity of a dualism; an "I" that is always confronted by a "Thou," an "I" that never creates reality or values, but recognizes them, as they *must* exist outside the "I."

Assuming this theoretical framework, which I have here loosely sketched to serve as a preliminary outline, it becomes clear why we should not suppose that the *Divine Things* was another work in philosophical theology, or a mere polemical pamphlet against distinct targets with opposing views (as in Schelling's crude response to it, the *Denkmal der Schrift von den göttlichen Dingen* (1812)).[15] Instead, the problem that Jacobi addresses is internal to systematic thinking in general, and idealism in particular. In it, the necessity of revelation is to be made apparent. Therefore, the notion of revelation will be the paradigmatic concept through which Jacobi can show how reason can escape the delusions of abstract rationalism and become the faculty that perceives the "realm of beings."[16] Jacobi pursues this endeavour via an analysis that conceptually assumes his opponents' positions (those of idealism) to demonstrate the weaknesses of their presuppositions and the invalidity of their results. His trajectory can therefore be deemed an analytical approach against the then

A STUDY

current system of thinking. We will see how Jacobi offers a philosophy that eventually reveals the powerful and healthy relation between analytical methodology and metaphysics. This relation, we shall see, eventually yields a distinct epistemology and a new philosophy of religion. In general, his philosophical doctrine of God, world, and divine things follows from the conceptual architecture that he elaborates in his interpretation of reason.[17]

It is important to understand that Jacobi does not possess a science of God. His contribution is closer to a doctrine that leans toward pietism.[18] Regardless of its characterization however, the *Divine Things* can be seen as the last and most progressive step that Jacobi takes in the exposition of what he believes all his writings are about: an exhibition of a doctrine of reason that is not systematic and that instead conveys a universal truth that opposes monism.[19]

From the beginning, the *Divine Things* proves to be inspired by Jacobi's hostility against the Enlightenment's impetus toward naturalism. In fact, the first instalment of Jacobi's text includes Georg Christoph Lichtenberg's prophecy: **"Our world will become so refined (*fein*) that it will be as ridiculous to believe in God,** as it is today to believe in ghosts."[20]

Lichtenberg (1742–1799), a mathematician and physicist, became well known for his contributions to the debate on religion while teaching at the prestigious University of Göttingen.[21] Lichtenberg was distinctly averse to anything that was not rationally explicable according to the paradigms of the *Aufklärung*. However, he did not reject the idea of unusual objects of intellectual investigation.[22] As a renowned physicist, his trained scientific mind encouraged him to both prudence and to constantly challenge the very laws of rationalism which led to his insight about the critical assessment of the limits of reason itself.[23] It is of no surprise, then, that Lichtenberg, who for many was an atheist, was in fact a "Geistverwandter" of Jean Paul.[24] Consequently, he is ideal for helping us introduce and understand where Jacobi stands within the spectrum of thinkers of his era. If Jacobi was a theist, then he was surely not a theologian. Moreover, Jacobi himself states, in a letter, that Jean Paul could finish the *Divine Things* on his behalf.[25] Thus, we can easily imagine a transitive connection of disposition (*Gesinnung*) that, according to Jacobi's own words, would match a general agreement between the three intellectuals.[26] These three figures have in common their hostility to the systems of thinking (*Systemfeindschaft*) and, as a consequence, their profound appreciation for aphorisms. This distinct literary style, so dear to Pascal as well, puts thinking on a diet, but it does not forego universality.[27] In the end, this specific morphology of aphorisms reveals more about the specific nature of thinking than about the form of truth itself; a thinking that only catches fragments of a truth never fully on display.

Though Jacobi's thinking also bears witness to the impossibility of knowing the full identity of the human world, his reasoning in the *Divine Things* is not consistent with Lichtenberg's unappealing skepticism. In reality, skepticism only provides Jacobi with a point of departure to further develop his theory of knowledge. This split between Jacobi and Lichtenberg is clear, especially when Lichtenberg explicitly refuses to follow Jacobi's thesis on *Glaube*, hypothetically taking Lessing's side in the *Spinozastreit*.[28]

The second section of the *Divine Things* focuses on a different thinker, one who is in stark contrast to Lichtenberg; Matthias Claudius. This not only because Claudius is an intimate friend of Jacobi, but also because of his impact on the era. Claudius is a *homme de lettres* whose ideas, at least in their general implications, Jacobi feels to be very close to his own theoretical and moral concerns.[29] After an encounter in Weimar in 1784, Claudius expresses his agreement with Jacobi on the necessity of an *"unmittelbare Gewissheit"* in matters of religion and plans to work on the issue, while Jacobi at this time is preparing to embark on his dispute with Mendelssohn.[30]

Jacobi notes that the Claudius-review was originally written as an account of the sixth volume of the complete works of the Messenger of Wandsbeck (which is Matthias Claudius' nickname, along with his penname Asmus). According to Jacobi's original plan, the review was to be published in Hamburg, as an article for the journal *Hamburgischer Unparteyischer Correspondent*. Yet as the length of the essay progressively increased, he resolved to re-edit and publish it as an independent text. The publication is finally announced for the third Sunday after Easter of 1798.[31] However, new obstacles present themselves on the path to its publication: Jacobi had to leave Hamburg and is invited to take part in the Fichte case that erupted that year.

Though less ardent than Jacobi in matters of religion, Claudius maintains that the human being needs a positive and external revelation to contrast with the revelation that is purely internal and subjective.[32] On the basis of this apparent concurrence, Jacobi developed the second part of the *Divine Things*. This makes explicit a fundamental divergence; in his view, an objective revelation does not imply that it should be foreign to the inner self or, worse still, that the very event of revelation should define the revealed object *only*. Contrary to what Claudius contends, Jacobi suggests that the immediacy of God's revelation does

A STUDY   11

not involve a complete transcendence. God himself leaves traces of his revelation within the human person and therefore the human person is defined according to this fundamental connection to the divine: revelation reveals both, the human being and the divine being concurrently.

As it is often the case during this period, elucidation evolves into misjudgement. In fact, Jacobi's explanation leads Claudius to misunderstand Jacobi's actual position on the matter of revelation.[33] Hence, explaining Claudius' criticism of Jacobi quickly becomes radical. Jacobi's proclivity to hold true an immediate and yet internal revelation would be for Claudius too idealistic, and his concept of revelation too subjective. Claudius therefore suspects Jacobi of "*Chimärismus, Phantasterey, Selbstgötterey,*" and eventually, "*Nihilismus.*"[34]

According to Claudius' assessment, Jacobi is at risk of being charged with nihilism just as Fichte was. In fact, Jacobi's defense of a subjective component to his conception of a revelation of the true may indeed appear to Claudius as a fatal claim that leaves neither independency nor objectivity to the revealed content. *Per contra*, in Jacobi's eyes the religious realism that Claudius defends mistakenly gives both scriptures and historical facts precedence over what lies inside the human spirit. According to Jacobi's observations this would make Claudius an idolater.

In general, the difference between internal and external revelation is that the internal does not require mediation. Nevertheless, in the *Divine Things*, Jacobi does not defend the internal view, nor does he aim at a negotiation between the two parties ("integral internalist" versus "integral externalist"), rather he claims a twofold rejection of both internalist and externalist in light of an analysis of the notion of existence and of the corresponding profile of the human being.

In this way, he separates himself from both Claudius (who embodies what Jacobi refers to as an externalist) and the idealists (whom Jacobi calls integral internalists, a categorization that would apply to thinkers such as Kant (at least, partially), Fichte, and Schelling). As a consequence, Jacobi's double refutation gives the *Divine Things* two targets that then serve the purpose of placing Jacobi's own doctrine in a third position which cannot be reduced to that of the other two. Thus, following this general plan, the second section of the *Divine Things* serves to dispute the *religious realism* of the integral externalists and shows the necessity for an internal element to the revelation of the divine things. The third and last section of *Divine Things* serves to confront *religious idealism* and attack the core of the integral internalist argument by aiming to clarify how the divine things are necessarily perceived by reason as factors that are independent of reason itself.

We will see that Jacobi shows that the internal or subjective element of revelation does not affect its objectivity and that, although divine things imply a subjective footing, they can only be acquired as mind-independent objects.

As noted earlier, Jacobi's confrontation with idealism occurs well before the publication of the *Divine Things* and spans over thirty years. However, the newest instalment in this confrontation, the one that concerns Schelling's identity philosophy, is what leads the volume to be more confrontational. At this point, I would like to caution the reader as this single segment in the development of Jacobi's philosophy may lead the reader to forget the importance of the organic wholeness of his treatise. Therefore, I must first clarify that Jacobi's criticism of Schelling's thought will prove coherent with his interpretation of the general traits of idealism. Jacobi's criticism of Schelling's philosophy should thus not be understood as something new in the overall account of Jacobi's thought or in the general economy of the text. The *Divine Things* provides Jacobi with the opportunity to further develop his ideas that do not stem solely from his confrontation with Schelling, for they also connect with Jacobi's previous disputes. This affinity notwithstanding, we will see that the ideas expounded in the *Divine Things* illuminate an important advancement in Jacobi's views on *reason* and *being*, which are described in light of the metaphysical foundation of his theism.

Apparently, the first meeting between Schelling and Jacobi took place in Munich in 1806, shortly before Jacobi became president of the Munich Academy of Sciences. The meeting is described as amicable, despite the fact that Schelling was already riled by Jacobi's "Letter to Fichte" (*Jacobi to Fichte*) and his *Lichtenberg's Prophecy*, due to the numerous references in these texts to the irreligiosity of post-Kantian philosophy.[35] The letters that describe their meeting indicate that Jacobi remained suspicious of Schelling's true feelings despite Schelling's affable approach.[36]

Jacobi's mistrust was not ill advised. A growing animosity between the two quickly ignited as Schelling suspected Jacobi of influencing some unfavourable reviews of his *System des transcendentalen Idealismus* (1800). In response, Schelling indicated that he intended to examine Jacobi's texts with greater attention and publish his evaluation of Jacobi's philosophy in the *Allgemeine Literatur-Zeitung*.[37] The situation escalated further with the publication of *Über das Unternehmen des Kriticismus, die Vernunft zu Verstande zu bringen, und der*

A STUDY   13

Philosophie überhaupt eine neue Absicht zu geben in 1802. Eventually, Schelling decided not to pursue his intentions to attack Jacobi, as Hegel published his *Glauben und Wissen oder die Reflexionsphilosophie der Subjektivität, in der Vollständigkeit ihrer Formen, als Kantische, Jacobische und Fichtesche Philosophie* (1802) which also offered an account of Schelling's ideas.[38]

At the time of Hegel's *Glauben und Wissen*, Jacobi was acquainted with mainly two essays by Schelling: *Ideen zu einer Philosophie der Natur als Einleitung in das Studium dieser Wissenschaft* (*Ideas for a Philosophy of Nature: as Introduction to the Study of this Science*) (1797) and *Erster Entwurf eines Systems der Naturphilosophie* (*First Plan of a System of the Philosophy of Nature*) (1799).[39] He later decided to read more of Schelling's speculative philosophy, to confirm his doubts about the real nature of the "Identity-System."

After his survey, Jacobi concluded that Schelling would disappoint the real *philosopher of nature*, because for the real philosopher of nature freedom or God are not an issue, and they are certainly not objects of inquiry in the natural sciences. However, this is not the case for the real *philosopher*, claims Jacobi, who recognizes that in Schelling's thought the "*transcendental creator*" is at work. For that "creator," Jacobi denounces, reality is just the expression of a self-sufficient impersonal ground, within which freedom, God and singular entities are wrongly attributed to identity and activity of that impersonal ground. In the end, real philosopher of nature and real philosopher would be both disappointed by Schelling's philosophy.

Thanks to the study of Schelling's more recent works, Jacobi arrived at the conclusion that Schelling's philosophy is the ultimate exposition of a system of *Unitotality*, where the structure of an absolute identity provides the architecture for both thought and nature.[40] Scientific naturalism – though intrinsically problematic in view of the annihilation of singular entities that it may assume – is, in Jacobi's view, not as questionable as Schelling's idealism. The latter gives shape to an advanced naturalism which adopts the methodology of systematic philosophy only to extract freedom from mechanical necessity, God from nature, and existence from possibility. Schelling's philosophy claims to deduce the divine things from the systematic "nothing" that transcendental philosophy provides. As a result, Jacobi's criticism becomes far more severe in the case of transcendental philosophy and its later developments (such as Schelling's philosophy) than in the case of scientific naturalism *tout court*.[41]

Consequently, Jacobi decided to make public his view of the then current development of German philosophy by publishing the so-called *Three Letters* to *Köppen* as a supplement to F. Köppen's *Schellings Lehre oder das Ganze der Philosophie des absoluten Nichts* (1803).[42] Some time will pass before either thinker begins to engage one another again. It is not until Schelling's address *Ueber das Verhältnis der bildenden Künste zu der Natur* at the Munich Academy of Sciences in 1807 that Jacobi is persuaded to return to his analysis of Schelling's thought. Schelling's address fuels new energy into Jacobi's polemic against transcendental philosophy.[43] If a prehistory of the *Divine Things* can therefore be seen in Jacobi's speech *Ueber gelehrte Gesellschaften, Ihren Geist und Zweck* (1807), then the overall design of the *Divine Things* evinces consistency in its analysis of issues that are both well beyond Schelling's philosophy and firmly anchored in Jacobi's earlier concerns about transcendental philosophy.[44]

It would appear that the personal relationship between Schelling and Jacobi remains more or less unaltered until the publication of the *Divine Things*. After its publication, the relationship between the two men becomes strained. Famously, Schelling replies in 1812 with his *Denkmal der Schrift von den göttlichen Dingen [et]c. des Herrn Friedrich Heinrich Jacobi und der ihm in derselben gemachten Beschuldigung eines absichtlich täuschenden, Lüge redenden Atheismus*. This response, as noted by Pauline Gotter, comes only a month after Jacobi's publication.[45] Jacobi for his part does not reply to Schelling's attack. Instead, he chooses to publish his views in his new preface to the dialogue of *David Hume* (1815) – which also represents the introduction to his collected works. Therein, Jacobi presents his unaltered ideas concerning Schelling's thought, despite Schelling's more recent *On the Essence of Human Freedom* (1809).[46] Schelling's paradigmatic assumption that the perfect develops from the less perfect, consciousness from non-consciousness, and free action from non-free actuality is what Jacobi challenged from the onset; ever since his meeting with Lessing.

It has been widely recognized that the dialogue between Jacobi and Schelling fuelled the polemical inclinations of numerous intellectuals. They include K.L. Reinhold, J.F. Fries, C.G. Bardili, Jan Paul, Friedrich Bouterwek, G.E. Schulze, Friedrich Schlegel, and A.K.A. v. Eschenmayer.[47] One may argue that the overall debate turned Jacobi into the representative of those who were unsatisfied with the evolution of post-Kantian philosophy, and turned Schelling into the spokesperson of a superseding form of transcendental thought. The more general dispute slowly solidified into a controversy of several issues surrounding these two thinkers. This may have affected the

A STUDY   15

assessment (this is true then more so than today) of the real relation between
Jacobi's and Schelling's philosophy, and may have generated a misleading
interpretation of the real intentions and *foci* of their respective efforts. At
least, this appears to be the case from Jacobi's viewpoint.

Furthermore, it may seem surprising that the new edition of the *Divine
Things* – which was ready between the end of 1815 and the beginning of 1816
– does not bear many traces of the so-called *Streit um die Göttlichen Dingen*
that ignited the German philosophical debate between 1812 and 1816. Besides
F.W.J. Schelling's *Denkmal* a series of other works appeared in response to
Jacobi's *Divine Things*, including: J.F. Fries' *Von Deutscher Philosophie Art und
Kunst. Ein Votum für Friedrich Heinrich Jacobi gegen F.W.J. Schelling* (1812)
and Jakob Salat's *Erläuterung einiger Hauptpunkte der Philosophie. Mit Zu-
gaben über den neusten Widerstreit in den wissenschaftlichen Ansichten der Hrn.
Fr. Heinr. Jacobi, F.W.J. Schelling und Fr. Schlegel* (1812). The reviews authored
by Friedrich Bouterwek, J.F. Fries, and Friedrich Schlegel complete the account of this controversy.[48] Notably, Jacobi seems to have considered all of
the above-mentioned works, even while ignoring Schelling's polemical essay.
This could be seen both as a testimony of Jacobi's dismissive detachment
from Schelling's reaction, or as a reasoned stance in agreement with the nature of Jacobi's true philosophical concern, which was necessarily broader
than a direct reply to Schelling.[49]

III THE BOOK: AN OVERVIEW OF ITS KEY CONCEPTS

I Introduction

In his treatise, *On the Sublime*, Pseudo-Longinus observed that sublime
thoughts belong only to the "loftiest minds," able to determine "τα δαιμόνια"
(divine things) and differentiate them from the things that occupy those with
illiberal thoughts and habits.[50] In the context of the *Divine Things*, the belonging of divine thoughts to certain minds can be regarded simply as an introductory metaphor about the distinct relationship between a certain kind of
mind and divine realities. Pseudo-Longinus' notion of belonging can thus be
regarded as a provisory introduction to what Jacobi's *Divine Things* also advances: a special quality of thinking is as responsible for the vision of "divine
things" as the "divine things" themselves, so that *both* the "divine things" and

the "loftiest minds" seem to be instrumental within the experience of a sublime vision. We will see that Jacobi's *Divine Things* focuses, in truth, precisely on this vision.[51]

Although he does not elaborate an explicit theory of the sublime, Jacobi adopts the term only with reference to human reason, which bears witness to an excellence that surpasses nature.[52] In this regard, the practical domain of human reason has proven critical to determining the sublime aspects of the human world. This idea, Jacobi acknowledges, owes its proper profile to Kant's writings on practical reason. Notoriously, Kant's practical reason had made it possible for the old metaphysical doctrines about God and the soul to become the subject matter of rational faith, according to which divine providence is perceived with rational "admiration," "respect," and "love."[53] Nevertheless, to stress more adequately his opposition to Kantian subjectivism, Jacobi claims that, contrary to Kantian philosophy, the thinking reveals not "*aus*" itself but "*durch*" itself. As Jacobi puts it: we do not see starting from the eyes, we see through the eyes.[54] In a sense, Pseudo-Longinus' notion of mutual belonging introduces us to the ultimate thesis of the volume, which maintains that "reason" does not fabricate the divine things but, instead, *finds* them.

Jacobi drafts this viewpoint long before the publication of the *Divine Things*. The idea of *finding* does not limit itself only to the divine things; rather, it is the operation that thinking performs in acquiring what really exists, which includes both finite and divine things (i.e., sensible and suprasensible objects). The idea of finding appears immediately clear to common sense when it concerns finite things, but the same idea may become obscure, and even arouses suspicions of mysticism, when the finding accounts for our relationship with divine things. In fact, the idea of finding things that belong to the divine horizon seems to suggest a mystical experience of some sort. We will see how Jacobi's so-called mysticism is, in truth, quite absent, and we will also see that the meaning of this finding requires further examination. As a general orientation though, it must be clear that his idea of finding perpetuates its validity throughout his works and eventually proves crucial for the economy of this final text; notions such as "revelation" and "faith" depend on it.

II Thinking as Finding

As an introductory simplification of Jacobi's philosophy, we could claim that divine things are the parameters of the metaphysical life of human beings. The divine things are: God, freedom, virtue, and the immortality of the soul. While

A STUDY 17

finite things are those objects that populate human sensible life, divine things are defined according to a suprasensible panorama that, while being distinct, exhibits connections with the former.[55] In fact, both divine and finite things are *found* and not generated by the human mind.[56]

As mentioned above, the general idea of a thinking that finds was clear to Jacobi from the moment he wrote the *Spinoza Letters*. There, he addresses the unbridgeable distance between his philosophy and modern philosophy, which is perfectly embodied by Spinoza's ethics: "I love Spinoza, because he, more than any other philosopher, has led me to the perfect conviction that certain things admit no explanation: one must not therefore keep one's eyes shut to them, but must keep them as one *finds* them."[57] This quotation attracts our attention because it not only states a theory of finding things, but it also states that there are things that are not found, but explained. In fact, beyond the distinction between finite and divine things, we also face the discrepancy between two different realms of objects included in two opposed descriptions of reality: on the one hand, we have those items that can be found, and on the other hand, we have those items that are known inasmuch as they are constructed according to explanations. As the *Spinoza Letters* shows, if a theory of reality assumes that *only* that which is justified by an explanation is real, then that theory produces a world of cosmic order that is defined by the reasons of its objects. Consequently, those objects are crafted according to the systematic reason that produces their theoretical profile, following a precise formal configuration: "all individual things mutually presuppose one another and refer to one another, so that none of them can either be or be thought of without the rest, or the rest without it."[58]

For Jacobi, this amounts to one, unavoidable end result: a cosmic monistic architecture, a product of intelligence that leaves no space for singularities. Spinoza, more than any other philosopher before him, makes clear that modern knowledge of reality aims at positing reality by way of justifications, so that reality turns into a theoretically universal framework. The resulting horizon is a plane of interconnections, the theoretical principle of which can be summarized as follows: "*gigni de nihilo nihil, in nihilum nil potest reverti*" (nothing is generated from nothing; nothing can revert into nothing).[59] Modern philosophy, in fact, has proven in the most convincing way that human intelligence provides explanations only in terms of a *mathesis*, which consists of a horizon whereby *determining* implies *relating*; in it, absolute singularities are inconceivable.[60] As a consequence, this infinite space of reasons provides only *immanent* mediations: no external transition is possible between one item and another, precisely because each determination of an item is reduced to the relation to its other.[61]

Jacobi seems to suggest that since this specific form of knowledge equates knowing to justifying, and justifying to the internal mediation of a whole, then the principle of explanation applies inevitably to any object that our modern intelligence concerns itself with. This leads to the aforementioned conclusion: "so that none of them can either be or be thought of without the rest, or the rest without it."[62] After Spinoza, Jacobi maintains, this approach to knowledge has in Kant and Fichte its ultimate expressions. On the one hand, Kant has translated Spinoza's *mathesis* into the intuitions of "space" and "time,"[63] while, on the other hand, Fichte's philosophy has showed that knowledge consists in the liberation from any contingency by way of a pure science, which reduces all multiplicity and relations to the principle of identity.[64]

Against this idea of science, Jacobi offers a different approach. For him, knowledge requires singular objects, and it is necessary that singular objects be *found*. In order to be found, objects (be them finite or divine) of real knowledge must present themselves as things that happen and that, simply put, are not determined by their conditions. In the end, they must not be determined by relations; hence, they are determined without implementing a mediation internal to the reality they are in. The only quality that determines them must be their singular *existence* (or being), which must be beyond conceptualization.

We will see how this argument unfolds and why existence is not a universal concept. For the moment it is essential that we keep in mind the clear distinction (despite it being explained in general terms) between two items of our thinking: on one side, we have the items (the objects of modern philosophy) of which we know the possibility; on the other side, we have items (the existing, real objects, finite and divine) of which we know their actuality.[65] Only the latter kind of items, Jacobi maintains, represents the true basis of our knowledge of both the finite and divine world. Instead, the former are just fulfilments of conceptual explanations.

As Jacobi has already made explicit in *Jacobi to Fichte*, the origin of knowledge must be found in the true being (the actuality or existence that the term *Wesen* implies) that performs the double function of being both the source of our knowledge and its limit.[66] The *Divine Things*, for its part, makes even more explicit the trajectory that was established in *Jacobi to Fichte*, and develops what the *Spinoza Letters* initiated: a severe criticism of the deduction of actuality from possibility, and a theory concerning the primacy of the former over the latter.

A STUDY

Hence, the *Divine Things* will have to focus on the divine things – leaving the theory concerning the finite things in the background – and show how, in ethics and religion, the opposition between the actual "true" and the merely conceptual "truth" is instituted.[67]

III Finding Things

To see what Jacobi denotes by a thinking that does not provide explanations but, instead, *finds* "things," we must identify what Jacobi calls the real "business of philosophy." Jacobi assumes that if we rely on the aforementioned principle of explanations, then we will obtain a knowledge that includes the conditions of possibility of things but not, he claims, their actuality. Instead, in order for our knowledge to be really objective, we need to know actual beings (*Wesen*).

The term Wesen is generally used by Jacobi to indicate something that exists independently of our subjective reasoning. And precisely to identify our relationship with what stands beyond our subjective reasoning that the notion of *Geschäft der Philosophie* arises. The service that true philosophy provides consists in defining and clarifying what lies beyond our subjective and conceptual understanding of things, hence philosophy is called on to assess *if* an *how* we can have access to objective reality; to being.[68] It goes without saying that we will need to understand if it is rational to assume that there is something beyond our subjective thinking – by looking at what Wesen and existence really mean in Jacobi's philosophy – and, once we can confirm such an objective being, we will have to assess the method to grasp it – by looking at our distinct relation to being as accommodated by the notion of *Glaube*. This plan may appear coherent with the general framework provided in the *Spinoza Letters* and *David Hume*, but we will have to articulate it according to an explicit implementation of the ethical and religious issues that concern the *divine things*.[69]

Let's start with a clarification of the notion of Wesen. To enter the ethical and religious horizon in which divine Wesen are placed, we must take a few introductory steps, beginning with the profile of our knowledge of finite things. In fact, it is in Jacobi's argument concerning the finite things that we will find the key to unlock his argument concerning the divine things.

By looking at *David Hume*, the outcomes of which resurface in the *Divine Things*, we may have the impression that Wesen are conceived primarily as pertaining to living beings: since "the [element of] individuality in a being" is "what determines its individuality, i.e., it makes the being into an actual whole," then "the organic natures all belong to this category." Notwithstanding this last remark, individuality does not belong to organisms alone. The same individuality belongs to any extended being, as they too exhibit "the same kind of unity" that belong to organisms.[70] Therefore, Jacobi appears to conclude that organisms call attention to a specific unity that defines the principle of individuality of any existing thing or Wesen.

To be sure, the living organism displays a kind of unity that does not show itself only by means of its "unity" and "impenetrability." The living being displays a specific *autonomy* that, surprisingly, grounds any knowledge: "the principle of all cognition is living being: living being proceeds from itself, is progressive and productive."[71] This passage, although short, is critical. It says that in order to be the basis of all cognition, unity and impenetrability do not suffice; they must pertain to a being that has the faculty to be a source of a motion, because cognition seems to arise only with reference to the specifics of an autonomous agent.

This last point alludes to the fact that a living being is not just an object of cognition but is rather the *paradigm* for cognition as such. We will return to this self-moving Wesen later, yet we now should stress a fundamental move that Jacobi has made in presenting the autonomous movement that lies at the basis of cognition. Cognition is not primarily something that deals with a way of defining objects. Rather, cognition pertains to the connection between the subject that finds things and those things that are found. In different terms, cognition results from the encounter between a living organism and its world of objects. Once we define the living organism and its world, we will identify what cognition in truth is.

We may thus assume that for Jacobi – at least according to these few introductory references – cognition is not conceived as something that presents the world in general; rather, cognition presents the world of and for a living organism. In Jacobi's opinion, the dream of describing the world as it is, independently of any presuppositions, even independently of the subject that finds it, may lead to a dangerous illusion: it may transform a scientific project into the hallucination of idealism. In point of fact, if the subject is removed from the process that determines the object, we may believe that we can arrive to a pure definition of objects; it would seem, in other terms, that once the influence of the subject is taken off, we would behold objects in their purity. Instead, if this was to happen, we would fall victim to the illusory knowledge that holds the reality of objects to be equal to their *possibility*. Our knowledge would be empty. Paradoxically, knowledge would be just the product of our thinking. Alternatively, Jacobi contends, cognition is based on what exists, and what exists is conceivable only in light of and within the concrete life of a living being.

We may further explain this last point by stressing that the Wesen is never conceived as a *Gewesen*. We may use the German term Gewesen, even though it is not used by Jacobi, to bring to light the quality of Wesen, the term that Jacobi often uses to invoke existence. Wesen does not show itself according to an abstract profile of the determinate negation through its other. It is rather an autonomous singularity. Jacobi seems to suggest that Wesen must not be interpreted according to conceptual parameters; instead, Wesen involves what is actual. In this sense, the service that philosophy provides consists in guiding our mind to something that *wirkt*, that moves, that produces effects. As Jacobi would state, Wesen is the origin of all knowledge because it is not posited by knowledge. Instead, Wesen occurs as something not-known that, while coming before knowledge, allows for it.[72]

Gewesen, instead, is something that has happened without being found, and as such is known. Precisely because its contours are established by its relations to what precedes it and what follows it, Gewesen is placed within a chain made of what is not actual. Gewesen, in a sense, is the ultimate brick of the reality whose explanation supposedly does not have any restriction, and it should thus be deemed abstract. The reality thus described expands as a whole making the Gewesen something that *is* only inasmuch as it *is known* within this framework. Gewesen is posited only insofar as it is conceived in the realm of explanations, because its identity is only based upon its other.

Wesen is never abstractly justified but is assumed as being independent of explanations. Conversely, Gewesen portrays an item within an indefinite chain of conditions, which substantiates its definition; hence, the item that is defined according to its justification is posited in the moment that the entire architecture of interconnections is posited.[73]

It may eventually appear in all clarity that Jacobi is presenting an entirely different way of thinking, that does not proceed by listing the conditions of possibility of its objects. This new way of thinking would instead necessitate a new way of conceiving of thinking itself, because a new way of thinking is necessary to describe what lies beyond justification. For Jacobi, this is the task that philosophy performs. Philosophy must concern itself firstly with a critical clarification of the nature of thinking in general, and secondly with the identification of the way in which this new thinking conceives of *being*.

In the end, it may seem as if Jacobi restricts the world that can be thought of to the world of living beings, and it may appear that in so doing he adopts a notion of both thinking (that finds) and being (the actual Wesen) that conform to that assumption. Nevertheless, the restriction of true knowledge to the knowledge of the world of living beings is quite modest. In truth, this restriction will be called *theism*.

For the moment, though, we must acknowledge that Jacobi does not dismiss discursive thinking as such. Nor does he reject the capacity of the cognitive faculty to create relations, justifications, and mediations. Rather, he claims that knowledge necessitates that something be *found* first. Only after this first and necessary step, can we potentially make connections and produce science. We need a faculty that perceives the Wesen first, and subsequently a faculty that elaborates upon it. We can call the first reason and the second understanding: "Reason is not grounded in the power of thought, a light that only later shone in the understanding; the power of thought is rather grounded in reason, which lights up the understanding wherever it is present and awakens it to *contemplation* – and upon contemplation there follows enquiry, distinct cognition, *science*."[74]

A problem arises only when the science of the understanding declares its self-sufficiency. This happens when we assume that we do not need to find anything outside the chain of conditions. Contrary to this, the *Beruf* of Jacobi's philosophy consists in defining the necessity and form of the "revelation" of Wesen.[75]

IV The Certainty of Existence

To move forward, we must now discuss, in a few steps, the definition of the thinking that thinks of existence; we will see that this also sheds light on the necessity of assuming the living being as a paradigm of our knowledge. Following these steps, we will be able to confirm that Jacobi promotes a single doctrine of thinking, which works for both finite things and divine things. In light of this doctrine, we will see that he also advances a specific idea on the connection between his ethics – that includes a discourse on divine things – and his epistemology – that concerns itself with finite things.

To start unravelling the matter, it is necessary to say something more concerning the nature of thinking in general and, more specifically, the nature of the thinking that finds being. As Jacobi contends, the basic distinction between an object of science and a truly existing Wesen lies in the *certainty* of our cognition of the Wesen. It is the certainty of our cognition that reveals to us a Wesen and distinguishes it from an object of discursive thinking.[76] The same

A STUDY

analysis of the notion of certainty seems to provide the principle for verifying the soundness of certainty itself, because the notion of certainty grants the criterion for judging what is contrary to certainty: "I am saying that representations (*Vorstellungen*) can never make the actual present *as such*. They only contain the properties of the actual things, not the *actual itself*. The actual can no more be presented outside its actual perception *than consciousness can be presented outside consciousness, life outside life, or truth outside truth*. The perception of the actual and the feeling of truth, consciousness and life, are one and the same thing ... This truth seems to me to be of the greatest importance, and for this reason I entreated you so urgently just now to hold firm to the ground of your knowledge of it, which is the ground of the knowledge of certainty itself and the only source of it."[77]

The soundness of his notion of certainty arises from the problems concerning the mediation between subject and object that discursive thinking inevitably falls into. In fact, the notion of certainty does not draw its authority from an updated, improved conceptualization of the mediation between subject and object. Rather, Jacobi's notion of certainty introduces a wholly different epistemological scenario, according to which the actual – the true, real existing thing – is not different from the subject's certainty of it. For this reason, the actual never becomes an object of representation; it remains an element of what Jacobi calls "life."

If we bring what we said about the "living organism" into the new scenario opened up by certainty, we could try to rephrase the whole idea differently: certainty does not refer to representation or discursive thinking because the subject's life is precisely that certainty. The form of the subject's life is the same as the form of certainty. As a consequence, only by unearthing the form of the subject's life we will then be able to appreciate the revolution that Jacobi's notion of certainty imposes on epistemology. However, we can approach a clear grasp of this thesis only gradually, since a few clarifications about Jacobi's realism are crucial to unwind the notion of certainty.

If we consider this notion of certainty within the realm of finite things, we see his criticism of Hume's idealism at work. Ultimately, Jacobi agrees with Hume by rejecting a) that experience starts with a subjective representation of the object of experience and b) that the existence of outer objects is inferred from an impression that the subject would passively receive from the external world.

However, Jacobi rejects the general stance of Hume's skepticism because Jacobi argues that a subject would not be aware of himself without opposing himself to something distinct than himself. He concludes that "there must be something in the perception of the actual which is not in the mere representations, for otherwise the two could not be distinguished. But the distinction concerns directly *the actual*, and nothing else. Hence *the actual itself, the objectivity, can never be made present in the mere representation*."[78]

The problem is quite simple: once we reject both representations of experience and deductions from the subject's passivity,[79] we find ourselves in need of clarity about how we should understand certainty. Jacobi's proposal arises from, and is supported by, the subject's awareness of itself as both affecting and being affected by another thing. This awareness gives shape to the subject's form of certainty. As he states in *David Hume*: "You know ... that for our human consciousness (and let me add right away; for the consciousness of each and every finite being) it is necessary that besides the thing that does the sensing, there is also a real thing which is sensed. *We must distinguish ourselves from something.* Hence, two actual things outside one another, or duality. Whenever two created beings (the one outside the other) stand in such a relation to one another that the one has an effect in the other, there we have *an extended being*."[80] Rejecting both deduction and representation of the object inevitably results in the assumption of an immediate manifestation of the two beings.

In the supplement to the second edition of the dialogue *David Hume*, entitled *On Transcendental Idealism*, Jacobi identifies the systematic spirit of Kantian philosophy precisely in that assumption: things in themselves, while being necessary to knowledge, do not affect the subject and, consequently, do not establish any real mediation with the subject. It is thus necessary for them to have an immediate relationship with the subject.[81] However, this immediacy cannot be digested by transcendental philosophy, hence it generates an unbridgeable distance that makes it impossible to enter the Kantian system of reason. Since transcendental philosophy seems not designed for that immediacy, then Kant eventually drives his endeavour directly into the paramount problem of transcendental philosophy, which grows into the accusation of egoism or subjectivism. Therefore, in order to win back objectivity, Jacobi suggests that we should not focus on the impossible project of refining the notion of *mediation* that the activity of representation implies. Instead, we must altogether reject the idea that an object is conceived as a content of representation; we should rather aim attention at the principal assumption of knowledge in general and accept the immediacy of the subject-object dialectic. Put it simply, we could contend that this theoretical manoeuvre re-introduces the

A STUDY   25

ontology that epistemology necessarily presupposes. Since the impossibility of a defined mediation between subject and object makes it impossible to speak about a justified knowledge, Jacobi accepts the immediacy of the subject-object dialectic and lays the foundations to offer a different way of defining objectivity. He reimages the role played by the object: the object is just one of the two elements involved in a twofold "revelation" that includes the subject – the living organism – too. This evades the limits of transcendental idealism without falling victim to a naïve realism.[82]

In this regard, we can list four remarks that Jacobi deems fundamental for overcoming Kant's transcendental idealism. These remarks supposedly analyze Kant's theoretical philosophy to show its internal tensions. They will eventually define the real ontology of the subject-object dialectic.

1   It is clear that the so-called represented object is not the external object that would affect the subject.

2   The presupposition of an object, conceived as the synthesis of one's representations, is built by the understanding, and is defined as a synthetic unity of the manifold of intuition. This is called an object=X. This too is not the object that would affect the subject. Rather, it results from the transcendental activity of the subject.

3   The only object that would be untouched by the subjective structure of representation must be thought in the form of a noumenon, and that must remain wholly unknown. Therefore, this too cannot be the object that affects the subject, as the subjective structure of representation does not apply to it.

4   The act of implementing transcendental categories beyond the subject's experience compromises the system of idealism. It is evident, then, that transcendental idealism deals with a very problematic notion of sensibility, because it cannot allow the affection of the subject. A thorough modification of the notion of sensibility in a more conceptual sense presents itself to Jacobi as a necessary endeavour.

As said, Jacobi's attempt does not yield an upgrade to the apparatus of transcendental idealism, nor does it substantiate an evolution of the structure of sensibility in the direction of a more sophisticated structure of mediation; rather, it represents a theoretical development that fully assumes the analysis of the internal tensions of transcendental idealism in order to transcend it; the failure of a mediating process between subject and object is indeed accepted.

The resulting impossibility of treading on the path of transcendental idealism is summarized in his famous dictum: "*Without* the intermediary between one real thing and another ... I could not enter into the system" of the transcendental idealism, "but with it I could not stay within it."[83] Consequently, even Kant's vocabulary needs to be revised; Kant might have claimed the "relative objective validity" of his knowledge, and he might have even called it "objectivity," but in truth, his epistemology ignores existence, which is what is "*truly objective*."[84] This mystification of the true meaning of words such as *objectivity*, *sensibility*, and *reality* leads to Kant's clear "egoism," according to which "our entire cognition contains nothing" of what is "independent of our representations."[85] In the end, it is impossible for transcendental idealism to work.

But instead of improving the logic of the mediation between subject and object, Jacobi suggests that, since we cannot solve the problems that arise in respect to the subject-object relationship because any solution brings with itself the incongruous dismissal of the object (idealism) or of the subject (materialism), we then need to acknowledge that what is "intermediary" between subject and object is *not* a relation or a mediation.[86]

At this stage, it should become clear that the kind of operation that modern thinking provides bears witness to a contradiction: the very notion of relation cannot be used to define the two elements involved in knowledge without annihilating their respective identities and, therefore, without creating a system of knowledge without being. The ruinous power of relating and mediating intensifies when it is conceived as the constituent paradigm of reality, not some subordinate aspect; Spinoza's system is, in this sense, emblematic. Nevertheless, Jacobi does not hold Spinoza (or Leibniz) as an inconsistent philosopher. Quite the contrary; Jacobi looks at Spinoza (and Leibniz) as the epitome of the consistent philosopher, the one able to provide "knowledge" in terms of the conditions of possibility of things.[87] However, Jacobi is adamant in his search for the boundaries of explanations, hence for what is "unanalyzable," "immediate," and "simple." Only if this simplicity is granted, we will be able to defy the reach of Spinoza's system, surpass mere possibility, and land on the safe shores of existence.[88]

It is no surprise, says Jacobi, that the first crack in Spinoza's system can be noted in the *Ethics* parts fourth and fifth, whilst Spinoza deals with human conduct and, necessarily, freedom. There Spinoza fails to sustain the same sharp insight he showed in the first parts of the *Ethics* and becomes less cogent and conclusive. This proves even more Jacobi's point, because as soon as

A STUDY   27

Spinoza approaches the problem of human freedom and identity, he fails to combine it together with the system that expounds the *causa sui*. The specific unity and autonomy of the human being is eventually overlooked.

Contrary to Spinoza, Jacobi intends to approach properly unity and autonomy by way of building a theory of the living being that he finds in Leibniz, who was also the one able to meet and amend the many inconsistencies of Spinoza's philosophy.[89] The principle according to which "life is the *principle of perception*" resonates in different forms in all Jacobi's writings and surfaces as he contends that "the *I* and the *Thou*, the internal consciousness and the external object, must be present both at once in the soul even in the most primordial and simple of perceptions."

Contrary to what may appear, the principle of the I-Thou simultaneity does not inhibit the unity of the human being, rather it promotes it. Leibniz must be deemed responsible for offering Jacobi a theoretical platform upon which to build the connection that leads from *life* and *perception* to *unity* of being and, eventually, *freedom*. "A true substance, such as an animal, is composed of an immaterial soul, and of an organic body; and it is the composite of these two that we call *unum-per-se*." The autonomous unity of the *unum-per-se* (as opposed to the unum through others) is the basis for perception as it consists in the faculty to resist against others.[90] This idea of resistance – that lies at the basis of the *Gefühl* that human beings have of finite things – expresses figuratively the contact between two mutually impenetrable beings, which can only interact through "action and reaction."

The straight line of continuity between principle of perception, notion of living organism, and autonomy of being stretches further out as Jacobi uses it to substantiate the impossibility for the human being to be described according to the laws of the system. Those laws – which only elaborates possibility over possibility – disregard the very notion of *unum-per-se*: "the *possibility* of absolutely autonomous activity cannot be known." In fact, as we consider possibilities, we are bound to the consideration of an *unum* through others, hence actuality, the *unum-per-se*, disappears into the systematic whole.[91] Conversely, once we dismiss the systematic approach to reality on account of its internal frictions, we win back the capacity to have knowledge of existence in the form of the dynamic of autonomous activity: only the "*actuality*" of absolute autonomous activity "can be known ... for it is immediately displayed in consciousness, and is demonstrated by the deed."[92]

V An Active Unum

We can rephrase what we have said so far in different terms to shed light on some different aspects of Jacobi's philosophy. We have seen that the principle of perception provides the basis to elaborate a progressively more precise definition of the autonomy of the *unum*, which eventually builds up to the proper definition of human being. At a first look the principle of perception seems to allude to epistemology only. It then becomes clear that the term "principle" does not allude to a faculty, or a proposition, but to the underlying notion that perception brings forth: the notion of the *unum-per-se*. This theory just states that the opposition between true substances must be granted to give knowledge an objective meaning. Through that theory, Jacobi adverts to the ultimate condition for the determination of the existence – the actuality – of the I and its Thou. In fact, the principle of perception allows the notion of the living being to enter the panorama of rationality without falling into a dangerously unclear theory about life. Instead, Jacobi sees the principle of life – the paradigm of all knowledge – as uniform with the principle of perception, as they both (life and perception) are based upon the *I-Thou* dialectic.[93]

In the end, as a reaction against Spinoza's philosophy, Jacobi intends to define a thinking that should present how things are independent of the subject's mind and why they must be singular entities confronted by a living being. His doctrine of *finding* aims at achieving both goals.

It has been shown that, if we assume that relations are all we can know of a thing, then "all individual things mutually presuppose one another, and refer to one another, so that none of them can either be or be thought of without the rest, or the rest without it."[94] The final outcome of this system consists in a total annihilation of content: mediation produces just an "empty weaving of its weaving" so that we can have "*all*," but ultimately, we do not have "*one*" or even "*something*."[95] Therefore, Jacobi seems to suggest, if we want our thinking to grasp reality, the actual, then we need to revise the notion of thinking at the outset and, to do so, we inevitably must start from our understanding of the relation between subject and object. This reform will eventually grow into the blueprint for the principle of individuation that modern philosophy lacks.

Yet, this revision can only be achieved by assuming that experience mainly consists of the fact that subject and object have an effect on each other. This point develops out of a special theory of the living, or, more precisely, a theory of an active living being, which aims at opposing the thesis that stipulates that

A STUDY

the existence of reality can be abstracted from the outside world or established on a subjective structure. The living being is in fact a self-activity: "I call *instinct* the energy which originally, without regard to not yet experienced pleasure and pain, determines the mode of self-activity, with which every species of living nature must be thought of as beginning and independently continuing the action of its own distinct existence."[96]

Notoriously, to give shape to his theory of action, Jacobi starts formulating a rectification of the notion of cause by cleansing it of any reference to the notion of ground. In this way, the cause of an event is not the ground of the possibility of that event. As he states in the Beylage VII of the second edition of the *Spinoza Letters*: "I have ... sufficiently established that, so far as the concept of cause is distinguished from that of ground, it is a *concept of experience* which we owe to the consciousness of our own causality and passivity, and cannot be derived from the merely idealistic concept of ground any more than it can be resolved into it."[97] The immediacy that ties an action to its effect is the pillar around which the relationship between subject and object starts taking shape.

This step also shows what Jacobi meant when he stressed that the living being is the principle of all cognition. We must interpret this remark from a distinct viewpoint. In fact, as stated above, Jacobi's epistemology does not proclaim to be the achievement of a *logos* of an objective reality independent of the subject. The theory of action of a living organism brings forth reality, thus Jacobi's notion of reality refers only to the reality of a living organism. Indeed, following Jacobi's footsteps, we may even challenge the idea of a reality-in-general. We could say that the idea of a reality-in-general is the product of the conditions of possibility of any reality, which presents itself in general terms, hence without being. But this missing part – the being – is not irrelevant to the definition of what reality is; it rather affects the definition of reality. If we take into account the notion of reality-in-general we need to acknowledge that it is not equal to the set of actual configuration of reality. The reality-in-general rather alludes to a reality that, in view of its own very constitution, would disregard existence altogether and, by doing so, would dismiss the paradigm that gives it shape.

The *Divine Things* will help us elaborate this thesis in detail, as it will present the definition and relevance of the living being's original action. We cannot detail the overall arc of Jacobi's criticism of the notion of ground – and of reality-in-general – as it would distract our attention to the *Divine Things*, but we may understand Jacobi's *pars destruens* against transcendental idealism by reviewing his *pars construens*, which he develops by following in Spinoza's footsteps. The *pars construens* will be presented in the following paragraphs and make more explicit the special relationship between subject and object. It will reveal one fundamental element in Jacobi's theory of action and lead us toward the definition of Wesen.

VI Glaube

At the dawn of modern era, the debate on the concept of causality took place when mechanical explanations failed to define causal transactions. For his part, Jacobi, while accepting Hume's "famous doubt about the reliability of the inferences that we normally draw from a necessary combination of cause and effect,"[98] interprets the transactions between a subject and the world *de facto* by accepting Spinoza's doctrine; this dictated a pure "*Scheidung*" without a "*Trennung*" between the two realms.[99] In simpler terms, Jacobi contends that the mind is not subject to any causal mediation with the world, because causal mediation cannot explain the fact that the mind has an image of the world. Instead, the peculiar transaction between mind and body arises immediately. It is thus not a transaction in the usual meaning of the term. This transaction rather assumes the contours of a "faith" (Glaube) which provides the alignment of a) the subject's idea about a specific thing, b) the existing thing, and c) the subject's consciousness of that thing that presents itself as a phenomenon in front of the subject.[100] The parallelism between the subject's mind and the extended world is enacted by Glaube and provides the answer to the problems that made Hume embrace a skeptical stance. But there is more to this Glaube.

Glaube alludes to something that connects with the notion of living organism that we have mentioned above. As said, Jacobi maintains that the certainty about a thing includes the fact that we know ourselves as subjects who know a thing outside of us. As the subject knows of the existence of a thing, the subject also knows that that thing is different than him. Thus, the subject assumes his own existence as opposed to the existence of the object. As the theory about the living organism has showed, any simple act of knowing eventually evinces a) the being of the subject, b) the being of a thing outside of the subject, and c) the subject's consciousness of the fact that that thing is a being-outside-of-the-subject. Jacobi's parallelism is indeed a thesis that involves a conscious act, i.e., a judgment that expresses the full content of Glaube.

Furthermore, Glaube does not merely represent immediate certainty. It also involves the representation that grounds a fundamental, mutual dependency.

A STUDY   31

In fact, Glaube grounds the mutual dependency of self-consciousness and consciousness, namely my consciousness of myself as a knower and my consciousness of the something that I know. In this sense, Jacobi assumes that I have knowledge of myself only inasmuch as I have knowledge of something that is opposed to me. But he also states that this mutual dependency consists of the subject having knowledge about himself knowing this mutual dependency. This last step is an important acquisition that helps define certainty. It shows that certainty is a conscious experience of the I.

According to this general picture, Jacobi's notion of knowledge does not include a description of the categories that can be used to describe an object. Instead, the subject-object relation merely involves the assumption of the existence of both. And this assumption – which represents the core of Jacobi's theory of knowledge – does not impact the content of the subject's experience.[101] This idea can be expressed in more radical terms: Jacobi does not describe the object of knowledge according to a table of categories; his epistemology is focused in describing the way that we must think of the manifestation of the existing reality. Although the subject performs a self-conscious judgment that reveals the being of both subject and object, the subject's Glaube does not dictate any description of the content manifested. Therefore, we could conclude that Jacobi's epistemology seems to ripen in nothing more than ontology.

Thus, Jacobi's Glaube is at the centre of a "twofold revelation": this revelation involves the subject on the one side, and a "thing" on the other side. Yet the only aspect that concerns the subject's thinking of the object is the existence of the object. This may look like a great limit of Jacobi's theory of knowledge; it rather constitutes the primary stumbling stone of modern epistemology and the first cornerstone required for a distinct and new perspective on our thinking. As a consequence, a different constellation of questions rises. Such a constellation draws on the recognition that our thinking seems to be assigned one task only; the revelation of being.[102]

Since this revelation does not result from our subjective apprehension or representation of external objects, since Wesen is not the source of affection of the subject – because there is no mediation between the subject and the object as far as their being is concerned – then how do we articulate the being that Wesen is? And how does this framework affect the definition of the divine things?

VII *Der Beruf der Philosophie*

The answer to the first question requires an investigation into the mission or Beruf of philosophy. Now that Jacobi's critical stance has cleared the way toward a definition of the genuine content of our immediate knowledge, we can determine the specifics of a thinking that unveils such a content. If our perception of the object's being is immediate, how do we conceive of this immediacy? Further: how do we immediately conceive of being?

In this context the notion of immediacy does not denote a sudden blaze of our understanding, a flash in conception. Sudden realization is, in the end, the opposite of knowing. Instead, Jacobi's notion of immediacy denotes a distinct way of knowing as it explicitly works alongside with discursive knowledge. More properly, Jacobi's notion of immediacy refers to a distinct way of defining experience as such. One could contend that immediacy is the way in which our thinking amends our knowledge by brining within our view what has always been before our eyes but never identified. As it happens, immediacy does not introduce new objects within our scope; it clarifies our understanding of our own vision.

Within this framework of intentions, Jacobi seems to confirm his alliance with J.G. Hamann on the equation between immediate revelation and experience,[103] but only to the extent that the "*erfahren*" of being implies an analytical definition thereof. In fact, Jacobi argues that the content of immediate knowledge is defined by means of an analysis of what our thinking holds true in any act of knowing. This may sound paradoxical, but Jacobi's notion of "erfahren" introduces us to an analytical clarification of the necessity and universality of the immediate source of discursive knowledge, which is not defined by discursive knowledge itself. In order to look into what lies behind discursive knowledge, Jacobi actually employs in the *Divine Things* the same method that he implemented in the *Spinoza Letters* and *David Hume* as he intended to unearth the content of a conceptual definition of being.[104]

Although *David Hume* can be seen as a treatise in the epistemology of the physical world, we may argue that it presents the method that we must use to investigate the premises of knowledge in general, finite as well as divine. The supposed universality of his method results from Jacobi's implementation, in the context of finite things, of a method that Kant used in the context of divine things, i.e., in ethics and religion. We could therefore conclude not only that in Jacobi's eyes the method is universal, but that *ethics* and *religion* appear to give the blueprint of our apprehension of all things, finite and divine. In the

A STUDY   33

end, for Jacobi, Kant's remarks on ethics and religion provide the ground to our epistemology, because they chiefly clarify the structure of our ontology.[105]

By following in Jacobi's footsteps, we can start defining his approach in respect to a conceptual definition of being by means of these two Kantian texts that he mentions in the *David Hume* and uses to build his ontology. The first is the essay that Kant submitted on the occasion of the famous *Preisfrage* at the Berlin Academy of Sciences (which was announced in 1761 and published in 1763): *Untersuchung über die Deutlichkeit der Grundsätze der natürlichen Theologie und der Moral* (1764). The second text is *Der einzig mögliche Beweisgrund zu einer Demonstration des Daseins Gottes* (1763).

In the 1764 essay, Kant, showed how metaphysics requires a specific method to certify its independence from mathematics. In contrast to mathematics, Kant observes that metaphysics proceeds via analysis: it performs a progressive scrutiny of the immediate premises of our knowledge and, by so doing, reveals the nature of those premises. The challenging part of this analysis consists in the nature of those premises: they are in fact always "given" to our thinking and never constructed by it.[106]

Contrary to mathematics, metaphysics deals with concepts that are not built by our intelligence. Rather, they consist in the simplest ideas that usually constitute the background of our understanding of reality. We could summarize by saying that the starting point of metaphysics coincides with its target: metaphysics is a science that only aims at defining its object. This can be seen with typical metaphysical questions, such as "what is being?" or "what is time?" This could leave the impression that metaphysics seems to cover a very short stretch: it does not progress beyond the clarification of what, for the other sciences, represents just a premise. Moreover, it may look like metaphysics is structurally unsound because it relies solely on the power of analysis.

One might get a similar impression while reading the *Divine Things*. The method that Jacobi implements is actually quite close to that of Kantian (precritical) metaphysics. Underneath the progressive structure of the *Divine Things* one can perceive the ambulatory nature of Jacobi's thinking, and yet the text often appears deprived of a clear theoretical development. It dwells, and keeps dwelling, in the very place where ethics and religion begin: the definition of being.

For these reasons, Jacobi's philosophy could be called a metaphysics: it does not evolve into a *doctrine* of divine being but rather manifests a way to *see* divine being. We have already seen that Jacobi claims this connection to metaphysics with reference to the pace of all his investigations. Surely, this holds true if we consider the *Divine Things*: the text asks questions that are bound to reveal what is embedded in our "heart" and needs to be unveiled.[107] Therefore, if the presupposition of cognition is what is at stake in all of Jacobi's inquiries, then in the case of the *Divine Things* Jacobi attempts at an unveiling of the presuppositions of our ethical and religious life following the same method. It does not go beyond that task.[108]

Moreover, Kant himself hinted at the universality and limits of this method, as he states that in metaphysics it is fundamental to start with "inner experience." This is an "immediate and self-evident inner consciousness" that prompts us to "seek out those characteristic marks which are certainly to be found in the concept of *any general property*."[109] However, metaphysics fails to provide the full architecture of notions concerning an object. It nevertheless achieves certainty concerning the characteristic marks of the object. In short, when we speak of certainty, then we refer to certainty of being. We do not refer to certainty of representation. From that specific kind of certainty, metaphysics eventually infers a reasonable description of the being of the object.

Jacobi follows this pathway in the *David Hume* as well as in the *Divine Things*; in truth, the *David Hume* and the *Divine Things* are not simply two treatises in two distinct fields. They are steppingstones toward a more general idea of reality. Hence, following Kant's approach, the *Divine Things* uncovers the principle of existence by delving deeper into the problem of all religion and ethics; something that Jacobi in the *David Hume* had only started to unravel with the help of (pre-critical) Kant's insight into religion and ethics. This will become more apparent as we continue to analyze the *Divine Things*.

We will also see that Jacobi neither provides a doctrine of God nor a doctrine of the human soul; rather, he inaugurates a metaphysical *logos* about their ground. In fact, metaphysics merely takes the first radical steps in the description of being, it does not bear the labour of describing a complex doctrinal code of belief. Jacobi's doctrines of God and soul remain obscure to some degree. Nevertheless, he can define how those few elements that he actually provides have an impact upon reality in general and the value of inner life in particular. We may thus start to understand how the investigation that aims at our "heart" teaches us how to investigate the revelation of the world in general and, above all, how to identify its existence. More will be said about the connection between the inner experience of certainty and the form of the world in the following sections.

The second text that Jacobi alludes to, *Der einzig mögliche Beweisgrund zu einer Demonstration des Daseins Gottes*, gives us more information about the

A STUDY   35

object that metaphysics and the *Divine Things* share. It focuses on the notion of being (or existence) in contrast to possibility. Famously, Kant demonstrates what existence is by subtracting from its concept all that it is not.[110] First, existence is not listed among the predicates that define an individual thing; for instance, we may know the definition of a thing by means of all the predicates that give to it a profile, but such a profile does not necessitate that that thing exists.[111] Second, existence is not the "copula" of a judgment; a copula describes the action of relating something (like a characteristic mark) to the subject of the judgment, but existence is not a relation – like the former thesis shows – because a non-existing thing is still describable. Moreover, existence is a "simple" concept; it does not have a characteristic mark and it cannot be attributed a predicate, hence it is (almost) not analyzable.

In the end, existence is neither the predicate, nor the copula, nor the subject of a judgment. In truth, this last argument relates and looks similar to the former, but it presents a new thesis concerning existence. This thesis explains the difference between existence and the copula: while the copula creates a relation, existence does not perform such an activity. Existence is not an activity that dictates a relation among the elements of a judgment. The rationale seems to be the following: since our understanding usually works by creating relations and by making them explicit in a judgment, we could claim that existence does not add anything to knowledge. Furthermore, we could state that existence is invisible to our understanding because existence falls outside the scope of our faculty of relating.[112] This does not mean that existence is an obscure matter that ultimately falls beyond our grasp. This simply means that existence demands both a special field of knowledge and a distinct faculty. In fact, we cannot dismiss the notion of existence from our knowledge of the world, because it makes a difference in our description of it.

Furthermore, if we assume that existence does not posit the relationship between possible things and their predicates, then existence must tell us something only about the things themselves. As a consequence, existence must be a special concept that defines the *way* a thing is posited. In fact, an existing thing is something more than the same thing conceived merely as possible.[113]

To understand what this last point really means, Kant introduces a fourth fundamental thesis: "if all existence is cancelled, then nothing is posited absolutely; all possibility completely disappears."[114] We can start analyzing this thesis by concurring with Kant when he admits that there is no contradiction in cancelling all existence. It can be done because, if it is true that the principle of non-contradiction limits existence (a contradiction cannot exist), it is also true that the principle of non-contradiction does not give rise to existence. All possible things fall under the principle of non-contradiction, but the principle of non-contradiction does not discriminate between the possible and the actual. This means that the relation between subject and predicate (i.e., when the principle of non-contradiction is granted) does not affect the way something is given. As we have seen before, the relation between a subject and its predicates does not inform us of whether the subject is merely possible or actually exists, because the principle of non-contradiction concerns merely the "copula" that establishes a relation of "agreement" between subject and predicate. At this point, Kant observes that we fall into conflict with ourselves if we claim that a possibility is given and, at the same time, deny existence in general. This happens, Kant claims, because possibility is given only in relation to existence.

To comprehend why possibility is given only in relation to existence, and what this relation means, we must first remember that like any other relation, the relation connecting possibility and existence is generally ruled by the principle of non-contradiction. But beyond this formal parameter, the connection between possibility and existence is not something that we can arbitrarily build under that parameter, analogously to the way we produce new laws in mathematics. The relationship between existence and possibility cannot result from the exercise of our intelligence; it must rather be something that stays behind the intervention of our thinking.

This evinces the real task of metaphysics, which consists in conceiving the connection of thinking with what is beyond the active production of thinking. In this case, our task in metaphysics consists in defining the relationship between existence and possibility. The solution to this problem is provided by an analysis of the only thing that is known in the relation between existence and possibility. Clearly, this cannot be existence, because existence is what lies beyond our discursive thinking; hence, beyond *relations*. Therefore, we need to analyze the notion of possibility, which represents the proper object of discursive thinking. We will then be able to define the notion of existence through the analysis of the relation that possibility has with it.

Kant suggests that we turn our attention to the fact that any possibility is a "*datum*" that, while being merely possible, is ultimately the result of a selection from what exists.[115] This can be conveyed when we consider the simplest elements of reality, which constitute the basis for any possibility. For instance, when we consider the notion of pure space – which is one of the simplest concepts, deprived of any relation – the only way for it to be still *meaningful* for

A STUDY   37

our thinking is by considering the way in which this simplest element is given to us. It is given by remodelling the elements of what exists. The notion of pure space is not a construction of our thinking; it is given to our thinking as a basis to constitute meaningful possibilities. On the one hand, pure space is given to our thinking; on the other hand, spatial possibilities result from the creative process of our thinking on the basis of that given.

At the same time, pure space is a distinct kind of presupposition of our thinking; it is not a formal parameter. In other words, pure space is given differently than is the principle of non-contradiction. The difference lies in the fact that pure space is not a relation. This happens for each elemental *"datum"* that represents a constitutive part of more complex concepts. This kind of presuppositions has to relate to something that our thinking receives as immediately given. At the same time, this presupposition does not have to be a mere formal parameter that connects possibilities. In this context we claim that pure space retains a meaning even though it does not have predicates.

Leaving aside the example of space, we can go back to the most basic of these concepts, which is existence. With regard to our thinking, existence is the absolutely given by virtue of the meaning that any thought must bear. In the end, following Kant's argument, we must claim that possibility just relates to a horizon of meaning that existence has previously established.[116] The relation between existence and possibility is therefore the only relation that stands beyond the horizon of possibility and constitutes the basis of meaning. From this point on, Kant's argument proceeds toward the notion of "absolutely necessary existence," but for the sake of interpreting Jacobi's text, we have already acquired what we needed.

We can indeed see that the relation between existence and thinking is something that, though still formally under the rule of the principle of non-contradiction, stretches beyond the formal connection between predicates and subject. It exceeds the perimeter of possibility as such, and steps onto the field of *meaning*. Existence shows itself as a relation that refers to the capacity to think something that is formally given, and thus it connects our thinking to a specific relation.

At the same time though, it is not the brainchild of our understanding; it is interesting to note that, if we think of mere possibilities (for instance, possible worlds), but reject the thesis according to which existence is the ground of possibility, we end up thinking of mere absurdities. In other terms, by rejecting the basis that existence provides, we leave the plane of meaning. Existence, in other words, is what we need if we want to think, and elaborate, every possible idea that is meaningful to us. Existence provides the absolute parameter of a meaningful intellectual horizon, but it is not given by means of a necessary relation. It can be said that existence is revealed because it precedes our capacity to elaborate any content, because existence grounds content. As mentioned above, Kant concludes: "if all existence is cancelled, then nothing is posited absolutely, nothing at all is given, there is no material element for anything which can be thought; all possibility completely disappears."[117]

The idea of existence representing the necessary presupposition of all possibility of thinking is a seed that Jacobi develops into a broader conception. The analysis of the presupposition of meaning for any scientific knowledge brings Jacobi to what he calls the "heart" of human being. There lies the faculty of connecting our thinking to what we hold true. One may conclude that on the one side, one possesses the freedom arbitrarily to represent any possible object; however, on the other side, rational thinking requires an unconditional *through which* everything must be thought.[118] That *through which*, that is existence, is the cradle of *meaning*.

Jacobi, in the context of the *David Hume*, understands that the real topic of Kant's *Beweisgrund* is not God's existence in the first place, but the very notion of existence; that *through which* our thinking thinks meaningfully. Therefore, he sheds light to the metaphysical problems that the notion of existence *per se* brings forth. The ultimate result is a theory according to which existence cannot be represented; rather, existence lies at the basis of the possibility of the representation of experience.

We can even state that existence does not appear in the representation of experience, but only in the analysis of it. With Kant's help, one can appreciate the Jacobian idea of the "business of philosophy" which aims at "analyz[ing] concepts which are given in a confused fashion, and to render them complete and determinate (*ausführlich und bestimmt*)."[119] According to this framework, Jacobi's analytical thinking points to make clear "the fundamental principle of our cognition," just as the pre-critical Kantian metaphysics did.[120]

As we now see in all its breadth, Jacobi's philosophy does not abstract existence from experience: his analytical investigation reveals the *through which* (or *durch*) that existence is, which must not be conceived as a *from which* (or *aus*). Metaphysics does not imply an abstraction from physics. Against the latter approach – which Jacobi identifies with Aristotle's philosophy – Jacobi advocates that a) the unconditional is not conditioned by its relation to the conditional, and b) the absolute is not the finite deprived of limits, because such an absolute would result in chaos. Instead, metaphysics provides an

A STUDY   39

analytical theory of existence according to which existence is conceived as the unconditioned.[121]

We will return to the latter question concerning the unconditioned when in the *Divine Things* Jacobi will deal with Schelling's philosophy of identity. For now, it is important to stress that existence represents the absolute unconditional that is accomplished by rejecting the deceptive aspiration of abstracting it from the conditional. This topic proves essential in Jacobi's essay *Über das Unternehmen des Kriticismus, die Vernunft zu Verstande zu bringen, und der Philosophie überhaupt eine neue Absicht zu geben*, which represents together with *Jacobi to Fichte* the second source that Jacobi draws from to draft the philosophical outline of the *Divine Things*.

After having investigated some of the topics that the *Jacobi to Fichte* shares with the *Divine Things*, we can now approach a different – though consequent – set of issues that arise from Jacobi's metaphysical approach to existence. This will bring us a step closer to the definition of the existence of the divine things.

Yet let us first stress one point that will help us define the connection between finite and divine things. We have seen that abstraction is always posited by relations: its content results from an intellectual operation that never goes beyond thinking. The genuine unconditional is instead given to knowledge by means of a kind of "intuition" that can either be the intuition of sense or the intuition of reason.[122] Sense and reason are two instances of the same faculty of acquiring what is presupposed, although they differ in the content of the specific unconditional being that they acquire. This difference notwithstanding, the existence of the two kinds of objects possesses the same "authority" – another term that Jacobi employs. They require, in other words, the same philosophical exercise to be identified. This can easily be proven by referring to the metaphysical imprint that Kant's essays give to the *conceptual content* of both sensible and supersensible things; they both exist. As stated above, Jacobi's use of Kant's ethical and religious writings in the context of the epistemology of finite things stresses that a certain metaphysical approach is necessary to deal with finite things too.

Moreover, if we consider that the definition of a subject's consciousness and self-consciousness results from the general definition of the existence of objects (because an "I" is defined only in relation to a "Thou"), then the same metaphysical form falls onto the subject as well. Furthermore, assuming the dialectic between the I and its object, we can maintain that the inner – religious and ethical – I is not less existent than the physical I, because the status of its existence is guaranteed by the same conceptual explanation. They only differ in terms of the activity that they perform. Or, better said, they differ in the nature of the inter*action* that their existence produces. The consciousness and self-consciousness of the religious and ethical I interacts through the metaphysical preconditions of its personality, as much as the physical I interacts through the metaphysical preconditions of its body.

The apparent discrepancy between two distinct horizons will eventually be dissipated by Jacobi's *theism*. The latter represents the final doctrine expounded in the *Divine Things* and mitigates the difference between the finite and the divine, senses and reason, body and personality. As we will see, Jacobi's theism describes how the personality of a free agent plugs into the physical cosmic order as created by an intelligent God. This connection implies the divine meaning of the concrete life of a person by giving factual and sensible identity to the moral autonomy of the person.

Following the perspective that Jacobi's theism opens, one may foresee how Jacobi is brought to believe that the Kantian distinction between the phenomenal and noumenal worlds would eventually collapse.

VIII Freedom

We have proposed an analysis of the historical and philosophical background that establishes the kinship between the *Divine Things* and the *Jacobi to Fichte*, together with some other related texts. Thus, we may now introduce a few remarks concerning the second text that Jacobi deems congruent with the *Divine Things, On the Undertaking of Critique to Reduce Reason to Understanding* (1802). If the former essay has proven critical to introducing and profiling Jacobi's metaphysical approach to the notion of being and the metaphysical vocation of philosophy, then the latter will provide the basic elements necessary to understanding the specific ethical and religious themes upon which the *Divine Things* elaborates.

In this context, Jacobi's rejection of Kant's distinction between moral and theoretical reason implies a more general interpretation of the notion of divinity. By deeming that distinction unsound, Jacobi will have to demonstrate the compatibility between the two dimensions without exposing himself to the problems afflicting Kant's philosophy. In fact, Jacobi's theism begins to take its proper shape as soon as he advances that the ideas of God, immortality of the soul, and freedom cannot be held true if theoretical reason regards them as unattainable or merely subjective. Instead, Jacobi claims, knowledge and

A STUDY   41

ethics must be in harmony, given that a proper dialectic between the living subject – the agent – and its world is established.[123]

In Jacobi's view, Kant's account of practical reason presents consequential problems that develop out of the subjective perspective of Kantian theoretical reason. This perspective turns religious and ethical objects – the postulates of practical reason – into empty concepts that are not objective, let alone real. These objects can surely be employed by the moral law, but they do not involve the existing, actual true.

Jacobi, in some sense, would agree with the opening remark that Kant wrote at the beginning of the *Critique of Pure Reason* according to which: "Human reason has the peculiar fate in one species of its cognitions that it is burdened with questions which it cannot dismiss, since they are given to it as problems by the nature of reason itself, but which it also cannot answer, since they transcend every capacity of human reason."[124] Reason is burdened with questions that are essentially *rational*. It concerns itself with those (divine) things that are at the basis of *existence*. But to answer these questions and achieve certainty about God, the immortality of the soul, and freedom, reason should transcend the jurisdiction of the understanding and prove to be a wholly different faculty. Only by doing so our reality remains rational.

Jacobi stresses that, while accepting the difference between reason and understanding, Kant clearly commits a fundamental mistake: he made of the limits of "experience" that the understanding provides those same limits under which the "metaphysics" of reason is assessed.[125] It is therefore clear that the moment Kant takes his first steps into transcendental investigations, reason's questions are tamed by the use of the understanding, which exercises its authority to dismiss the question concerning the real existence of the postulates.

The authority of the understanding in transcendental philosophy can be glimpsed as soon as we recognize that Kant's practical reason deals with its unconditional objects as if they were just an extension of the conditional.[126] In the Kantian framework, reason is therefore an ancillary authority under the restrictions that the understanding enacts, so that its necessary postulates are merely subjective functions with no real content. In Jacobi's opinion, Kant's intention is to save the objectivity of the postulates of practical reason by differentiating them from theoretical objects, protecting its postulates from the charge of being mere subjective creations. But Kant eventually fails, so Jacobi argues, because according to his account of practical reason he cannot but confirm the priority of the understanding over reason and therefore build the ideas of God, the immortality of the soul, and freedom following what the system of transcendental philosophy is based upon: an egoism that disregards what the understanding considers impossible to know. Hence those postulates become empty of reality. Jacobi even implies that they are toxic to proper metaphysical thinking because they represent an unconditioned that is defined according to the conditioned. The infinite becomes just the finite deprived of its limits.[127]

This represents the general framework of Jacobi's criticism of Kant's practical reason. But Jacobi goes even further. The "things" that Kant's practical reason holds true belong to two different groupings. On the one side, practical reason posits *freedom* as the condition of the moral law. On the other side, practical reason needs to posit the conditions for the necessary object of a will to be determined by the moral law. Hence reason needs to assume the *immortality* of the soul and the existence of *God*. Therefore, if we assume Kant's perspective on the postulates of practical reason, we must conclude that all postulates do not refer to existing objects per se. Admittedly, they are necessary presuppositions of reason's need to comply with the moral law. They are either conditions of the implementation of the moral law (freedom) or conditions of the connection between the moral law and human will (the immortality of the soul and the existence of God).[128]

Everything – stresses Jacobi – revolves around the assumption that the moral law – being a fact of reason – imposes the purely (abstract) universal identity of the free agent and reveals the postulates for what they are, i.e., presuppositions; the reality of which must remain unknown and the definition of which is constructed on the basis of the conditioned.

Eventually, practical reason shows itself to be "barren, desolate and empty."[129] The utter "void" that the moral law generates promotes the "*nothing, the absolutely indeterminate*" that has no existence whatsoever. Even the agent, the singular bearer of the moral law, is referred to only by means of the moral law; the agent reveals itself as an instance of the moral law, so that its individuality disappears.[130] As a consequence, one may easily acknowledge that the ethical and religious objectivity that a subjective structure of thinking provides will contrast with actual existence. Terms such as objectivity or universality become ambiguous, for they just translate subjective outcomes. This amounts to Kant calling "something" what in reality is "nothing." From Jacobi's standpoint, the entire architecture of practical reason boils down to an abstract intellectualism that may well be called nihilism.[131]

A STUDY   43

Notwithstanding his critical remarks, Jacobi admits that Kant's practical reason manifests the original metaphysical disposition of humanity: it makes human beings ask questions about the unconditioned, even though Kant himself deems them unanswerable.[132] In truth, those rational questions need to be scrutinized. They appear unanswerable only if we assume that the quality of their objects, i.e., the unconditioned, is achieved by abstracting from the perimeter of the conditioned, which is set by the understanding. This fatal manoeuvre prevents the unconditioned from being properly determined. Jacobi would thus claim that, once the unconditioned is properly recognized as something that remains unknown under the framework of the understanding, the unconditioned can and must then be determined as something actual and true, hence beyond the horizon of the conditioned.

Jacobi observes that Kant's basic mistake consists in the fact that, in truth, those postulates are not objects of reason, for they derive from a categorical extension of the conditioned *as infinitum*.[133] Let us take for instance the postulate of the existence of a creator God. Kant explains the context within which this arises:

> in the preceding analysis the moral law led to a practical task that is set by pure reason alone and without the aid of any sensible incentives, namely that of the necessary completeness of the first and principal part of the highest good, **morality**; and, since this can be fully accomplished only in an eternity, it led to the postulate of *immortality*. The same law must also lead to the possibility of the second element of the highest good, namely **happiness** proportioned to that morality, and must do so as disinterestedly as before, solely from impartial reason; in other words, it must lead to the supposition of the existence of a cause adequate to this effect, that is, it must postulate the *existence of God* as belonging necessarily to the possibility of the highest good (which object of our will is necessarily connected with the moral lawgiving of pure reason).[134]

According to Kant, the highest good is attainable only if we assume a proportion between morality and happiness. This proportion is granted only by the existence of a God conceived as a ruler that is "morally perfect" and "all-powerful."[135] At first, it seems that the existence of God is a postulate that serves the purpose of harmonizing the natural order – which disregards freedom – with the moral order of reality – which grants freedom.[136] But Jacobi stresses that the existence of God serves also the purpose of harmonizing human will with the moral law.[137] More properly: if we assume, as Kant does, that there is a discrepancy between natural disposition and virtue, then that discrepancy cannot be solved within the horizon that the understanding dictates. In fact, the understanding admits the objectivity of the order of nature in contrast to the subjectivity of the postulate of freedom. And this discrepancy cannot be bridged.[138] For this reason, to win back the will for freedom, the architecture of the highest good must be upheld by postulating the existence of God which, together with the postulate concerning the immortality of the soul, allows the object of the will to be determined by the moral law. Kant, in other words, tries to disregard what he has established with the understanding by giving authority to reason; but this happens only under a subjective point of view. This strategy – as we have seen above – is thus not only deprived of any actual value, but it works only under the assumption that objective reality is granted by the understanding alone.

Moreover, the same strategy reveals that Kant's ethics is not as autarchic as it has been deemed to be. As Jacobi confirms in the *Divine Things*, the lack of autarchy in Kant's notion of virtue is further manifested by the admission that the fulfillment of the moral law is tied to the sentiment of duty. In fact, the good deed is not done for the reality that it manifests, but only as a reflection of an abstract aspiration that needs to be fulfilled in a plane of reality that, in truth, is deemed merely subjective.[139] The ideality of Kantian moral virtue mirrors that of the postulates, which are built to rectify the assumed finitude of a subject involved in moral action. To Jacobi this appears to be quite the opposite of an autarchic ethics, which should be based on the concrete identity of the subject. Therefore, if we assume the Kantian practical framework, virtue neither expresses the objective order of reality nor is it desirable for its own sake, because virtue does not pay off in view of its exercise only.[140]

Contrary to Kant, Jacobi's notion of virtue is based on the true existence that the free agent executes. The real free agent exercises an authority over nature, thus manifesting and validating the reality that the subject and the world substantiate.[141]

Notwithstanding this criticism though, Jacobi acknowledges that Kant successfully demonstrated that the unconditioned cannot be known from the conditioned.[142] Kant's *summum ius* consists in the exclusion of the postulates of practical reason from the realm of demonstrative science; this proves that Kant approves a noetic apprehension of the ideas of freedom, immortality of the soul and God.[143] Kant admits the impossibility of a justi-

A STUDY 45

fied knowledge of these ideas. Yet this – in Kant's opinion – jeopardizes the objectivity of the postulates. Hence, Jacobi admits, Kant is prone to agree with an "immediate cognition" of those ideas, though he also rejects the appropriateness of that knowledge.[144]

In truth, Jacobi sees himself in a conceptual affinity with the noetic character of Kant's practical reason: in the panorama of modern thinking, Kant alone (with Jacobi) recognizes that the postulates are not demonstrable, and he (again, in agreement with Jacobi) also deems them to be the true objects of philosophy.[145] Kant's spirit is led by the purpose of having to run this philosophical "business"[146]: he confirms the value of the postulates of God, freedom, and immortality of the soul, and prevents them from being included within the science of the understanding by making them objects of a non-knowledge.[147] As Jacobi rephrases: the postulates of practical reason are acquired immediately and noetically. But contrary to what Kant presumes, their distinct nature does not jeopardize their reality and objectivity. It rather defines them.[148]

However, to meet his need to claim the objectivity and existence of the divine things, Jacobi must counter Kant's deduction of the unconditioned from the conditioned on the one hand, and to elaborate upon Kant's noetic approach to the divine things on the other hand. In short, Jacobi must unearth the structural justification of the divine things' objectivity. Additionally, let us remind, this justification must account for the existence of both the empirical and the ethical worlds, making explicit the bond that connects the theoretical and practical dimensions of the human being.

This would eventually define the true unconditioned and its relation to the conditioned. Therefore, we will have to investigate how Jacobi presents the knowledge that belongs to the *Seele* of a knower of the "divine things." This investigation will reposition also the finite I within the horizon of the divine I.

IX Final Remarks about the True

At this point, some concluding remarks may help draw perimeter and limits of our investigation into the *Divine Things*.

a) We can state that the Wesen are objects that are defined according to the subject that finds them: insofar as the living organism is determined as a free agent, it constitutes the paradigm to define that which is actual and true. This definition is implemented to determine the physical as well as the ethical/religious world. We have explored the argument for the necessary existence of physical objects only to the extent that it makes our argument for the existence of the "divine things" clearer.

b) If divine Wesen are reduced to mere subjective parameters, then the existence of the ethical and religious subject disappears. Within this framework, the subject becomes a mere implementation of a universal law without a self, hence producing the paradox of an ethics without real free agents.

c) Since the "divine things" are found and not constructed, they must possess the same autonomy as any other real object, the identity of which needs to be conceived as having precedence over knowledge. Moreover, to the same extent that finite objects are determined on the basis of the free, living agent that finds them, so too ethical and religious Wesen are posited within the panorama that a free, living agent introduces. Hence, they always refer to the autonomy that a free agent is deemed to possess: "freedom is inextricably rooted in the human mind as true concept of the unconditional, and compels the human soul to strive after a cognition of the unconditional that lies beyond the conditioned."[149]

d) As said, the idea of autonomy works as a fundamental paradigm for all kinds of existing things; it shows that an ethical norm – autonomy – dictates the paradigm of existence in general. Based on this common paradigm, we may assume that Jacobi does not describe two realities, practical on the one side and theoretical on the other. Rather, the definition of reality is determined by the same, single rational paradigm. Moreover, Jacobi uses Kant's texts on the metaphysics of ethics and religion in a treatise on the epistemology of finite things (the *David Hume*); this shows that Jacobi addresses the problem of knowledge in general according to an ethical and religious viewpoint.

e) This common paradigm notwithstanding, the existence of the divine things is clearly not the same as the existence of the finite objects. We will thus have to investigate on the one hand, the uniformity of the practical and the theoretical, and on the other hand, the specifics of the practical domain. In fact, since autonomy appears to be the basis for cognition in general, Jacobi shows some affinity with Fichte's philosophy, as he himself stresses in *Jacobi to Fichte*. In that context, Jacobi shows that he agrees with Fichte: autonomy provides the intrinsic relation between epistemology, ethics, and religion, and grounds the constitution of our consciousness.[150] But, as I noted above, it has not yet been explained how the existence of finite objects (of our *outer* world) differ from the existence of infinite objects (of our *inner* world). The autonomy seems to provide the basics of the definition of existence, but we have not yet been able to discern the "divine" from the "finite" with due precision. We must therefore conclude that the metaphysical method that has been used to define existence is apparently not fit to discern the difference between the two horizons.

f) We have seen that the identity of the divine things is the one element that is clearly stated in *Einleitung in des Verfassers sämmliche philosophische Schriften* (1815): God, freedom, the immortal soul, and virtue. This becomes progressively more evident from the moment we study Jacobi's references to Kant's pre-critical essays; the divine things have a distinct metaphysical denotation. We may in fact maintain a few critical hypotheses from the analysis of those metaphysical texts: freedom expresses the unconditional autonomy that grounds the very notion of existence; God and the immortal soul are the I and the Thou which, "from eternity to eternity," reflect each other to constitute the ethical and religious domain; virtue reveals the divinity of the I within the concrete dimension of finite things.[151] As a consequence, we can deem freedom the constitutive trait of the subject that both exercises authority over conditions and gains existence by way of its free actions.

I believe we must come to terms with the fact that our investigation will never completely resolve the puzzle of existence. Considering the precedence of autonomy over knowledge, existence remains opaque. In fact, the opacity that the metaphysical investigation has left on the notion of existence is mirrored by the notion of the subject's autonomy. With reference to Fenelon's allusion to Augustine, Jacobi admits: "we stand too high above ourselves, and shall not be able to comprehend ourselves."[152] This opacity demonstrates the limits of comprehension of the identity of a free agent, but it simultaneously defines the absoluteness of its Wesen, which can only be a presupposition of our knowledge. In this sense, both the subject's life and its objects (finite as well as divine) must be explained within the limits that Jacobi's metaphysics dictates.

A second set of conclusions refers specifically to the practical domain.

a) In general, we can claim that the autonomy of the Wesen lies beyond temporal or spatial coordinates. We could even say that their *being* opposes *time* and *space* insofar as time and space are conceived as transcendental conditions. These transcendental conditions would dissolve the Wesen in the sequence of possibilities and place them within a transcendental realm, *de facto* annihilating their individuality. If considered only through the analytical approach of metaphysics – hence in light of their existence – Wesen oppose spatio-temporality.[153]

b) As a consequence, the I is primarily established within a-temporal and a-spatial horizon. This is reminiscent of the view *sub specie aeternitatis*, which in fact represents the "heart" of the human being. In other terms, this horizon is where freedom constitutes the a-temporal and a-spatial order of reality.[154] Within the same order, the ethical and religious reality reveals itself.[155]

c) As the a-temporal and a-spatial thesis shows, we should not forget that the paradigmatic dialectic of the I and the Non-I does not involve any kind of mediation. Jacobi's dialectic does not fall into the transcendental structure of consciousness. Nor can it be deduced from our experience. Rather, Jacobi's dialectic is conceptually defined by means of a metaphysical method that posits (existential) experience behind discursive knowledge. Jacobi refers to Plato's *Philebus* to express this idea; as hunger is not determined by the experience of food, so too knowledge is guided by a disposition of our soul to recall the dialectic that determines the realm of beings. Within that realm, the soul and its objects are posited. As Plato concludes, we seek food before we know it; the same happens to the subject: it "has a glimpse of what an opposite sensation would bring about."[156] This *memory* is the "mystical way" that Plato uses to define what Jacobi has already found in Kant's metaphysical writing, whereby philosophy is the investigation of what must be *speculated from*.

d) Notwithstanding Jacobi's criticism of science and knowledge, the rejection of spatio-temporality would ultimately jeopardize meaning: if it is true that the source of meaning (which is existence) is conceived as being beyond a spatio-temporal framework, it is also true that meaning is only accomplished when we connect, relate, and mediate existence by forming judgments upon its basis. Therefore, if metaphysics defines what our faculty of perception (reason) reveals, then the faculty of judgment (the understanding) makes the subject aware of what has been revealed by connecting existence with its possibilities. Hence, we need the unconditional Wesen to be mediated with spatio-temporality, because "without

A STUDY
49

concepts no 'repeat-consciousness' is possible, no consciousness of *cognition*; hence, no distinguishing or comparing of these cognitions, no weighing of them, no pondering, no appraising; in a word, no actual *taking possession* of any truth whatever."[157] The understanding is therefore necessary to give form (also in a spatio-temporal fashion) to our cognition of being.[158]

e) In truth, Jacobi observes that the understanding rules over the forms of all human activity, so that "philosophy too obtains its form from the understanding" in virtue of "distinguishing or comparing."[159] This should not come as a surprise. The Kantian writings on metaphysics that we have analyzed are indeed examples of what the "consciousness of *cognition*" consists of: it does not disregard the mediation that science deploys. Instead, metaphysics arises in combination with science, as much as immediate knowledge works in alliance with mediation.[160]

f) There has been some fluctuation in Jacobi's way of expressing the connection between *Vernunft* and *Verstand* in his texts. This fluctuation can be seen in contexts where "reason" and "understanding" join forces with or exclude each other. However, *David Hume* and the *Preface* (1815) express clearly that the Verstand is the faculty that gives form to self-consciousness. Therefore, if (1) autonomy is not only an ethical feature of the I but the conceptual ground of knowledge in general, and if (2) autonomy of being in general is perceived by reason and metaphysically defined, then (3) we will need to establish the role of *mediation* within the ethical and religious realm to know that realm.

We must therefore conclude that, if metaphysics guides our investigations about the immediate experience of being, and if Jacobi's notion of autonomy provides the rational foundation of being, then we will have to define the twofold role of *mediation* in the religious and ethical dimension to discern two fundamental unsolved issues (one internal to the ethical and religious dimension, one external to the ethical and religious dimension): the specific relation between the I and the divine things on the one side, and the general relation between the ethical/religious dimension and the finite dimension on the other side. These tasks can only be completed by looking at the relation of the I with God.

However, the autonomy of the I merely expresses the general condition of meaning. It does not, as of yet, include a definition of its specific content. This has a direct impact on the religious and ethical horizon, as noted by Jacobi in *Jacobi to Fichte*.[161] The investigation of the mediation between the I and God will eventually provide the answers we are looking for.

A last detail may have become clear to the reader: to bring together the theoretical and the practical dimensions, Jacobi will have to reconcile the two frameworks for the dialectic between the I and its objects (epistemology on the one side; ethics and religion on the other). This will provide greater clarity to the thesis according to which the paradigm of existence is one and the same for both. Therefore, we could maintain that the purpose of the *Divine Things* is to justify the unclear equation between the "good" and the "true." As Jacobi says in the *Fliegende Blätter*: if the "good" and the "true" are not taken together, then everything turns into contradiction.[162]

X Toward Theism

The first remark concerning the connection between the I and the divine things is introduced at the beginning of the *Divine Things* by means of a reference to Pascal. Pascal's text sheds light on one more textual source of the locution "divine things" – which appears to be a term common to many philosophers – and suggests the priority of immediate attainment over justified knowledge.[163] The excerpt referred to is a paragraph from Pascal's *Art of Persuasion*. This has loosely been quoted by Jacobi as follows: "Divine truths (*vérités divines*) are infinitely superior to nature; God alone can place them in the soul (*l'ame*). He wanted them to enter from the heart into the mind (*l'esprit*), and not from the mind into the heart. Hence, if human things (*choses humaines*) have to be known before they can be loved, you have to love divine things (*choses divines*) in order to know them." Right at the beginning of the volume, these few lines make explicit the proper place occupied by the "divine things." Love is the feeling of connection between the I and the divine things, and it shows the priority of our immediate relation with them over our knowledge of them.[164]

We must recall that at the beginning of the volume Jacobi puts Lichtenberg's prophecy in clear contrast to J. von Müller's motto, which is demonstrative of Jacobi's general viewpoint: "there are unreceptive times, but what is eternal always finds its time."[165] The decision to place Pascal's words in this context seems to suggest that, in our heart, the "time" of the eternal faces a major hostility in the modern era, even though the strength of divine things is not wholly obliterated in our heart. Jacobi finds himself in the midst of unreceptive times

A STUDY   51

because philosophical science is unreceptive to what is truly unconditioned, nevertheless the divine things eventually find their means of revelation.

Further enriched by the reference to Pascal, Müller's pronouncement somehow echoes the necessity of an immediate access to divine reality, which is true, good, beautiful, and ignites our love. The search for the beautiful – which is evident, for instance, in Jacobi's brief *Ueber und bei Gelegenheit des kürzl ich erschienenen Werkes, Des lettres de Cachet et des prisons d'état* (1783)[166] and in the *Allwill* – is also presented as an act of love.[167] This reference to love signals a greater framework of notions that Jacobi uses to counter the rationalistic science of God, to which he does not oppose sheer sentiment of the divine: love is not just an emotion, it instead matches the requirements of an immediate awareness of the unconditioned. More properly, love is the feeling that a subject feels when it recognizes honorable traits in existing objects; similar feelings such as *Hochachtung, Dankbarkeit* or *Ruhe* magnify the quality of the dialectic that arises between the subject and the object that possesses those honourable traits.[168] However, these feelings are not felt in the solitude of one's heart. For instance, we recognize the presence of "divine things" in the persons we meet and in the person we are. Only in light of the ethical values that are enhanced in this relationship, do we feel love. Feelings of love are basically the representation of a Glaube that is directed toward the recognition of the ethical and religious determination of a Wesen.

It might be clear how those feelings are incited by our relationship with other people; it may remain unclear how those same feelings may be caused by our experience of ourselves. The solution to this problem resides in our awareness: we are aware of ourselves only as free agents, hence only as we act in contrast, or in relation, to others. The awareness of our virtue brings about the basis for the respect we *feel* for ourselves as well as for other free agents. Only as free agents do we feel ourselves as distinct Wesen. Therefore, Jacobi seems to suggest that love is a direct consequence of our self-awareness. Within this dialectic – which is quite simple and yet loaded with rich metaphysical implications – the ultimate unconditioned manifests itself.[169] In general, "love" involves an immediate relation that neither possesses nor produces what is loved.

But this initial certainty contrasts with a clear restriction. Jacobi's paraphrase of Pascal's writing and von Müller's motto constitutes the true point of departure of Jacobi's treatise only inasmuch as it disputes Lichtenberg's prophecy. As much as the former (Pascal/Müller) gives hope, the latter (Lichtenberg) gives perspective. The latter sets forth the anti-systematicity of love and thus presents Jacobi's restriction upon both religious feeling and religious thinking.

Jacobi further elaborates on Lichtenberg's aphorism, showing what he sees in Lichtenberg's eschatological stance.[170] Jacobi foresees an appalling truth: he believes that contempt for faith in an existing, personal God will not reveal the end of human intellectual involution. Jacobi seems to imply that the erasure of true religion and true faith is not the lowest intellectual chasm that human history can reach. Next in line lies exploitation: the regality of a person and the majesty of a personal God turn into the authority of a moral principle; religious devotion changes to a creed about the human faculty to produce order. *Hochachtung* is turned into the respect for a non-existent postulate, and religious piety turns into deference toward a ghost. The dissolution of religion is thus assimilated into a revolution that brings forth a religion marked by a minus sign. The pillar of this new religion is an unconditioned that our thinking produces from the conditioned. As the text reads, the prophecy continues by announcing that at "**the highest summit of refinement … once the peak reached, the judgement of the wise men will turn once again**" until "**we ourselves will be like God. We will know that being and essence are – and can only be – ghosts.**"[171]

Jacobi would unquestionably support an overturning of modern refinement, but what is presented here merely announces a progressive annihilation. It represents the spreading to all human knowledge of the religious subversion that nihilism fostered, whereby the existing God, together with all true beings, is turned into a ghost. In that moment, refined and enlightened thinking seems to obliterate not only the absence of God; it also obliterates everything that, in Jacobi's view, depends on the existence of God, i.e., all ethical and religious subjects.[172] Jacobi reads in this prophecy the manifestation of the *nothingness* that nihilism produces.

This point explicitly connects the *Divine Things* with a thesis expressed early in *Jacobi to Fichte*, where Jacobi observes that as soon as God is defined according to the systematic performance of the understanding, "everything gradually dissolves for him into his own nothingness. Man has the choice, however, and this alone: Nothingness or a God. If he chooses nothingness, he makes himself unto a God, that is, he makes a *phantom* into God, for it is impossible, if there is no God, that man and all that surrounds him should be anything but a *phantom*."[173]

The only escape from this nothingness consists in the *realm of beings* that the ethical and religious I perceives. Therefore, if reason is the faculty for per-

A STUDY   53

ceiving it – for it perceives the actual and true – and if reason is "the grasping of, the true, whether internal or external,"[174] then reason must be the source of a metaphysical certitude in this realm as well. The understanding will, for its part, define the possibilities of the relation between the Wesen, but only after reason has revealed their ethical and religious identity.

To make this collaborative enterprise explicit, Jacobi embarks on the investigation of the nihilistic eradication of the true God, whose structure and design would reveal an alternative: either a personal God or nothingness. As Jacobi concludes later in the text: "The human being has only one alternative: either he derives everything from **One** or he derives everything from **nothing**. We prefer the **One** over nothing, and we name it **God** because this **One** (*Ein*) must necessarily be a **personal one** (*Einer*), otherwise it would be the same universal nothing but differently named, essentially undetermined yet all-determining."[175] Again, the alternative shows that Jacobi does not promote some immediate sentiment or emotion of the divine. This is not what love indicates. As we mentioned while referring to the analytical approach implemented by Kant, Jacobi's theoretical exercise shows itself in a thoroughly critical consideration of the intellectual proficiency of his adversaries – those who annihilate God – to demonstrate the necessity of taking the opposite route, i.e., the assumption of the existence of a personal God.

No doubt that Jacobi's analysis of the opposing thesis works as a historical qualification of the background onto which Jacobi projects his own manoeuvre. However, this strategy – the historical qualification – does not work as a *justification* of divine things.[176] Divine things reject justifications, for they depend on the immediate revelation of the existence of God that is defined by means of the investigation into the necessary presuppositions of knowledge. In this sense, the necessity and profile of the certainty of divine things will become manifest only after philosophy has unearthed the function that the existence of a personal God fulfills.[177] This has not yet been presented but is precisely what we should expect from our next steps into the investigation of Jacobi's theism.

In short, in this new section of our investigation we have seen that (a) reason reveals what (b) the understanding elaborates and (c) the feeling of love imposes as a representation. For its part, philosophy must present itself as a form of theism because it deciphers, through the metaphysical method, the systematic unity between (a), (b), and (c). The systematic unity is achieved by stating what existence involves. This could help avert (at least in theory) the charge of irrationalism that Jacobi suffered and, to some extent, still suffers.

We could state that, on the one hand, Jacobi does not justify his theism via a merely positive endorsement of it; any sort of justification would make of it a product of the Enlightenment theology he was so critical about. On the other hand, Jacobi approximates the intrinsic value and implications of his theism via an analysis of what its denial would entail.[178] Within this constellation, the *Divine Things* presents an essay whose target is a modern intellectual deterioration, countered by disclosing the profile of a rational theism.

XI Measure and Rational Being

The dilemma, of either a personal God or nothingness, gives Jacobi the opportunity to express his reasons for siding with theism. And he does so by means of an unbroken confrontation with the opposite theory: *naturalism*. Jacobi seems to state that, on one side, theism gives consistency to knowledge by determining true existence (the bedrock of knowledge), while, on the other side, naturalism provides a system that includes incongruities because it neglects true existence. We must then understand what it means to derive everything from God.

As Jacobi states in the dialogue *David Hume*, his realism is based on an inquiry into the foundation of knowledge that accounts for human faculties in general. And these faculties do not limit themselves to physical reality, because the definition of physical reality requires something that is not physical: "the perfection of sensation determines the perfection of consciousness *with all its modifications*. As the receptivity is, so is the spontaneity; as the sense, so the understanding. The degree of our faculty for distinguishing ourselves from external things, extensively and intensively, is the degree of our personality, that is, the degree *of elevation of our spirit*. Along with this exquisite property of reason, we receive the *intimation of God*, the intimation of HE WHO IS, of a being *who has its life in itself*."[179]

As Jacobi states: "Such is his **reason** that a God's existence (*Daseyn*) be more manifest (*offenbarer*) to him and more certain, than his own. There is no reason where this revelation (Offenbarung) is not."[180] This anthropological note leads *David Hume* to its inevitable conclusion and seems to qualify the ontological scope of Jacobi's investigation into human's heart. With this reference to Aristotle's *Nicomachean Ethics*, we have finally reached the point where Jacobi's theism becomes visible, so that the theoretical and the practical start connecting.

A STUDY   55

As *David Hume* closes, the *Divine Things* opens: "[the human being] finds himself as a being completely dependent, derived, concealed to himself: yet, he is enlivened by a drive to inquire into his origin, to recognize himself in it, to experience by himself **the true** (*das Wahre*) **through** this origin and **from** this origin. He calls **reason** this drive that identifies his genus."[181]

This last quotation prompts us to try to connect these three topics: the investigation into the consistency of knowledge, the nature of reason, and the essence of human being. We will see that these themes come together as the profile of the notion of *origin* arises.

To be human is to be rational, affirms Jacobi, echoing a long-standing equation. But rationality is not a firm possession. It seems as if rationality depends on the way human beings think: rationality is a drive (*Trieb*) to perform a specific investigation. This restriction shows once again that Jacobi's thesis concerning knowledge is grounded on his thesis concerning ethics and religion: on one side, there is the notion of existence which is grounded on the notion of autonomy; on the other side, there is rationality, an impulse to find the origin of that autonomy.

None of this is new. Already in the *Woldemar*, Jacobi draws on Aristotle to make explicit the essence of the notion of this rational drive: this "Instinkt des Menschen" is what precedes experience and makes human being comprehend the definition of being.[182] Therefore, though his restriction might look arbitrary, Jacobi imposes it because reason is universally understood as the faculty that dismisses subjective thinking to achieve objectivity. Consequently, the ultimate endeavour of reason consists in the determination of the objective limits of the subject's thinking. Under this very general and, presumably, universal assumption, we could claim that in the act of defining our origin, we are not determining any temporal circumstances, rather we are defining the objective perimeter of our own rational activities. Moreover, given the equation between this investigation and human nature, we may draw the decisive conclusion that human nature is an interrupted intellectual relation to its own origin.[183]

The same argument seems to apply to all existing things. The act of reaching back to the origin does not illuminate the definition of humanity only. In fact, the "true" does not extend beyond rationality, but complies with it. Therefore, all Wesen must make explicit their relation *with* and *through* the origin of reason by means of their very existence. In the end, any being is "true" and does not disappear into nothing only so long as it relates to the origin.[184] The act of *deriving* from the one personal God starts revealing its contours.

These two important results disclose important details of Jacobi's theism. Though the relationship to the origin is universal, the investigation into the origin is a privilege of human beings: the "being able to know something higher and better than himself" is the way in which human beings acquire knowledge in the first place.[185] But, as is well represented in the destiny of the eponymous character of Jacobi's first novel, *Allwill*, the notion of this immediate moral impulse – that we can also call *Gewissheit* – can dangerously turn the Aristotelian virtuous act into the self-sufficiency of the moral genius. The moral genius is the figure that errs precisely in considering himself the author of virtue, inasmuch as his impulse is only defined according to his *need*. By considering himself the Alpha and the Omega of virtue, Allwill commits a moral suicide. He forfeits his dependency on the real source of the true, good, and beautiful: the Origin, God. In the end, as rational impulse is turned into mere rational need, nihilism appears on the stage.[186]

As long as the necessary investigation into the origin is considered as a mere need – and not as the manifestation of our connection to the origin – the human being will perceive its own subjectivity as something arbitrary and, in the end, meaningless. Only the confrontation with an objective limit makes the investigation – hence, reason itself – meaningful. And this happens precisely because the human being – and reason itself – shows its substantial limit.

Jacobi's criticism of nihilism gains strength in one more way. God, the Origin, must not be conceived as equal to the infinite being, because the infinite being does not have any existence or form; Jacobi here clearly equates "finite" with "definite" and "infinite" with "indefinite." Hence, God must be finite; yet the finitude of God is of a special kind. Jacobi's rejection of the infinite All-One is rooted in his siding with ancient philosophy. He goes as far back as Plato, who in the *Philebus* shows how the infinite being does not have any being because that which is not limited is shapeless.

But Jacobi's theism can also be said to be reminiscent of Parmenides' enmity against the *apeiron*: the *apeiron* is the infinite shapeless being which is contrary to truth and contrary to being because it lacks identity. This is the great error in which those who draw the notion of infinite from the notion of finite fall into. They imagine the origin, God, the unconditioned, as notions that result from the negation of the limits of the finite. But Jacobi shows that when the unconditioned is conceived as the unlimited *apeiron*, then it does not escape the limitedness; it just loses being. Hence, under the tutelage of Plato and Parmenides, Jacobi maintains that since the infinite being, the *apeiron*, cannot have being, then God must not be conceived as infinite being, for *apeiron*

A STUDY

clearly implies the equation of God with the "All," i.e., the equation between God and nothing.[187]

The "All" – like in *All-will* – is a concept that carries in itself the necessary annihilation of being because it is the negation of *peras* – the limit – thus implying the obliteration of identity. The annihilation of limits that the *apeiron* so clearly represents corresponds to the annihilation of the determination of any reality: "Its image is the hallucination of the shapeless, of a pre-being nonthing (*Unding*) that would be a First; First of all, yet not of any singly – it is the non-thing (Unding) itself."[188]

Since the limitless is non-thing, Jacobi concludes that the general rule to define being is *peras* (limit). This last point must be clearly restated so as to avoid a misunderstanding: being is conceived neither as a principle of emanation of the actual nor as a ground upon which the possible is sustained. Rather, it shows itself through peras. From this follows that different relations to peras define different ways in which being reveals itself; on one side animals are beings that know the *measured* through the sense perception of limits, on the other side, humans are those beings who know the *measure* that defines limits through reason. Animals and humans share the sense perception of the measured, but humans possess something that animals do not: humans possess the capacity to act according to the measure that defines beings. Human beings are defined according to their capacity to relate to measure actively and receive knowledge from this activity.

Eventually, God is the one that *creates* measure by creating *peras*: since everything that exists must have measure, then measure is the fundamental feature of any Wesen. Hence also God has an essential relation to measure: "he himself is measure."[189] In opposition to measure is the infinite: "Plato declares himself in a remarkable way on this subject. In the progression of things, he boldly assigns the lowest place to the infinite; the highest, to *measure*, which unites the finite with the infinite and gives birth to the *actual* things first. He presupposes a *God*, who is a *spirit*, a *discerning* personal being, as the author – *through the perfection of his will* – of all things."[190]

According to the *Divine Things*, Jacobi's God is the God of creatures, the God-Creator, the measure-giver. Although in Jacobi's view, God is the only one that can defeat the dialectic I-Thou, as he can declare "I am WHO I am," the explicit reference to measure makes Jacobi's God different from the one of the Christian mystics, whose notion of God has a different profile than the relationship between Creator and creatures.[191] As human beings, we can only have a relationship with God through created order of reality, be it morally or bodily conceived. We could therefore presume that this relationship through the notion of measure determines a distinct definition of God. Nevertheless, the relationship between the measure Giver and the measured retains a certain invisibility.[192]

Yet in general, we must say that this invisibility does not jeopardize the investigation. Instead, this invisibility provides the parameter to differentiate between absolute origin and conditional beginning. Absolute origin needs to be conceived without reasons, because it must consist in something that has no justification. This origin is invisible precisely because it is never an object of a systematic thinking. It thus shares with the finite Wesen the quality of being that is never "given," but rather "gives." On the contrary, conditional beginning consists in an arbitrary final point in our backward search for justifications.[193]

The special status of the absolute origin may look like an unparalleled objection to the possibility to seeing what *gives*. It seems that we are in the impossibility of understanding the profile of the origin in clear terms. And this danger has vast consequences, since the definition of the true, beautiful, and good depends on it. However, invisibility does not dismiss the *logos* about the origin; if this was the case, then we would face a great danger. In fact, as stated above, the essence of reason is tied to the activity of investigating the origin and is shaped according to it. The invisibility of the origin would thus represent a major threat to the definition of ourselves.[194]

Yet, the apparent impossibility of defining God seems to stem from the impossibility that our thinking go beyond its systematic ability to connect and compare concepts, an ability that Jacobi demands that authentic rational thinking reject. Hence, the *logos* about the origin makes us encounter a great challenge, because the quality of intuitive, non-systematic thinking is put to an important test. Regarding the knowledge of God, Jacobi needs to reply to the question about the relation between human reason and the origin of measure. If this relation is invisible and, as a consequence, we cannot state what connects reason to origin, then it would appear that Jacobi's intuitive thinking may not be able to bring to a clear end the path it has commenced. If this relation is not defined, then reason would become an enigma to itself.

In light of this riddle, the definition of the origin provides the steppingstone that unfolds the most surprising outcome from Jacobi's theism. We may say that the definition of the origin of being has brought to light, with great urgency, problems concerning the definition of rational thinking.[195] Yet, this correlation is something that is not new in the panorama of Western thinking. It represents a topic that is ingrained in Western philosophy, as it represents

A STUDY   59

a major point of reference for all ancient philosophers. We can appreciate the magnitude of this topic by looking at Aristotle's *Metaphysica*, which can be seen as a collection of ancient theories about the *arché*.[196] In some sense, Aristotle can help us find the proper background to grasp Jacobi's proposal concerning the relation between reason and the origin of being.

Aristotle writes that the origin is 1) "that part of a thing from which one would start first" (as in the beginning of a line); 2) "that from which each thing would best be originated" (like it happens when learning: we must sometimes begin not from the first point of the subject, but from the point from which we learn the subject most easily); 3) "that from which, as an immanent part, a thing first comes to be" (as in the foundation of a house); 4) "that from which, *not* as an immanent part, a thing first comes to be, and from which the movement or the change naturally first begins" (like a child from his father and mother, or a fight from abusive language); 5) "that at whose will that which is moved is moved and that which changes changes" (like the magistrates in cities, as well as the oligarchies, monarchies, and tyrannies, called *archai*); and 6) "that from which a thing can first be known, – this also is called the beginning of the thing" (that is, the hypotheses are the beginnings of demonstrations). Aristotle eventually summarizes as follows: "it is common, then, to all beginnings to be the first point from which a thing either is or comes to be or is known."[197]

On the one hand, Aristotle's framework seems to defeat the invisibility of the origin. Yet, on the other hand, we should ask ourselves whether this framework turns the absolute origin into a conditional beginning. In fact, Aristotle seems to approach the problem of the origin systematically, as if he conceives the origin only according to the conditions of systematic possibilities that the notion of beginning would fulfill in a system of interrelated items. If this is the case, we would lose the absolute autonomy of the origin in exchange for a thread of conditions. Unexpectedly, systematic thinking seems to gain the upper hand one more time. This short detour of our investigation seems to confirm that Jacobi was right when he rejected Aristotle's metaphysics to reinvent our theoretical relationship to the absolute origin anew.

However, as this first impression fades, one can see that Aristotle seems to be aware of the danger of eradicating the autonomy of a being from the notion of origin. In fact, he stresses the necessity that the origin include "being" and "unity"; "for these might most of all be supposed to contain all things that are, and to be most like principles because they are by nature; for if they perish [if a principle is not, and is not one] all other things are destroyed with them; for everything *is* and is one."[198] Surprisingly, this remark brings us back to what Jacobi's philosophy is expounding. The characteristic mark of the origin functions as the characteristic mark of all things, so that the autonomy of the origin works as the condition for all Wesen. To be, means to be one. Therefore, the origin is present in all things as their formal condition.

We may then assume that metaphysics (the Aristotelian too, not only the pre-critical Kantian or the Platonic) has connections with Jacobi's way of understanding issues concerning the origin. This leads us to an additional thesis about the origin: the origin seems to be bound to a profound law, which is expressed in the locution "from which" stated in the aforementioned summary. While Aristotle claims that all things *are* and *are unities* according to the formal condition of their being, he also stresses that the investigation into the origin needs to search for what lies behind all things. To understand what the origin is, we are therefore invited a) to include everything that is a beginning in the ultimate profile of the origin (the six definitions), b) to refer to the origin in order to justify how a thing is (is and is one), and c) to include the origin in the realm of beings, because the origin must be, hence it must be one. Jacobi, just like Aristotle, conceives the origin as something that reverberates in the formal condition of *every* Wesen: "For a being without selfhood (*Selbstseyn*) is absolutely and universally impossible. But a being-oneself without consciousness and, conversely, a consciousness without self-consciousness, without substantiality and at least an attributed personality, is wholly impossible: the one as well as the other are nothing but empty words. Therefore God is not, is the non-being in the highest sense if he is not a **spirit**."[199]

This thesis may look less surprising, now that the Aristotelian background has helped us focus our attention onto the relation between origin and being. Insofar as reason is the activity which finds itself in what it seeks, reason will eventually find itself in this original being and it will give shape to the ultimate quality of the "Who" that (1) gives measure and (2) makes of all realities its own reflections.

We can conclude that Jacobi performs a twofold operation: he includes the origin in being, and he makes the origin the "through which" everything "is or comes to be or is known." This makes the origin the blueprint of rationality itself and designs the "through which" everything must be defined: this is the deduction from the "one" that Jacobi was referring to.

As a consequence, origin, being, and soul share the same nature: "Call **Him** the one who **gives** measure, in which the measure **originally** is set – it is said:

A STUDY   61

he himself is measure! – call Him creator by means of giving measure to every
actuality (*Wirklichkeit*), every **existence**, worlds and beings; the creator in every
being, by **determining measure**, of its strength, the proper relations, and its
own living **soul** that gives **support** and guidance."[200]

Obviously, this last point projects a series of problems concerning the identity of God. The first of those includes the impossibility of God's not-being.
The origin is not free from being, because it is conceived only as the measure
of created beings; if the origin could not be, it would not be the Who that gives
measure. A measure that does not give measure, an origin that does not originate, is not. Creator and creature are necessarily tied together within the dialectic of creation. Nor they would be conceivable otherwise. If this dialectic
between creator and creature is not granted, then the phantom of mere for-
malistic conceptualization of the origin would rise back. It would thus annihilate the only necessity upon which our rationality and our being rest.[201] A
merely potential origin would destroy the very ground of its definition (being)
and would annihilate its creatures.[202]

XII M. Claudius and the Externalists

Now that the overall theoretical outline of Jacobi's philosophy of the divine
things has become clearer, we may proceed towards its implementation within
a narrower perimeter.

The second part of the *Divine Things* grows out of a review of the edition
of Matthias Claudius' complete works. This part of the *Divine Things* could
be divided into two sections: a first section which includes the analysis of Claudius' so-called positive (or historical) approach to the revelation of God, and
a second section that contains a more general analysis of the post-Kantian
philosophy and its notion of God. While the former represents an explicit
critique of the "integral externalists" and discusses pros and cons of historical
revelation, the latter considers the notion of God in general and unveils the
complex argument against the "integral internalists."

As it is now clear, Jacobi faces two opposing parties: on the one side the "integral externalists" and on the other side the "integral internalists." The former
believes in the essential role played by the historical revelation of God. The
latter presents the position held by transcendental philosophy in general and
idealism (whose ultimate form is naturalism) in particular. As we shall see, the
position of the internalists is not wholly clear without an explicit description

of the position held by the externalists. The externalists, however, dive into some key issues that Jacobi uses to define his own ideas about immediate access to absolute truth.

Jacobi's analysis of Claudius' position gives Jacobi the opportunity to unmask a fundamental tendency of the "integral externalists:" they assume that an external source – in the form of a historical happening – is essential for the revelation of divine things as it grants objective superhuman origin. To the externalists, who intend to surpass the risk of subjective delusion with the affirmation of an historical objectivity, Jacobi replies by holding that only human inner nature, or "spirit," provides the necessary ground for any apprehension of the true.[203]

The confrontation between Claudius and Jacobi is not that simple though. Its subtlety lies in the fact that, unlike integral externalists, Claudius does not uphold a completely passive human attitude toward an outward influence. Rather, he claims that historical examples are necessary to awake our inner, spiritual virtue. Claudius is convinced that we need Christ, Confucius, and Socrates because they teach us that the human soul is immortal; if we did not have those examples, he continues, we could not learn what we are. In opposition to this conviction, Jacobi aims at showing that it is necessary to have an immediate, personal, and innate apprehension of the idea of the good, true, and beautiful; this indeed has priority over any external teaching. Only through this idea we are able to recognize it in the world. In truth, he does not exclude an experience of it; he just claims that in order to have experience of it, we first need to know what it is.

Matthias Claudius was a writer and a poet with a religious education. His pietistic ideas resonate in his treatise *On Immortality*, where he claims that the highest truths neither come from outside us nor are they human artefacts, for they proceed from within us. More precisely, the highest truths emanate from us although they are not subject to our desires; they are rather independent drives. These supersensible ideas and concepts raise the human being over nature and its necessity, eventually making the human being reflect its model: a free, personal God.[204]

Jacobi would share this thesis with his friend Asmus, yet Jacobi's understanding of the innate connection with the divine does not comply with the idolatrous reliance on Christ that Claudius professes. In fact, Christ is, for Claudius, a fundamental tool. Nevertheless, this does not make Claudius an integral externalist, rather, he could be deemed a mild externalist. But to understand Claudius' view with greater accuracy and to assess its difference

A STUDY   63

from Jacobi's theism, we need to look at Jacobi's analysis of Claudius' theology in detail.

Jacobi agrees with Claudius' idea of the revelation of divine things in the following ways:

1 Jacobi claims that divine things are innate concepts of our inner self. As the reference to Pascal conveys, we find them immediately in our "heart"; they are embedded in our "spirit," before we know them. In fact, only because they are in us, can they guide our search for them; but since they are paradigms of our research, they remain beyond justified and discursive knowledge.[205] The overall activity of human rational investigation is summarized by a reason that searches the origin of its own activity, which is both distinct from human reason and yet rational.[206] This thesis – that we developed in the preceding section – represents a point further advanced by Jacobi after the publication of *Divine Things*. In the *Fliegende Blätter* (1817), for instance, he gives an account of the distinct epistemological status of the divine things, which are comprised within rationality and yet beyond description. In a sense, this distinct feature of the divine things grounds and provokes rationality because, following the guiding light of the divine things, reason tells prophecies and poeticizes. Claudius would agree with Jacobi on this point for Claudius also believes that an innate element is necessary. In this sense, the reference to "prophecy" does not imply that reason foresees the future; rather it suggests that reason displays what pertains to the origin, remains unknown, and yet affects our knowledge. This rational "drive" gives direction toward a life of higher degree and archetypical profile, which substantiates human "dignity" (*Würde*).[207]

2 Another shared thesis concerns the self. The definition of the self by means of its inner relation to divine things gives it authority over natural phenomena and provides human beings with autonomy. As can be perceived in Kladde IV and Kladde VI, Aristotle is responsible for giving Jacobi the coordinates of this notion of virtue: according to Aristotle's teaching, virtue is the faculty that overcomes obstacles, hence it is the ultimate tool through which the soul (Seele) reaches happiness.[208] Yet, freedom does not refer to free will or human behaviour only. Rather, freedom constitutes the manifestation of a distinct instance of autonomy, which is the fundamental paradigm according to which we think of reality and act upon it.[209] The autonomy of the self is the key to

understanding human virtue, but it also represents the bedrock upon which reality rises. This makes of ethical autonomy the only sacred thing in human being. Successfully contrasting the lower scene of reality, dominated by mechanical causes, does not translate in a division between two distinct realities: horizon of freedom and horizon of mechanism. It merely means that as human beings reveal the actual being of reality with their freedom, they also describe its internal connection in a manner that is congruent with scientific, discursive knowledge. In this sense, we may state that mechanism is rejected only insofar as it assumes that it can define the individual constituents of reality, while it is accepted when it turns into a fair scientific enterprise that describes the connections of such individual constituents.[210] Within this picture we can understand that virtue becomes the manifestation of the original order of reality where final causes shape the being and give rise to the human world, whose account is displayed by the ethical and ontological authority (not autocracy) over nature.

3 Jacobi has extensively treated the topic of the final causes in the *Spinoza Letters*. In that text, he stresses that if one assumes that explanations are only those offered by the understanding (the power to produce discursive knowledge), then final causes become unrealistic, even if they represent the source of both thought and action.[211] But Jacobi also adds in the introduction to the complete works that the understanding provides a fundamental function in mediating the content of both finite and divine things, hence providing a proper basis to natural sciences and ethics.[212]

4 A further thesis that Jacobi and Claudius share consists in having God as model of virtue. Defeating the necessity of nature through his will, he not only becomes a model for all human beings but shows that virtue is what human beings and God share.[213] **Yet this connection with the divine** is not the product of some sort of elaborate deliberation, rather it represents the first "feeling" we have of God: through our internal eyes we experience the presence of the order he establishes upon human beings and the world. This last thesis connects Jacobi and Claudius quite clearly, in fact they both acknowledge that no experience is closer to the experience of God than the experience we have of a righteous man. The feeling that the righteous man inspires in us is, in fact, the same as the feeling we could have in a direct experience of God.[214]

5 As already stated, the first experience that human beings have of divine things occurs when they experience their freedom from nature. Both

A STUDY

Claudius and Jacobi contend that freedom provides the first instance of an agreement between external events and internal will. Although freedom coincides with the ethical status of the human being, it cannot become reality unless it is exercised in contrast to the brute natural mechanism. This makes explicit the measure-giver character of the human being.[215]

6 Since the experience of freedom provides the foundation for Jacobi's philosophy of religion, we have yet more evidence of how ethics provides the ground for the suprasensible. Claudius would concur that the experience of the autonomy of their will makes human beings realize that they are a bridge between two realms, one dominated by nature and the other established by freedom. Hence, the act of revealing this suprasensible dimension translates into the act of revealing the ethical nature of human beings.[216]

7 God provides the model for all human beings; this is the original and internal revelation from which any other instance of the revealed religion follows. Once this thesis is granted, Jacobi concludes that in all ages the idea of God mirrors human ethics. Hence perfect ethics assumes and necessitates perfect religion or put differently, human freedom mirrors the profile of a personal God. Claudius and Jacobi seem to suggest that autonomy provides the archetype of the definition of God to the extent that we can draw the profile of a God from the ethical principles that a rational subject possesses.[217]

8 The common features between Jacobi's theism and Claudius' philosophy include the claim that the extraordinary event of God's incarnation can be interpreted as an allusion to the ordinary event of the awakening of the inner divine nature in human beings. As stated above, humans seek a God that corresponds to their own characteristic ethical mark.[218]

In contrast to Claudius' position, Jacobi holds a few fundamental points that lead him to reject the *integralism* of externalists:

1 Claudius believes that human beings need the example of Christ to learn what freedom is. He believes that only through the example of Christ could we acquire the morals that show us how to overcome natural necessity. Instead, Jacobi maintains that human beings first need to have an idea of freedom to recognize when freedom is brought about. Only with that innate knowledge, human beings are in the position to identify

and value a free agent (be it Christ, Confucius, or Socrates). So, an immediate and internal experience of freedom is the necessary presupposition of our knowledge of historical instances of freedom. This argument elaborates a point that we have already seen at work: Jacobi observes that we have an immediate relationship to "measure," because we possess it in our "heart." Knowledge is therefore never a discovery of something that we do not possess, it is rather a recognition of what our reason intimately affirms. Cognition is thus an event that happens through a metaphysical reconsideration of our rational activities, a recollection and memory of the presupposition of our existence. Only in light of this reexamination, can we broaden our understanding of divine things.[219]

2 Jacobi believes that it is irrelevant whether Christ existed or not, because the ground of our immortal soul consists in the divine autonomy of our being. This is what gives life to anything alive.[220] Therefore, it is Jacobi's opinion that confusing the historical Christ with this innate Christ leads Claudius to "religious materialism."[221] Claudius, for his part, goes as far as to charge Jacobi with the accusation of turning God into a mere subjective projection or a ghost, that merely complies with human desires.[222]

In general terms, Jacobi claims that we need to assume that divine things are inborn because they constitute the necessary paradigms for our knowledge of them or, better said, for our identification of them in the historical plane of reality. This theory provides the model for all divine things, which represent the principle *through which* we become aware of, or perceive (*vernehmen*), both our own and God's nature. The opposing thesis, according to which revelation can manifest something foreign to our reason, entails the idea that reason can identify something that it is not fit for, as if our eyes could perceive a colour that it is not within the range of visibility.[223] In light of his confrontation with Claudius, Jacobi confirms the great distance that separates him from those religious thinkers who, in his opinion, fulfil the simple maieutic role of freeing human beings from strict naturalism, i.e., from the tempting but wrong belief that the deterministic essence of nature is all there is to know about reality. But beyond this role, these figures cannot teach the real ethical essence of the human being. Only our "heart" can.[224]

Notwithstanding his clear stance, we will see that Jacobi is not a religious idealist. He does not accept the approach of the philosophers who treat God as an inborn, subjective experience. According to Jacobi's terminology, these philosophers provide the portrayal of the "integral internalist," who is un-

A STUDY   67

moved and unperturbed before God precisely because they intimately know
that God has merely grown inside human intelligence as nothing more than
an idea.

XIII The Internalists

A long review of *naturalism* follows Jacobi's criticism of Claudius' position.
In this last part of the text, Jacobi equates naturalism with the second daughter
of transcendental thinking: Schelling's philosophy. Since in the previous
chapters we touched upon many of the relevant issues that this last part of the
volume also covers, we will now investigate what has not yet been discussed,
while referring to a few ideas that have proved instrumental for our analysis.
In a sense, in this last section I will aim at clarifying the systematic unity of
Jacobi's theism.

In Jacobi's opinion, the main thesis of Schelling's naturalism is expressed
in his notion of the absolute, which is conceived as an original point of indifference between subject and object. This absolute union of what Jacobi would
instead hold as the projection of a necessary dualism posits the irrefutable accomplishment of a systematic approach to reality. The philosophical architecture that upholds this point of indifference is first presented in the *Darstellung
meines Systems der Philosophie* (1801), although its main thesis can be briefly
summarized with reference to subsequent texts.[225] Schelling, as it has happened
with Fichte, provides a regressive path toward the principle from which multiplicity emerges. This principle establishes an original point of indifference
from which every possibility can be drawn: "since we make the identity of all
opposites our first principle, unity itself along with opposition will form the
highest pair of opposites. To make unity the supreme principle, we must think
of it as comprehending even the highest pair of opposites, and the unity that
is its opposite as well, and we must define this supreme unity as one in which
unity and opposition, self-equivalence and non-equivalence, are one."[226]

These words, from *Bruno oder über das göttliche und natürliche Prinzip der
Dinge* (1802), provide a concise picture of what Jacobi has in mind when he
thinks about the ultimate form of naturalism. In light of this supreme principle, Jacobi sees a direct line of continuity between Schelling's philosophy of
identity and Schelling's early texts, which can be regarded as the idealistic re-
interpretation of some of Spinoza's systematic ideas. As Jacobi states in the
second letter to Köppen, he interprets texts such as *Erster Entwurf eines Systems
der Naturphilosophie* (1799), *Einleitung zu seinem Entwurf eines Systems der*

Naturphilosophie (1799), and *Darstellung meines Systems der Philosophie* (1801) as instances of a continuous, coherent line that leads to what the last section of the *Divine Things* tackles.[227]

That said, we must also stress that there are profound affinities between Schelling and Jacobi. Like Jacobi, Schelling claims that the main interest of philosophy lies in the definition of the origin, whose relevance emerges in light of the initial question that Schelling posits: "was ist das Existierende?"[228] Therefore, starting from the mutual interest in the question concerning *existence*, Schelling, just like Jacobi, observes that true existence needs to surpass the Kantian discrepancy between a deterministic nature and a spontaneous subject. A consistent notion of existence requires a distinct account of a genesis that is apt to coordinating both freedom and nature within the same principle. This problem appears in all clarity as soon as we acknowledge that human existence is the conflictual horizon upon which freedom and nature contend their jurisdictions; as both Jacobi and Schelling admit, the subject is free and autonomous even though exposed to deterministic nature. Hence the subject needs to be conceived as an agent that brings together opposing norms.[229]

Like Schelling, Jacobi shows in the *Spinoza Letters* that the problem concerning the specific identity of the subject is deeply intertwined with the problem of *determining* in general. However, unlike Schelling, Jacobi is concerned about the great peril that may present itself in an idealistic way of determining (through mediation). In order to avoid the nihilistic outcome of idealism, Jacobi adopts a different model of determination (through immediacy) by accepting a diverse interpretation of the spontaneity of the subject: freedom is the immediate act that functions as a paradigm of all determination. It is only in light of the subject's existential autonomy that Jacobi defines the true determination of existence.[230] This consists in the activity of a person that gives measure by rationally acknowledging the source of measure. In Jacobi's view this is the theoretical point where metaphysics, ontology, and ethics meet. Contrary to this approach, Jacobi is convinced that Schelling's monistic account of nature is elaborated in a way that makes the subject emerge from a point of indifference, leaving no possibility whatsoever to differentiate the subject from its origin. Schelling's subject cannot and must not reveal true freedom, because it cannot define real individuality.[231] In this sense, Schelling's inclusive whole, Jacobi observes, is not just the initial stage of reality, rather it constitutes the true and eternal shape of reality. This whole is thus considered as a productive activity that never produces anything different than itself. Eventually, the activity of this whole is supposed to bring forth existence but,

A STUDY

Jacobi claims, the activity of the whole does not generate true being, because it does not generate a true individual agent.[232]

The result is thus quite overt: this absolute portrays the profile of a God that "is the equivalence of necessity and freedom; for the negation, in virtue of which necessity appears to the finite soul as independent of freedom and opposed to it, disappears in Him. But He is equally essence of freedom and necessity [and] since God is the absolute harmony of necessity and freedom, *yet this harmony can only be expressed in the whole, not in individuals, so history too occurs only as a whole.*"[233] Schelling elaborates on this thesis not only in the writings that lay the foundation for his philosophy of identity, but also in the talk that he gave in 1807 at the Academy of Sciences of Munich.[234] As said earlier in this introduction, in respect of its focus on the activity of the I the Munich conference marks an important turning point in the pre-history of the dispute between the two philosophers, although a more elaborate and precise composition of the disputation will only appear in the *Divine Things*. Nevertheless, in his 1807 speech Schelling clearly states that nature is the only inspiration for artists, because nature is "the holy, eternally creating, primordial force of the world that begets and laboriously brings forth all things from itself."[235] The idea cannot be clearer than in this quotation: it helps us see what Jacobi sees as the most controversial and disputed of Schelling's theses. The conflation of spontaneity and determinism, of freedom and necessity within a whole that does not only brings everything forth, but it is that everything that is brought forth.

According to Schelling, the productivity of the all-including movement unearths the finite being's true existence, which matches the necessary movement of the whole. Nothing is above this whole: it includes the All-Unity of existence and introduces the sole actuality of an all-encompassing life. All this can be re-phrased differently by following what Jacobi seems to have in mind: since Schelling claims that we have access to proper cognition only if we determine properly, and since proper determination consists in defining the original connection between autonomy and determinism, the key to proper cognition seems to result from the bridge between the unconditioned and the conditioned. This approach ends either with turning any determination into a conditioned *ad infinitum*, or with accepting an unconditioned that brings to an end the chain of determination, or with accepting that any determination is just a conditioned that associates within an unlimited unconditioned. Since the first option leads to an untenable regress and the second option to an unjustified principle, Schelling accepts the latter option.

The resulting monistic conception of reality calls for thinking to be conceived as a *Subjektivität* that solely defines an anonymous activity of the absolute. From this new conception of the I, Jacobi draws his famous thesis concerning Schelling's philosophy: such a subjectivity is a mere I that does not possess any real existence.[236] The unconditioned that Schelling theorizes is a subjectivity that is not a subject, because it merely portrays the activity of the principle of indifference. It is a primordial force that does not unearth a world of finite, existing objects, it never produces an objective other-than-itself, as it just grows out of itself and in itself. The activity of this whole is rather an internal process of self-ontogenesis.[237]

Hence, Jacobi re-defines the whole *logos* of the determination of existence via a re-habilitation of those paradigms that concern the I and its relation to its other. Jacobi then establishes the determination of existence according to the rational nature of the I which, this time, is conceived as a person. On the one side Jacobi needs to avoid the contradictions of an I that is not a real I, while on the other side he also must overcome the frictions of a notion of existence that does not refer to anything existing. To solve these problems, he does not define the I in systematic terms. Rather, he focuses on the autonomy of the I's being because the I's being alone grants real freedom and real existence.

The autonomy of the I's being is therefore not defined as a mere finitude. If the I's being were conceived as a mere finitude, it would bring back the *mediation* to others and, by the same token, the two nihilistic alternatives: (1) it would be related to the unlimited chain of the conditioned, or (2) it would necessarily lead to its obliteration into the unconditioned. Instead, the I's being is defined according to the traits of a person, which is a rational activity that reveals the metaphysics of being and shows – by means of this very rational activity – what is the "true." In the end it is the person the only catalyst that reveals the necessary connection between three elements: the free agent, the determination of being in general, and the profile of a divine origin.[238] Within this connection one can see how the distinct activity of the person is the virtue that defines autonomy and provides the concrete determination of a world of finite, autonomous Wesen.

Truth be told, the connection of the human being with the objects of nature, hence the connection between freedom and determinism, unconditioned and conditioned, is not entirely defined in Jacobi's texts. But Jacobi fully accepts the inexplicability of the connection between the conditioned and the unconditioned because this connection dwells within the person. Moreover, Jacobi

A STUDY   71

shows the rationality of this inexplicable connection: real being is defined following a specific metaphysical method that brings forth the identity of being, like Kant did in his pre-critical texts. At the same time, Jacobi makes explicit that *rationality* itself is the specific human "drive" that manifests the "realm of beings" and shows their connection to their origin. The person, by acting as a rational agent, shows the original connection between unconditioned and conditioned for it embodies the principle by means of which everything should be conceived.

The *Divine Things* can be interpreted as a return to issues already discussed in the *Spinoza Letters*. No doubt, Spinoza furnished the paradigm of the All-One that orients systematic philosophy with regard to both thinking and action. It is also clear that idealists like Schelling do not perceive the *en kai pan* as an oppressive principle that annihilates individualities, but as the original impulse that enlivens them. However, Jacobi would claim that this life is no one's life, because no individual really exists within that universal totality.[239]

As has been shown, Jacobi's notion of origin does not correspond to the whole that the *en kai pan* describes. The origin is rather an *Einer* that limits itself and constitutes the measure of existence. In light of the *logos* that explains existence, the specific activity of a God-creator is repeatedly depicted in the final pages of the *Divine Things*, where God's self-sufficiency (he is the one that can declare "I am who I am," without reference to a Thou) is associated with a clear echo of human free agency and its specifics, so that God's absolute solitude is connected to human ethical profile.

In these pages, we can see how the fundamental aspects of Jacobi's criticism of Schelling's naturalism are consistent with the three Letters to Köppen.[240] In these letters, Jacobi shows how modern thinking is unable to solve the problem that the Kantian antinomy presented in respect to the origin of the world. Jacobi is then able to convey the idea that the problem concerning the origin of existence has shown the way we need to walk if we want to assess the real character of rationality. Rationality is challenged on its very foundation when the origin of the world is taken under consideration: how our thinking should perceive the link between the unconditioned to the conditioned, how our thinking should conceive of absolute creation, and how our thinking must define free action. These are the questions that the antinomy brings to the fore, but they are also those questions that must remain beyond the reach of discursive thinking. As Jacobi has tried to contend, those questions are better defined only within a different idea of reason and a different idea of knowledge.[241]

72 PAOLO LIVIERI

Jacobi's theism is thus the basis of his ontology as well as his theory of rationality, because both God's existence and his creative action are revealed in the absolute measure that produces both the cosmic order of being and the very *logos* that reveals that same being.[242] This shows how Jacobi's theism upholds the primacy of the *true* over the *beautiful* and *good*: the *logos* concerning God and his freedom reveals that existence – hence, what is true – and manifests just the measure that God has given.[243]

IV CONCLUDING REMARKS

A very general description of Jacobi's motivation to write the *Divine Things* can be summed up by considering the problem of defining existence.

Apparently, we cannot know existence per se, for it becomes available to our knowledge only through its systematic qualifications; it never appears as it is. Nevertheless, we need to define a way to connect intellectually with what dwells behind our knowledge: a place that is immediate accessible to us, yet resistant to all qualification and seemingly impossible to relate to. This situation calls for an analysis of this original antecedent, which looks like the object of a "faith" that can never be doubted because extends where knowledge has yet to arise.

I have described what I called *recollection* by means of a metaphysical approach, which proves both necessary and insufficient to describe what existence is. Jacobi seems to maintain that pre-critical Kantian and Platonic metaphysics must help us unearth the right route towards existence; just as much as Aristotle comes to the aid of our investigation concerning the notion of origin. However, this method proves insufficient, for it does not bring about a successful explanation of existence.

This failure notwithstanding, the insufficiency of the metaphysical investigation manifests the nature of existence itself, which eludes definitions and explanations. In a sense, this method is insufficient, but not deficient. Jacobi's theism addresses precisely this conundrum, as it demands we decide whether to deduce everything (all existence) either from one or from nothing. To be more precise, Jacobi does not really ask us to *deduce* from one, as if to infer from an absolute principle. Rather, he requires that we see all that is endowed with true existence through (*durch*) the One or through the Nothing. In other terms, Jacobi wants us to decide whether to define the actual through the

A STUDY

autonomy of an individual agent – that his philosophy describes – or through the Nothing – that naturalism, idealism, and systematic philosophy impose with their doctrines of immanent connections.

According to the *Divine Things*, deciding for the One mainly implies two arguments: (a) reason displays the autonomy of our practical nature and makes it explicit what objects populate our experience, and (b) reason connects us with our origin. Jacobi's deduction thus rests on the fact that a free agent becomes the concept that gives access to true being. Based on his practical profile, the human being describes a reality in which the profile of the ultimate *you*, God, is reflected not only in the profile of the agent, the I, but also in the definition of everything that populates the human world. In this sense, describing existence equates with defining our relationship with our ultimate origin.

Though merely human, Jacobi would claim, existence is not subjective: the human element rather makes the revelation of existence possible and its origin rational. If the human element were subtracted, we would fall victim of an abstraction, that would pave the way for the idealistic approach to reality. The human element must hold true: both human reason and human activity allow for the revelation of the markers of existence, e.g., God creator, the immortality of the soul, and the existential autonomy. They are the three factors that ground Jacobi's realism. But only a person can reveal these markers; and it does so by revealing its own rational self. In short, as we execute what makes us a person, we reveal to ourselves the divine order of existence.[244]

Nevertheless, existence remains partially invisible, because it depends on those markers that never fully become phenomena.[245] God himself never explicitly appears in phenomena; he does not incarnate. Jacobi may call himself a Christian, but his creed remains within the limits of this specific perimeter, which rejects both historical epiphany and rational proof. In fact, Jacobi claims that God neither comes to us in the form of his son nor in the form of the conclusion of a reasoning.[246] Instead, God is immediately revealed to us by our *personhood*, which perceives the divinity of being and executes this divinity. Our reason embodies our personhood and rightfully becomes the "Priesterin des Gottes."[247]

Beyond this delicate equilibrium, one more issue seems to present itself. A person needs to *relate* to the world of finite objects. Following Jacobi's reasoning, one must admit that existence necessitates a dialectic between the world of conditioned realities and the dimension of unconditioned authority. Jacobi is aware of this dialectic: his theism assumes that the connection between God and creation, absolute unconditioned and conditioned, is the same as the relation between a free agent and the natural world. This dialectic "is an inconceivable presupposition because, while it apodictically claims a relationship of all that is conditioned to a single unconditioned, it does not in any way reveal the real interconnection between the two."[248]

Based on this recurrent remark, we must admit that human intellect cannot really investigate the depth of the unconditioned, though it cannot reject it. If we were to reject it, then individuals would vanish and existence would disappear: "there has arisen a world of qualities without a man to them, of experiences without anyone to experience them, and it almost looks as though under ideal conditions man would no longer experience anything at all privately and the comforting weight of personal responsibility would dissolve into a system of formulae for potential meaning. It is probable that the dissolution of the anthropocentric attitude ... has finally begun to affect the personality itself; for the belief that the most important thing about experience is the experiencing of it, and about deeds the doing of them, is beginning to strike most people as naïve."[249]

If at this point Jacobi's theism should have become clearer, it remains partially problematic its general profile. We must indeed remember that this God is just the God of Jacobi's distinct theism. I do not want to claim that this limit is necessarily a defect, but I would like to pinpoint that Jacobi conceives of God only in contrast to modern nihilism. It seems that Jacobi's God and its realm of beings cannot cope with the many manifestations of annihilation that Western religious tradition would welcome, including the idea that the eradication of the rationality of God's personhood is part of God's revelation. Eventually, the salvation that Jacobi's notion of freedom yields only accommodates those specific issues that systematic philosophy introduces.

NOTES

1   Hegel's interpretation of Jacobi's thought evolved from a negative critique, as in
     Faith and Knowledge (1802), to a general, yet thorough analysis, as in the *Encyclopaedia* 1830 (§§ 6–178). For a study of their limited interaction and an understanding of their respective positions see: Buée, *Savoir immédiat et savoir absolu*; Franks,
     "All or Nothing"; Halbig, "The Philosopher as Polyphemus?" George di Giovanni
     had indicated to me that Jacobi acknowledged that "he [Hegel] may well be right,
     and I would dearly love to undertake with him, once more, a thorough research

A STUDY   75

into what the power of thought can yield itself, were not the head of the old man too weak for the job." Letter to Johann Neeb, 30 May 1817. See Roth, *Friedrich Heinrich Jacobi's auserlesener Briefwechsel*, 2:467–8. More recently, Schick, "Möglich, Wirklich oder Notwendig?"

2 See Cassirer, *Das Erkenntnisproblem*, 3:18. For a more contemporary discussion see Snow, "F.H. Jacobi and the Development of German Idealism," 399. As Snow points out, proof of the undeniable value of Jacobi's analytical interpretations and reformulations of prominent philosophical perspectives is in the fact that even those who devalue Jacobi's philosophical stature, nonetheless recognize his critical position in the development of post-Kantian philosophy, see Summerer, *Wirkliche Sittlichkeit*, 226. This also seems to be the position assumed by Baum, *Vernunft und Erkenntnis*, 1.

3 See Essen and Danz, *Philosophisch-theologische Streitsachen*. The *Theismusstreit* usually dates from 1811 through 1812; by way of a different time reference, I would like to stress the relevance of texts included in Jacobi's *Divine Things* that dates back to the conclusion of the *Atheismusstreit*, hence more than ten years before. However, the *Theismusstreit* concerns the very limited time frame 1811–12 in terms of the actual controversy.

4 Roth, *Friedrich Heinrich Jacobi's auserlesener Briefwechsel*, 2:303.

5 See Roth, *Friedrich Heinrich Jacobi's auserlesener Briefwechsel*, 2:467–68. In what follows I will use the terms "existence" and "being" as synonyms.

6 In this introductory study the "Letter to Fichte" will always be mentioned as *Jacobi to Fichte*, following the English edition by George di Giovanni in *The Main Philosophical Writings*, 497–536. However, in my translation of Jacobi's *Divine Things*, I will use "Letter to Fichte." On this topic see Nuzzo, "Nachklänge der Fichte-Rezeption Jacobis in der Schrift von den göttlichen Dingen und ihrer Offenbarung (1811)."

7 See the letter 11 May 1811, in Roth, *Friedrich Heinrich Jacobi's auserlesener Briefwechsel*, 2:177. In this letter Jacobi refers to this text as focusing on "Philosophie und Christenthum." Accounts of the publication can be obtained in Jean Paul's letter to Jacobi (13 August 1811), where one finds a surprisingly early report of the issue, see Paul, *Sämtliche Briefe*, 6:218. Jacobi's letter to Goethe from 1 September 1811 refers to the printing process, see Goethe, *Briefe, Tagebücher und Gespräche*, 1, 6:58, 22, 39, and 43. According to the editor of the critical edition, the *Divine Things* must have been published at the end of October or beginning of November 1811, see Jaeschke, "Editorischer Bericht," 175–6. We can offer even greater precision in terms of dating by taking into account that the issue of the *Morgenblatt für gebildete Stände*

published on Thursday, 10 October 1811, advertises that a new book by Jacobi, the *Divine Things*, has been released. This information appears to be based on the list of new publications made at the Michaelis-Messe.

8 See Jacobi's brother's *Taschenbuch für das Jahr 1802*. The text will return to being an independent essay in the second edition of the *Divine Things*.

9 See Jaeschke, "Kommentar," 191. In 1797 Jacobi accepts a commission from the *Hamburger Correspondent* to review the 6th volume of M. Claudius' collected writings.

10 Roth, *Friedrich Heinrich Jacobi's auserlesener Briefwechsel*, 2:413.

11 It is worthwhile to notice that Jacobi includes in a letter to F. Perthes (4 May 1811) an eight-page manuscript written by Jacobi's half-sister Lotte which presents a copy of the final component of the *Divine Things*. Jacobi, in his own hand, titles the excerpt "Philosophie und Christenthum/Beschluß." Therefore, the title *Von den göttlichen Dingen und ihrer Offenbarung* was given to the text later in 1811. See Jaeschke, "Editorischer Bericht," 186–7. For further discussion on the different titles that Jacobi gives to his work on revelation see Fries, *Aus seinem Handschriftlichen Nachlasse*, 318. And also Jacobi, *Briefe an Friedr. Bouterwek*, 130.

12 See Jacobi, *Werke. Gesamtausgabe*, 3:139. On the exact date of the publication (the official 1802, instead of the actual 1801), see Jaeschke and Piske, "Editorischer Bericht," 485.

13 Roth, *Friedrich Heinrich Jacobi's auserlesener Briefwechsel*, 2:414. Italic added.

14 See Verra, "Jacobis Kritik am deutschen Idealismus."

15 See Schelling, *Sämtliche Werke*, 18:53–230. On Jacobi's true intentions see the *Vorbericht* to the second edition (1816) in Jacobi, *Werke. Gesamtausgabe*, 3:153, and Jaeschke, "Kommentar," 191. Jacobi himself states that he sees the four texts (*Jacobi an Fichte, Ueber das Unternehmen, Weissagung Lichtenbergs*, and *Von den göttlichen Dingen*) as one single essay, see the *Vorrede* in *Werke. Gesamtausgabe*, 3:139. Jaeschke observes that Jacobi might have meant to include the *Misslungener Versuch* (the Claudius review) instead of *Von den göttlichen Dingen* in the list. However, Mues argues that there is no reason to contradict what Jacobi himself affirms. See Mues, "Editionspraxis," 169.

16 Jacobi, "Jacobi to Fichte," 508–9. On the notion of Jacobi's true rationalism as opposed to idealism, see Franks, "All or Nothing," 95–116.

17 As early as Leo Strauss' dissertation on F.H. Jacobi's philosophy, the relation between *Wahrnehmung* and *Vernehmung* became critical to the interpretation of Jacobi's thought. See Strauss, *Philosophie und Gesetz*, 3–123.

18 On the opposition between science and the doctrine of God see Cerutti, "Présentation," 13. See also Höhn, "F.H. Jacobi et G.W. Hegel," 129–50. Jacobi equates his doc-

A STUDY

77

trine with pietism in his letter to Voß, 16 October 1809. Notwithstanding Jacobi's self-portrait, one should consider the differences between pietism and Jacobi's thinking as they have been introduced by Hammacher, "Ein bemerkenswerter Einfluss," 327–47. On the religious motivation of Jacobi's first writings see Lorenz, "Sur la portée historique," 111–18.

19 Important to this particular discussion is the letter to F. Jacobs in March 1813. See Hammacher, "Ein bemerkenswerter Einfluss," 327–47.

20 Jacobi, *Divine Things*, 109.

21 Lichtenberg was renowned as critic of culture (more so than a systematic thinker) mainly for his contributions to both the *Göttinger Taschen Calender*, of which he was the editor since 1778, and the *Göttingeschen Magazin der Wissenschaften und Litterature*, that he founded in 1779 together with G. Foster (the first issue was published in 1780). He left a great number of aphorisms, excerpts, and notes that were published between 1800 and 1806 in nine volumes under the title *Vermischte Schriften*. The above-mentioned aphorism was included in Lichtenberg's first volume, see Lichtenberg, *Vermischte Schriften*, vol. 1 (Göttingen: J.Ch. Dieterich, 1800), 166. A more accessible edition of his writings can be found in Lichtenberg, *Vermischte Schriften*, vol. 1 (Göttingen: Dieterischen Buchhandlung, 1844), 58. A letter by Lichtenberg sent in 1793 bears witness to the esteem that he had for the "sage from Pempelfort." See Lichtenberg, *Schriften und Briefe*, 4,2:615–17. For a comprehensive portrayal of both Lichtenberg and his position in regards to the religious turmoil and uprising at the end of eighteenth century, see Sautermeister, *Georg Christoph Lichtenberg*.

22 See Promies, *Georg Christoph Lichtenberg*, 83–4. And also Verrecchia, *Georg Christoph Lichtenberg*, 162.

23 See Promies, *Georg Christoph Lichtenberg*, 126.

24 About Lichtenberg's rather elusive figure, see especially Zubke, *Georg Christoph Lichtenberg*, and Butler, "Fielding's Panzaic Voice," 189–206. See also Mengaldo, *Zwischen Naturlehre und Rhetorik*. For topics that are relevant for this context see also Löhnert, *Sitz und Stimme in Gottes Unterhaus*. The complexity and ramification of Lichtenberg's ideas cannot be detailed here because he is not one of Jacobi's direct interlocutors in the *Divine Things*. Jacobi uses Lichtenberg's aphorism only to set the initial tone and sketch the dramatic evolution of his age. In fact, Jacobi uses Lichtenberg's ideas to give to himself enough room to elaborate upon them according to his own vision.

25 See Roth, *Friedrich Heinrich Jacobi's auserlesener Briefwechsel*, 2:413.

26 Ibid., 260.

27 See Requadt, *Lichtenberg*, 2:9–19. Lichtenberg connects aphorism to a *Philosophie*

des Lebens that originates from the encounter of the biblical tradition with ancient Greek and Latin cultures. See Lichtenberg, *Vermischte Schriften* (1844), 1:274. On this see Requadt, *Lichtenberg*, 2:133–66.

28 See Verrecchia, *Georg Christoph Lichtenberg*, 186.

29 We have a clear instance of this affinity in 1778. After consulting with Wieland, Jacobi turns to Claudius for the education of his two sons, Johann Friedrich and Georg Arnold. See Roedl, *Matthias Claudius*, 215.

30 Ibid., 268. In 1786 Claudius writes two reviews about the dialogue between Jacobi and Mendelssohn which, while being impartial, shows his appreciation of Jacobi's exceptional analyses. See Claudius, *Werke*, 431.

31 See Jaeschke, "Editorischer Bericht," 178.

32 See Roedl, *Matthias Claudius*, 363–4. On this see also Cerutti, "Présentation," 10–11.

33 See Roedl, *Matthias Claudius*, 362–3. Jacobi hopes a final clarification will come in the *Vorrede* to the third volume of his *Werke*. According to Perthes, 1796 is the year when the first disagreement between Jacobi and Claudius occurs. See Cerutti, "Présentation," 11. See also Perthes, *Friedrich Perthes' Leben*, 1:62. This confirms that the letter to Jan Paul refers to the time of inception of the *Divine Things* project.

34 See Jacobi, *Werke. Gesamtausgabe*, 3:48. Italic added. This divergence notwithstanding, the locution "Göttliche Dinge" comes from Claudius, see Claudius, *Werke*, 557. On this issue the French editor of the *Divine Things* P. Cerutti refers to Claudius' letter to Fürstin von Gallitzin sent on 12 February 1792. See also Hammacher, "Biographie als Problemgeschichte," 112, n44. And also Kranefuss, *Matthias Claudius*, 182.

35 See Tilliette, *Schelling im Spiegel seiner Zeitgenossen*, 1:98. See also Sommer, *Zwischen Metaphysik und Metaphysikkritik*, 93–108. Currently there are plans to devote an edited volume on the relationship between Jacobi and Schelling, which will fill a gap in the scholarship devoted to classical German philosophy. The present analysis, however, is dedicated to the *Divine Things* only, whose focus is not a confrontation with Schelling's philosophy. As said above, Jacobi's intention is to tackle a problem that surpasses Schelling's thought and goes back to Jacobi's study of Spinoza's ethics and Kant's transcendental philosophy.

36 See Henke, *Jakob Friedrich Fries*, 311. See also Weischedel, *Jacobi und Schelling*, 20–1.

37 See Brüggen, "Jacobi, Schelling und Hegel," 210.

38 See Schelling, *Aus Schellings Leben in Briefen*, 346 and 351. See on this Brüggen, "Jacobi, Schelling und Hegel," 211.

39 See Jacobi and Bouterwek, *Briefe an Friedr. Bouterwek*, 28.

40 See ibid., 28–9. Italic is mine. I here refer to Schelling's *Darstellung meines Systems der Philosophie* (1801), see on this Ivaldo, "Sul teismo: Jacobi versus Schelling," 139.

41 See Jacobi's *Einleitung* in Jacobi, *Werke. Gesamtausgabe*, 2, 1:375–433.

A STUDY

79

42 Jacobi gives a report of his interaction with Schelling's philosophy of nature in Jacobi and Bouterwek, *Briefe an Friedr. Bouterwek*, 51. In this letter, dated from 1808, Jacobi explicitly identifies all Schelling's phases as stages of a coherent evolution of his Identity-philosophy.

43 See Jacobi and Bouterwek, *Briefe an Friedr. Bouterwek*, 124.

44 See Ivaldo, *Filosofia delle cose divine*, 207–9. See also Brüggen, "Jacobi, Schelling und Hegel," 217.

45 In a letter dated 14 January 1812 Schelling speaks of "offner Krieg," a war waged on him by Jacobi, which started raging as early as 1803 when J.Fr. Köppen published his *Schellings Lehre oder das Ganze der Philosophie des absoluten Nichts* together with three letters by Jacobi in which the term "Krieg" is overtly mentioned. This literary war was not confined to Munich but reached Goethe in Weimar as noted by Jaeschke, *Religionsphilosophie und spekulative Theologie. Quellenbd.*, 318. See also Wenz, *Von den göttlichen Dingen*, 3–19, especially nn 4–8.

46 On Schelling's early philosophy and its relation to Jacobi's criticism see Sandkaulen, *Ausgang vom Unbedingten*.

47 See Jaeschke, *Transzendentalphilosophie und Spekulation. Quellenbd.* And also Jaeschke, *Religionsphilosophie und spekulative Theologie*. A quick look at the letters of some of the figures involved in the philosophical disputes in Germany in the early nineteenth century makes us appreciate the degree of anticipation that surrounded the publication of the *Divine Things*: Jean Paul and Friedrich Schlegel were eagerly expecting (the first expressed in a letter sent on 13 August 1811, and the latter in a letter dated 23 November 1811) this last work by Jacobi; whereas Schelling in a letter to K.J.H. Windischmann (12 November 1811) inquired whether the book had yet been issued. See Jaeschke, "Editorischer Bericht," 174–5. Among the many reactions, one of the most significant can be found in F. Schlegel's review of Jacobi's *Divine Things*, which is included in the French edition of the text. Schlegel, "Recension (1812)," 157–71.

48 We can also mention Georg Ellinger's *Der Werth der positive Offenbarung, aus der Unhaltbarkeit der bisherigen philosophischen Bemühungen*, published in *Deutsches Museum* (1812), though it merely repeats Fr. Schlegel's position. See also Wenz, *Von den göttlichen Dingen*, 76–80. It is important to note that a large group of scholars and intellectuals stood by Schelling's *Naturphilosophie/Identitätsphilosophie*, for instance J.A.G. Schaffroth, H. Steffens, and J.W. Goethe among others. By the time the second edition of the *Divine Things* appeared (1816), the so-called *Streit um die Göttliche Dingen* had already ceased. A last, important fallout was attested in F. Schlegel's review of Jacobi's *Werke*, in Schlegel, *Kritische Friedrich-Schlegel-Ausgabe*, 8:585–96.

49 In a letter to Jean Paul dated 13 September 1809, Jacobi mentioned that he was trying to bring to conclusion his work "on Revelation" without even alluding to Schelling's philosophy; the same happens in the letter that Jacobi sends to the editor Perthes in May 1811, where he announces the conclusion of the manuscript: no mention of Schelling is made. See Roth, *Friedrich Heinrich Jacobi's auserlesener Briefwechsel*, 1:413. And also ibid., 1:177n14. Jacobi's reference to Schelling comes explicitly to light in the second, third, and fourth volume of the *Werke* (1815, 1816, 1819).

50 See Pseudo-Longinus, *On the Sublime*, chapter 9.

51 See Doran, *The Theory of the Sublime*, 185. In Kant, the "supersensible existence" is defined "sublime" (*erhaben*) with reference to its immediate access to a dimension of freedom. See Kant, *Gesammelte Schriften*, 5:88. Concerning the sublime aspects of human life, one must keep in mind that Jacobi does not conceive his enterprise as a positive evaluation of the sublime in nature. There is no such an "enthusiasm" for nature in his philosophy, as opposed to other philosophers and artists of his time. See Sandkaulen, "Zur Vernunft des Gefühls bei Jacobi," 358–9.

52 Cf. Jacobi, *Divine Things*, 184.

53 See Jacobi, "Preface (1815)," 556 and 559–60.

54 See Körner, *Briefe von und an Friedrich und Dorothea Schlegel*, 155.

55 See Jacobi, "Preface (1815)," 555 and 564.

56 On this distinction, see Baum, *Vernunft und Erkenntnis*, 131–2.

57 Jacobi, "Concerning the Doctrine of Spinoza (1785)," 193. Italic is mine.

58 Ibid., 227.

59 See di Giovanni, "The Unfinished Philosophy," 74. The translation from Latin is di Giovanni's.

60 See Jacobi, "Concerning the doctrine of Spinoza (1785)," 218.

61 See ibid., 226.

62 See ibid., 227.

63 See ibid., 218.

64 See Jacobi, "Jacobi to Fichte," 502–5. See Acerbi, "Commento," 251, and Sandkaulen, "Oder hat Vernunft den Menschen?," 421–2.

65 On this issue, the distinction between "Abstraktion" and "Intuition," is essential. It is made as early as 1773 in Jacobi's essay entitled *Betrachtung Über die von Herrn Herder in seiner Abhandlung vom Ursprung der Sprache Vorgelegte Genetische Erklärung der Thierischen Kunstfertigkeiten und Kunsttriebe*, in Jacobi, *Werke. Gesamtausgabe*, 4, 1:13–25.

66 See Jacobi, "Jacobi to Fichte," 512.

67 See ibid., 506.

A STUDY

68   See the letter to Hamann dated from 16 June 1783. Jacobi, *Briefwechsel*, 3:161–4. The term *Geschäft der Philosophie* is used in the *Fliegende Blätter*, see Jacobi, *Werke. Gesamtausgabe*, 5, 1:415.

69   See Jacobi, "Concerning the Doctrine of Spinoza (1785)," 370.

70   Jacobi, "David Hume," 294.

71   Jacobi, *Werke. Gesamtausgabe*, 2:229.

72   See Jacobi, "Jacobi to Fichte," 514–15.

73   On this see Baum, *Vernunft und Erkenntnis*, 108.

74   Jacobi, "Preface (1815)," 584–5. See on this Ivaldo, *Filosofia delle cose divine*, 87–9, and Baum, *Vernunft und Erkenntnis*, 113–15. Baum claims that the common misunderstanding that puts *Vernunft* and *Verstand* in conflict has grown out of Jacobi's early terminological inconsistency, which has thus nourished those interpretations that saw in Jacobi's philosophy a cardinal model of the so called *Lebensphilosophie*. This, as Baum detailed, has its focus upon what cannot be objectified (which includes what cannot be scientifically approached) and is instead defined only to the degree that it fits a teleological framework. See Baum, *Vernunft und Erkenntnis*, 5 and 118. For general references see Bollnow, *Die Lebensphilosophie F.H. Jacobis*. A more precise account on this can be found in Harms, *Über die Lehre von Friedrich Heinrich Jacobi*, 14–15, and Crawford, *The Philosophy of F.H. Jacobi*, 48–9.

75   See Baum, *Vernunft und Erkenntnis*, 18–19.

76   I use "discursive thinking" and "science" as synonyms.

77   Jacobi, "David Hume," 305.

78   Ibid. As it has often been confirmed ever since the publication of the volume by L. Bruhl, Jacobi referred to D. Hume's philosophy to elaborate a fully different theory about the *Glaube*, which, in Jacobi's case, yields an objective definition of the existence of the object outside of the subject. See Lévy-Bruhl, *La philosophie de Jacobi*, 107.

79   The problem with abstraction consists in the fact that abstraction connects subject and object according to a relation that is ultimately subjective. Therefore, this process inevitably results in the annihilation of any difference between subject and object, which causes the eventual abolition of reality as such.

80   Jacobi, "David Hume," 293–4.

81   See ibid., 335.

82   See Sandkaulen, *Jacobis Philosophie*, 184–5. Sandkaulen offers a sophisticated analysis of Kant's notion of *thing in itself* in relation to Jacobi's realism. The following remarks draw from Sandkaulen's text.

83   Jacobi, "David Hume," 336.

84   Ibid., 337.

85 Ibid., 334–7.

86 See Jacobi, "Jacobi to Fichte," 502.

87 See Jacobi, "Concerning the Doctrine of Spinoza (1785)," 191.

88 Ibid., 194.

89 See Jacobi, "David Hume," 277, especially footnote 15.

90 Ibid., 295.

91 Recently on this topic, see Agamben, *L'irrealizzabile*, especially ch. 3. *Il possibile è il reale.*

92 Jacobi, "Concerning the Doctrine of Spinoza (1785)," 345. One should not pay attention to the use of the term "demonstrated" (*beweist*) in this context. One would run the risk of interpreting the apparent contradiction between immediacy and demonstration as a symptom of a broader theoretical fallacy. Jacobi might well have used the term "revealed" in this context.

93 See Jacobi, "David Hume," 301.

94 Jacobi, "Concerning the Doctrine of Spinoza (1785)," 227.

95 Jacobi, "Jacobi to Fichte," 510.

96 Jacobi, *Werke. Gesamtausgabe*, 2, 1:252. It refers to the second *Anhang* to the letter to Fichte, whose text has been first published in the 1792 edition of the *Eduard Allwill*. See on this Jacobi, *Werke, Gesamtausgabe*, 6, 1:89–90.

97 Jacobi, "Concerning the doctrine of Spinoza (1785)," 371–2. See Sandkaulen, *Grund und Ursache*, 103–30.

98 Jacobi, "David Hume," 269.

99 Jacobi, *Divine Things*, 189.

100 See Bowman, "Notiones Communes und Common Sense," 166. Bowman provides a detailed analysis in support of the thesis that Jacobi was inspired by a Spinozistic understanding of the notion of certainty, which only subsequently found a backing in Th. Ried's philosophy. On the notion of *Fürwahrhalten* in the context of and in opposition to systematic philosophy see Sandkaulen, "Fürwahrhalten ohne Gründe." Sandkaulen shows that Jacobi assumes Spinoza's system as the ultimate results of a coherent architecture of philosophy as opposed to Mendelssohn's flawed rationalism, which inappropriately seeks to rise to the knowledge of the biblical God by way of demonstration. As Sandkaulen shows, Jacobi's notion of *Glaube* is independent of any religious representation; it rather takes place act in the form of a grounding the immediate certainty of being.

101 See Baum, *Vernunft und Erkenntnis*," 97–8.

102 On the twofold revelation of the I and the opposite Thou in all aspects of the I (finite and divine), see Hamann, *Schriften über Philosophie, Philologie, Kritik*, 73.

103 See Jacobi, *Briefwechsel*, 3:385–90.

A STUDY

83

104 M.M. Olivetti offers a sophisticated account of Jacobi's theory of knowledge, which would bring forth a bridge between epistemology and hermeneutics. As Jacobi's reading of Lichtenberg's prophecy would show, knowing would translate into comprehending the traces of being in our own intellectual activities. See Olivetti, *L'esito teologico della filosofia del linguaggio di Jacobi*.

105 See Jacobi, "David Hume," 281–5. On Jacobi's philosophical apprenticeship see Pistilli, *Tra dogmatismo e scetticismo*. On the topic of the Kantian method implemented by Jacobi, see Livieri, *Metafisica dell'esistenza*.

106 See Kant, "Inquiry," 250.

107 Cf. Jacobi, *Divine Things*, 100.

108 See Jacobi, "Preface (1815)," 568.

109 Kant, "Inquiry," 259. Italics added.

110 In the English translation of Kant's text, the term "being" (*Sein*) is identical with "positing in general," while "existence" (*Dasein*) is the "absolute positing," which is equivalent to Jacobi's notion of "existence" (Dasein/Wesen). See Kant, "The Only Possible Argument," 119 and 124.

111 See Kant, "The Only Possible Argument," 117–19.

112 See ibid., 119–20.

113 See ibid., 121.

114 Ibid., 123.

115 See Ibid., 125.

116 See Ibid., 124–5.

117 Ibid., 123.

118 See di Giovanni, "The Unfinished Philosophy," 82–3.

119 Kant, "Inquiry," 250.

120 See ibid., 256.

121 See Jacobi, "Preface (1815)," 571–3.

122 See ibid., 563. Baum's whole interpretation of Jacobi's philosophy can be regarded as both a theoretical and historiographical analysis of the distinction between *Intuitio* and *Abstractio*. Baum deems intuition the pivotal notion of Jacobi's realism, which stands against those epistemologies that claim that knowledge draws its content from an alleged external reality (as it is the case in Aristotle, Locke, Condillac, Bonnet, etc.). See Baum, *Vernunft und Erkenntnis*, 26–7.

123 See Jacobi, *Werke. Gesamtausgabe*, 2, 1:322–3.

124 Kant, *Critique of Pure Reason*, 99.

125 See ibid., 99.

126 See Sandkaulen, "Letzte oder erste Fragen?," 57.

127 See Jacobi, *Werke. Gesamtausgabe*, 2, 1:325.

128 See ibid., 325–6.

129 See Jacobi, "Jacobi to Fichte," 517.

130 Ibid., 519.

131 See Jacobi, *Briefwechsel*, 4:277. On this topic see Feldmeier, "Der Mensch, ein 'krummes Holz?,'" 162.

132 See Feldmeier, "Der Mensch, ein 'krummes Holz'?," 325. On this topic see also Sandkaulen, "Letzte oder erste Fragen?," 49–58.

133 See Sandkaulen, "Letzte oder erste Fragen?," 57.

134 Kant, *Critique of Practical Reason*, 100.

135 See ibid., 104.

136 See ibid., 103.

137 See Jacobi, *Werke. Gesamtausgabe*, 2, 1:325–26.

138 See Rohs, "Was ist das Problem," 68–69. Rohs shows how from a notion of freedom that is not compatible with determinism follows a series of issues that arise when determinism itself is assumed to define the laws of nature. This inevitably leads to Jacobi's criticism of Kant's concept of cause. See ibid., 75.

139 See Jacobi, *Divine Things*, 149.

140 See ibid., 148–9.

141 See ibid., 147–9.

142 See Jacobi, "Preface (1815)," 551–2.

143 See Jacobi, *Divine Things*, 149.

144 See ibid., 168–9.

145 See ibid., 158–9.

146 See ibid., 171–2.

147 As stated above, Kant does not recognize the epistemological value of the postulates, hence he does not leap into a metaphysics of non-knowledge. According to this perspective, Kant shows dissatisfaction with the relevance that may wrongly be bestowed on the postulates. See for instance Kant, *Critique of Pure Reason*, 674. Jacobi, while taking a different route, is well aware of it. See Jacobi, *Briefwechsel*, 4:277. See Sandkaulen, "Letzte oder erste Fragen?," 54.

148 See Jacobi, *Divine Things*, 163–4.

149 See Jacobi, "Preface (1815)," 572.

150 See Baum, *Vernunft und Erkenntnis*, 108.

151 See Jacobi, "Preface (1815)," 561 and 555.

152 Jacobi, "Jacobi to Fichte," 497.

153 See Baum, *Vernunft und Erkenntnis*, 112.

154 The parallel between Jacobi and Kant cannot be underestimated. One can establish a parallel between Jacobi's aspatial and atemporal notion of Wesen and what Kant

writes in the *Critique of Practical Reason*: "the same subject, who is also conscious of himself as thing in himself, considers his own existence, *so far as it does not stand under conditions of time*, as itself determinable only through laws that he gives himself through reason, and in this his existence nothing is antecedent to his determination of his will, but every action and every determination of his existence changing in accord with his inner sense, even the entire course of his existence as a sensible being is never to be regarded in his consciousness of his intelligible existence as anything but the consequence and never the determining ground of his causality as a *noumenon*." Kant, *Critique of Practical Reason*, 79. The consonance holds true only if we assume that reason *finds* and does not produce its laws; hence the determination of the existence of the Self surpasses the transcendental forms of intuition only to define existence according to the autonomy that the ethical Self shows.

155 See Calker, *Urgesetzlehre des Wahren*.

156 Jacobi, "Edward Allwill," 492.

157 Jacobi, "Preface (1815)," 562. On the connection between *Vernunft* and *Verstand* see Ivaldo, "Sul Teismo: Jacobi versus Schelling," 139–50. The Kladde VIII makes even more explicit the positive cooperation between reason and understanding. See Jacobi, *Die Denkbücher*, 2:317–77.

158 On the notion of *Zeitlichkeit* in Jacobi, see Sandkaulen, *Jacobis Philosophie*, 271–88.

159 Jacobi, "Preface (1815)," 562.

160 On the analytical method as the one proper to philosophy, see the letter to von Fürstenberg on 17 July 1771. See Jacobi, *Briefwechsel*, 1:118–22. See also Ivaldo, *Filosofia delle cose divine*, 187, and Lauth, "Nouvelles recherches sur Jacobi – II," 499–500.

161 See Jacobi, "Jacobi to Fichte," 514–15.

162 See Jacobi, *Werke. Gesamtausgabe*, 5, 1:403.

163 The term "göttlichen Dingen" was used by M. Claudius in a letter to Princess Gallitzin dated from 12 February 1792. See Jacobi, "David Hume," 281–5.

164 See Jacobi, "Preface (1815)," 570.

165 Jacobi, *Divine Things*, 100.

166 See Jacobi, *Werke. Gesamtausgabe*, 4, 1:377.

167 See Jacobi, "Edward Allwill," 132 and 173–5.

168 See Bowman, "Die Wirklichkeit des wahren Gewissheit," 41–3. The author provides textual references concerning Jacobi's criticism of the proofs for the existence of God. No doubt that Jacobi's criticism of the ontological proof is quite different than Kant's criticism, at least in consideration of Jacobi's understanding of the status of existence in contrast to possibility. Jacobi rejects those proofs for God's existence is immediately perceived, while Kant rejects them for God's existence

86   PAOLO LIVIERI

is a condition for the possibility of one's will to be determined by the moral law. See ibid., 35–6.

169   See Sandkaulen, "Wie 'geistreich' darf Geist Sein?," 55–70.

170   Jacobi quotes G.Ch. Lichtenberg's actual text until "Gespenster" (ghosts); after that, Jacobi elaborates autonomously. On this see Hammacher, "Jacobis Schrift," 129, footnote 1; see also Jaeschke, "Kommentar," 193–4. With the reference to the prophecies, Jacobi might mistakenly have referred to Johann Lichtenberg, not Georg Christoph Lichtenberg, see Hammacher, "Jacobis Schrift," 131, n23.

171   Jacobi, *Divine Things*, 107.

172   See Wenz, *Von den göttlichen Dingen*, 21.

173   Jacobi, "Jacobi to Fichte," 523–4.

174   Ibid., 514.

175   Jacobi, *Divine Things*, 121.

176   See Jacobi, *Werke. Gesamtausgabe*, 5, 1:415.

177   See Jacobi, *Briefwechsel*, 1:118–22.

178   The strategy implemented is common to all of Jacobi's works. The reason for this frequent implementation lies in Jacobi's almost Platonic way of examining all possibilities of thinking about a distinct problem. As a consequence of this examination, Jacobi always produces an outcome that shows the necessity of a solution together with the immediate evidence of its principle, which shows itself by reducing the opposite to absurdity. If not taken as it should be, which means as a constituent part of Jacobi's broad understanding of the possibilities of thinking (e.g., systematic versus non-systematic), this dialectical approach may appear as if it was just a token of Jacobi's polemical attitude. This last interpretation has been hinted at by the otherwise very positive assessment of Fries, *Von deutscher Philosophie*, 40–1. This reading can also be found in Cassirer, *Das Erkenntnisproblem*, 17 and 33, and Busch, *Die Erkenntnistheorie*, 4. See also the introduction by Jan Ulbe Terpstra in Jacobi, *Allwill. Textkritisch herausgegeben*, 5, and also Wieland, "Friedrich Henrich Jacobi," 508–9.

179   Jacobi, "David Hume," 329.

180   Jacobi, *Divine Things*, 108. We can further discuss the problem of certainty as it appears in the first pages of the *Divine Things* with the help of Agrippa's trilemma. In his book *All or Nothing: Systematicity, Transcendental Arguments, and Skepticism in German Idealism*, Franks identifies the problem of the foundation of knowledge according to a critical view of the relation between systematicity and skepticism, and places Jacobi's efforts within this problem. Jacobi's project is to escape the dilemma by abandoning altogether the idea that both Agrippa's trilemma and its

A STUDY

87

responses assume: the idea that the principle of reason provides explanatory conditions of existence. On this see Albert, *Traktat über kritische Vernunft*, 9.

181 Jacobi, *Divine Things*, 108.

182 See Jacobi, *Werke. Gesamtausgabe*, 7, 1:249–50. On this see Stolzenberg, "Was ist Freiheit?," 19–36, and Ivaldo, "Jacobi, Kant (e Aristotele) sulla virtù," 50–60.

183 Through this self-analysis reason recognizes the limits of thinking and ascertains the need for thinking to relate to something that precedes it. This last point was elaborated by Jacobi as early as 1788 in connection to what he calls the "Siegel unserer Unvolkommenheit" which, on one hand states our indebtedness, while one the other hand confirms our superiority to animals. See Jacobi, *Werke. Gesamtausgabe*, 5,1:120–3.

184 Cf. Jacobi, *Divine Things*, 108–9.

185 Cf. ibid., 109.

186 See Lauth, "Friedrich Heinrich Jacobis Allwill," 54–62.

187 Cf. Jacobi, *Divine Things*, 112. Though Jacobi identifies Anaxagoras' teaching with the beginning of a philosophical consideration of the supersensible – as he says in ibid., 175 – he uses Plato's *Philebus* and *Sophist* to establish a notion of supersensible that on the one hand provides a limit to the understanding (e.g., when it comes to the definition of freedom), and on the other hand gives access to the proper definition of God as a free creator of a world populated by finite things. See Acerbi, "Osservazioni sulla lettura Jacobiana di Platone," 54–5. Acerbi stresses that from the Kladden it results that Plato was not the object of extensive study, albeit Jacobi draws from Plato's philosophy in consideration of the issues related to the notion of infinite. See Jacobi, *Die Denkbücher*, 107–8.

188 Jacobi, *Divine Things*, 172.

189 See Plato, "Laws," IV, 716c, and Plato, "Theaetetus," 151d–152a. See Sayre, *Plato's Late Ontology*, especially chapter 2; and White, *Plato on Knowledge and Reality*, especially ch. 1. See Jacobi, *Divine Things*, 112.

190 Jacobi, "Edward Allwill," 494.

191 Among the many examples, one can look at the sermon *Beati pauperes spiritu* in Meister Eckhart, *Deutsche Predigten und Traktate*, 3.Aufl. (München: Hanser, 1969). See Flasch, "Predigt 52: Beati pauperes spiritu," 163–99. Jacobi's notion of God gives evidence of the profound difference between Jacobi's thinking and Christian mysticism, hence the accusation of mysticism was at least technically unsound. However, Jacobi does mention mysticism, for instance in a letter to Stolberg (29 January 1794), but only to emphasize a direct apprehension of the true that Jacobi sees in Plato's philosophy. See Jacobi, *Briefwechsel*, 10:308–20.

192 Jacobi, "Edward Allwill," 489.

193 On the paradox of cosmology see *Beylage VII*, in Jacobi, *Gesamtausgabe, Werke*, 1, 1:253–4.

194 What follows comes from my essay "On the Necessity of Origin in F.H. Jacobi's Last Work," in *Una Filosofia del Non-Sapere. Studi su Friedrich Heinrich Jacobi*, eds P. Valenza, G. Frilli, and F. Pitillo, Archivio di Filosofia (Roma: Serra, 2020), 151–63. I thank the editors for their permission to publish an excerpt of it in this chapter.

195 Cf. Jacobi, *Divine Things*, 104, 114, and 115–16.

196 I need to remind that Aristotle is one of those philosophers whom Jacobi criticizes for confusing abstraction with real knowledge. At the same time though, Jacobi praises Aristotle for his ethics, which ultimately provides a fundamental support to Jacobi's ontology. See Ivaldo, "Jacobi, Kant (e Aristotele) sulla virtù." However, beyond Jacobi's negotiations with Aristotle, in what follows I would like to present a few passages from the *Metaphysica* only to better introduce an important maneuver that takes place in the *Divine Things*.

197 Aristotle, *Metaphysica*, 1013a.

198 Ibid., 1059. See Franco Chiereghin, *Sul principio* (Padova: CUSL, 2000).

199 Jacobi, *Divine Things*, 125.

200 Ibid., 112.

201 Cf. ibid., 113–14.

202 In the *Critique of Pure Reason*, Kant warned that: "the unconditioned necessity, which we need so indispensably as the ultimate sustainer of all things, is for human reason the true abyss. Even eternity ... does not make such a dizzying impression on the mind; for eternity only *measures* the duration of things, but it does not sustain that duration. One cannot resist the thought of it, but one also cannot bear it that a being that we represent to ourselves as the highest among all possible beings might, as it were, say to himself: "I am from eternity to eternity, outside me is nothing except what is something merely through my will; *but whence* then am I?" Kant, *Critique of Pure Reason*, 574.

203 No other concept suffers a refined censorship like the notion of spirit (*Geist*), because Jacobi assumes that it is through a non-discursive power of thinking that spiritual reality is known. Cf. Jacobi, *Divine Things*, 108–9. In the same fashion, in the *Spinoza Letters*, Jacobi draws attention to the same topic by quoting Herder and making Herder's words about the clear eye that sees the true his own. Jacobi equates the Greek *daimon* with the Christian "clear eye" that dwells in our heart: "We have a friend in us – a delicate sanctuary in our soul, where God's voice and intention has long since resounded, sharp and clear. The ancients called it the *daimon*, the *good genius* of man, whom they revered with so much youthful love,

A STUDY

89

and obeyed with so much respect. This is what the Christ meant by the *clear eye* that is the light of life and enlightens the entire body. David asks for it in prayer, as the *Spirit of Life* that leads him on the straight and level path, etc. Let's call it *conscience, inner sense, reason*, the *logos* in us, or what you will." Jacobi, "Concerning the Doctrine of Spinoza (1785)," 247–8. Jacobi used and uses other terms in different works, but all converge to mean the same thing: the reason [*Vernunft*] of man's spirit, the place where God reveals himself. Cf. Jacobi, *Divine Things*, 108. On Jacobi's notion of reason opposing a kind of rationalism see Franks, "All or Nothing."

204 Cf. Jacobi, *Divine Things*, 130–2.

205 Cf. ibid., 129–30.

206 Cf. ibid., 129.

207 See Jacobi, *Werke. Gesamtausgabe*, 5, 1:396–8. Reason reveals to us the divine things (God and our freedom in particular) together with our ignorance. See Iacovacci, *Idealismo e nichilismo*, 112.

208 See Jacobi, *Die Denkbücher*, 235, 140, and 152.

209 An example of Jacobi's epistemological dualism. Even before the publication of the *Spinoza Letters*, Jacobi claims that the human being is only properly defined insofar as it is conceived as a subject able to perform free actions. Without the faculty to act freely, the human being cannot determine itself; instead, it is determined by nature and thus lowered to the animal status. See Jacobi, *Werke. Gesamtausgabe*, 4, 1:306–7 and 315. In this context Jacobi includes some interesting remarks on the necessity for the human being to live in a civil society where lower instincts are surpassed. The society would therefore represent an institute of reason, an *Anstalt der Vernunft*, that gives a safe and stable environment for the human being to thrive.

210 Cf. Jacobi, *Divine Things*, 130–1.

211 See Jacobi, "Concerning the Doctrine of Spinoza (1785)," 193.

212 See Jacobi, "Preface (1815)," 547–9. On this topic see Ivaldo, *Introduzione a Jacobi*, 121–2.

213 Cf. Jacobi, *Divine Things*, 131.

214 See Jacobi, "Preface (1815)," 588. It is worth quoting the whole paragraph: "Just as this spirit is present to man in his highest, deepest, and innermost consciousness, so also is the Giver of it, *God*, present to him – more present to him through his heart than nature is to him through his external senses. No sense object can so seize upon mind, and so invincibly establish itself before it as true object, as can those supersensible objects that are only seen with the eye of the spirit – the True, the Good, the Sublime, and the Beautiful. Hence we may well have the courage of our audacious language: we believe in God because we see him; though we cannot see with the eye of the body, he appears none the less to us in every upright man.

The appearance itself, however, is not God; and often can even deceive us. Yet the feeling aroused in us by it did not deceive us, and the inner countenance we beheld was a vision of the true. 'Nothing is more like God,' Socrates says according to Plato, '*than the most righteous among us.*'"

215   Cf. Jacobi, *Divine Things*, 131–2.

216   Cf. ibid., 131–3. On this see Frank, *Friedrich Heinrich Jacobis Lehre vom Glauben*, 131–2. By identifying the nature of faith in the overall body of Jacobi's work, Frank defines three different phases: faith as feeling of the truth (1771–82), faith as the experience of freedom and faculty of the supersensible (1782–94), faith conceived as rational activity whose organ is reason itself (1794–1819). We may see that the second and the third phase are necessarily connected insofar that the experience of freedom (phase 2) coincides with the rational acknowledgment of the true (phase 3). See also Schick, *Vermittelte Unmittelbarkeit*, 255.

217   Cf. Jacobi, *Divine Things*, 133–4. See preceding point 3) and its footnote.

218   Cf. ibid., 134–5. On this see di Giovanni, "Hegel, Jacobi, and 'Crypto-Catholocism,'" 53–72.

219   Cf. Jacobi, *Divine Things*, 135.

220   See Jacobi, *Werke. Gesamtausgabe*, 4, 1:309.

221   Jacobi, *Divine Things*, 136–7.

222   Cf. ibid., 137.

223   The content of the entries listed in the common/contrast framework between Jacobi and Claudius reminds of some passages from the New Testament that deliver an orientation toward God and divine things that seems similar to Jacobi's. For instance: A) "How blest are those who know their need of God; the kingdom of Heaven is theirs," Matthew 5:3; B) "And so I tell you this: no sin, so slander, is beyond forgiveness for men, except slander spoken against the Spirit, and that will not be forgiven. Any man who speaks a word against the Son of Man will be forgiven; but if anyone speaks against the Holy Spirit, for him there is no forgiveness," Matthew 12:31; C) "When he had entered Capernaum a centurion came up to ask his help. 'Sir,' he said, 'a boy of mine lies at home paralysed and racked with pain' Jesus, said, 'I will come and cure him.' But the centurion replied, 'Sir, who am I to have you under my roof? You need only to say the word and the boy will be cured. I know, for I am myself under orders, with soldiers under me. I say to one, 'Go,' and he goes; to another, 'Come here,' and he comes; and to my servant, 'Do this,' and he does it,'" Matthew 8:5. Finally, the pivotal point that the conclusion states echoes Matthew 13:15: "you may hear and hear, but you will never understand; you may look and look, but you will never see. For this people's mind has become gross; their ears are dulled, and their eyes are closed. Otherwise, their eyes might

A STUDY 91

see, their ears hear, and their mind understand, and then they might turn again, and I would heal them." All quotations are taken from *The New English Bible: The New Testament*. Obviously, the difference between the New Testament and Jacobi's philosophy is paramount. One could appreciate the distance between the two just by considering the specifics of the doctrine of incarnation, the idea of sin, the practice of exorcism, the Christian notion of love, and the Christian God's transcendence. On this topic see Ivaldo, *Filosofia delle cose divine*, 181. These differences make explicit that Jacobi's thought is solely grounded upon the principle of freedom that adapts and customizes the transcendent aspects of Christianity to meet the requirements of a theory of the finite, but autonomous, agent. The most noteworthy of those aspects is probably the identification of the nature of human being with traits that are supposedly exclusive to Jesus. This move consequently deprives Jesus of all transcendent features and makes him ethically equal to any human being. See the letter to Reinhold dated from 19 January 1817.

224 See Jacobi, *Werke. Gesamtausgabe*, 1, 1:335–53. See also the letter to Fries on 24 December 1808. On the relation between Christian doctrine and heathen wisdom Jacobi shows some ambiguity, that can only be solved if we assume that Jacobi's understanding of transcendence is tempered according to a Kantian perspective on practical reason. See Ivaldo, *Filosofia delle cose divine*, 156–7.

225 A volume entirely dedicated to the confrontation between Jacobi and Schelling from a purely philosophical perspective is yet to be written (although an edited volume is currently in preparation). However, studies that touch upon the subject include Sandkaulen, *Grund und Ursache*, especially 200–56, and Sommer, *Zwischen Metaphysik und Metaphysikkritik*, 93–108. An exception is the study by Weischedel, *Jacobi und Schelling*, 1969. See also Ike, *Das Gefühl*.

226 Schelling, *Sämtliche Werke*, 1, 4:236. For the English translation of this excerpt I refer to di Giovanni's in Jacobi, *The Main Philosophical Writings*, 632.

227 See Sandkaulen, "System und Zeitlichkeit," 282–4.

228 See Buchheim, "Die Idee des Existierenden und der Raum," 37.

229 A more confrontational opposition than that with Jacobi could be seen elsewhere, as presented in Berger, *The Schelling-Eschenmayer Controversy, 1801*."

230 See Jacobs, "Von der Offenbarung göttlicher Dinge," 146.

231 See Jacobi, *Divine Things*, 163–4.

232 For a clear understanding of the tight connection between Jacobi's idea of systematic thinking – that refers back to Lessing's Spinozism – and Schelling's philosophy see Danz, "Wir 'halten mit Lessing,'"127–48. For an overview on this topic see Danz and Stolzenberg, eds, *System und Systemkritik um 1800*.

233 Schelling, *Sämtliche Werke*, 1,6:56–7. For the English translation see Jacobi, *The Main Philosophical Writings*, 632. Italics mine.

234 See Hammacher, "Jacobis Schrift," 133.

235 Schelling, *Sämtliche Werke*, 1, 7:293. For the English translation see Jacobi, *The Main Philosophical Writings*, 633. Cf. Jacobi, *Divine Things*, 161.

236 See Sandkaulen, "Dass, was oder wer?," 100.

237 Cf. Jacobi, *Divine Things*, 176–7.

238 Jacobi does not seem in favor of a distinction between two forms of knowledge, knowledge of the absolute and knowledge of the world. This distinction is instead the core of D. Henrich's interpretation in his "Der Ursprung der Doppelphilosophie," 13–27, especially 17. Jacobi is rather involved in the scrutiny of thinking in general, both of the world and of God, and his thesis tries to make explicit the ties that connect knowledge of God and proper knowledge of worldly reality while discarding any theory of systematic thinking that abstains from the idea of an absolute singularity of things. On this see Sandkaulen, "'Ich bin und es sind Dinge außer mir,'" 169–96. This idea of connecting both natural world and God is at the centre of Jacobi's conception of man as being a Vowel (*Selbstlaut*) between Consonants (*Mitlaute*), God and Nature. On the *conditio humana*, see Hammacher, "Jacobis Schrift 'Von den göttlichen Dingen,'" 129–41.

239 See Sandkaulen, "Dass, was oder wer?," 107.

240 See Jacobi, *Werke. Gesamtausgabe*, 2, 1:332–73. See especially the second letter. Schelling reads Jacobi's letters as an attempt to protect the finite. He believes that in Jacobi's philosophy lies a contradiction, because Jacobi apparently acknowledges both consistency and necessity of systematic philosophy, while opposing it. But, as is now widely recognized, that apparent contradiction highlights precisely the core of Jacobi's theoretical efforts. See Sandkaulen, "System und Zeitlichkeit," 282.

241 Cf. Jacobi, *Divine Things*, 185–6. See Valenza, "Naturalismo e teismo," 128–9. As Valenza has noted, Jacobi seems to accept a notion of science that Anaxagoras introduced by stating that the principle of nature lies outside nature, so that the study of nature does not include an investigation of its principle. Therefore, the unconditional value of existence does not represent a value that science can assess, for it exceeds the conditional value of the causal connection that science admits. See also 130 for the overall evolution of Jacobi's position pro and contra Kant's theism.

242 Cf. Jacobi, *Divine Things*, 176–7. See also Jacobi, "Concerning the Doctrine of Spinoza (1789)," 368–71. There is no such thing as a third-middle thesis between theism and Spinozism, as is posited by Herder. See Valenza, "Naturalismo e teismo," 135–6.

A STUDY

243 This measure is not a yardstick. Rather it exhibits an actual world, in which the rational I-person reveals God's project. This project is good and beautiful only inasmuch as it represents the ground of reality. See Jacobi, *Divine Things*, 149–50. See also Jacobi, *Werke. Gesamtausgabe*, 5, 1:403–9.

244 Cf. Jacobi, *Divine Things*, 194.

245 About the immanent relationship that God has with the human being and the distinct nature of Jacobi's theism see Catia Goretzki, "Jacobis Denken," 125.

246 Cf. Jacobi,, *Divine Things*, 195–6.

247 Jacobi, *Werke. Gesamtausgabe*, 5, 1:114. See Goretzki, "Jacobis Denken," 131.

248 Jacobi, *Divine Things*, 186.

249 Robert Musil, *The Man without Qualities*, 175.

Note to the Translation

The present translation is based on the critical edition of *Von den göttlichen Dingen und ihrer Offenbarung* (1811), edited by W. Jaeschke (Hamburg/Stuttgart: Meiner/frommann-holzboog, 2000), which has been published as third volume of Friedrich Heinrich Jacobi's *Werke* edited by Klaus Hammacher and Walter Jaeschke.[1]

Three more translations are currently available, one Italian and two French: *Le cose divine e la loro rivelazione*, edited by G. Sansonetti (with partial contribution by N. Bobbio) for the collection *Et-Et/Aut-Aut* (Torino: Rosenberg & Sellier, 1999), and *Des choses divines et de leur révélation*, edited by P. Cerutti, for the collection *Textes et Commentaires* supervised by Jean-François Courtine (Paris: Vrin, 2008). The older French translation included in *Œuvres philosophiques*, edited by J.J. Anstett (Paris: Aubier, 1946) is the textual basis from which Cerutti draws. While the Italian translation resulted unserviceable, Cerutti's work has been a point of reference to unravel many intricacies of Jacobi's text. Many notes to the texts come from the French edition.

Since both the German edition and the new French translation already provide precise *apparatus* to assist detailed analysis of the work, this English translation does not have editorial notes. Instead, the present publication presents a book-length analysis of Jacobi's text; the French translation provides just a general *Présentation* that does not go into the many details of Jacobi's philosophical endeavour. A book-length analysis of Jacobi's *Divine Things* was published in Italy, Marco Ivaldo's *Filosofia delle cose divine. Saggio su Jacobi* (Brescia: Morcelliana, 1996).

I decided to present the text *On Divine Things and Their Revelation* together with the text *On Lichtenberg's Prophecy*; these two texts are intimately connected as Jacobi shows in his own edition of the complete works. The reader will also find the first and second foreword. Unlike the critical edition and the French translation, I decided not to include the introduction to the third volume of Jacobi's complete works (1816), for two reasons. First, I wanted to preserve the compact unity of the *Divine Things* in the form Jacobi imagined and accomplished it. Second, the 1816 introduction is a text that, while being thematically relevant to the *Divine Things*, maintains its autonomy.

Within in-text square brackets [...] are numbers referring to the critical edition page numbers; they also present textual additions that have been introduced to facilitate the English flow. The reader will find square brackets also in the footnotes: they provide short notes of the translator, bibliographical references to English editions (e.g., I. Kant) or current German editions (e.g., Fr. Schlegel) of the texts that Jacobi mentions. In some cases, as in the case of Fr. Schlegel's quotations, I decided to translate the German instead of referring to extant English editions; in these cases, I simply do not refer to any English edition in the footnote. Square brackets also refer to internal reference to other parts of Jacobi's critical edition. They also present elucidations concerning names and topics that may be unknown to the reader.

Bold and <u>underlining</u> are used to highlight what Jacobi himself highlights, while *italic* is used for titles and foreign words. At the end of the volume the reader will find a glossary. Some terminological decisions must however be made explicit in the present note.

If not differently stated, Wesen has been translated with "being," while *Dasein/Daseyn* has been translated with "existence." This decision has been taken in view of the non-abstract/intellectualistic meaning of Wesen, which Jacobi introduces. The more common English translation "essence" would have suggested a reference to a realm of mere universals that Jacobi's notion of Wesen instead criticizes.

Unbegreiflich has been translated with "non-conceptually." Passages like the following: "He communicates Himself non-conceptually (unbegreiflich) to the human being through sensation (*Empfindung*) transformed into **devotion** address a specific issue. God is rational, although not defined through concepts" (Jacobi, *Werke. Gesamtausgabe*, 3:11). Other possible translations, e.g., "inexplicable," would have made of Jacobi an irrationalist, which he was not. A rational, but non-conceptual God makes Jacobi's point against the Enlightenment clear. Nevertheless, in different contexts I translate differently.

NOTE TO THE TRANSLATION

For instance, at Jacobi, *Werke. Gesamtausgabe*, 3:13 the term unbegreiflich is translated with "inconceivable": "There are propositions in current use at **every** level of knowledge that hover over the inconceivable on mere faith, with no further support." The same happens at Jacobi, *Werke. Gesamtausgabe*, 3:18, and again at Jacobi, *Werke. Gesamtausgabe*, 3:31, where I translate with "inconceivable" and "incomprehensible."

I decided not to use the quite vague English term "belief"; I instead translate Glaube with "faith" (which retains the risk of ambiguity – as in German – but it also heralds Jacobi's philosophical originality and ensuing motivation to write the *David Hume*) and *Überzeugung* with "conviction."[2]

The terms "human being" (*Mensch*) and "God" (*Gott*) have been referred to as masculine.

Jacobi's English glossary has been established by George di Giovanni's *The Main Philosophical Writings and the Novel* Allwill, Montreal: McGill-Queen's University Press, 1994. In some cases, I draw also from *The Cambridge Edition of the Works of Immanuel Kant*, edited by P. Guyer and A. Wood, Cambridge: Cambridge University Press, 1992–.

NOTES

1 On critical aspects of this German edition see A. Mues, "Editionspraxis." I decided not to veer from the critical edition.

2 On the translation of the term Glaube see di Giovanni, "The Unfinished Philosophy," 90. Moreover, the following passage would become unintelligible, had Glaube not be translated with "faith:"

He: What's that jolly book you have there?

I: Jolly book? Why do you say that?

He: The way you looked when I came in.

I: I was reading some reflections about faith.

He: You mean in the May issue of the Berlin Monthly?

I: Are they so jolly? Have a look at my book! It is Hume's *Enquiries*.

He: It's against faith, then.

I: No it is for faith.

F.H. Jacobi, "David Hume," 258.

On the Divine Things and Their Revelation

FRIEDRICH HEINRICH JACOBI

[1] "There are unreceptive times, but what is eternal always finds its time."
Joh. von Müller

[2] "Divine truths are infinitely superior to nature; only God can put
them into the soul. He wanted them to enter from the heart into the mind,
and not from the mind into the heart. Hence, if human things have to be
known before they can be loved, you have to love divine things in order
to know them."
Pascal

Foreword to the Present New Edition

[157] The spirited animosity that the publication of *On the Divine Things and Their Revelation* widely generated upon its first appearance, and the furious insults his author suffered amidst this animosity, are universally known. Now, as then, I stand by my resolve to let the work defend itself and its author. Accordingly, the *Divine Things* appears again here in the complete edition of my works as it did on its first appearing, with no change in it, not even a syllable. Thus and not otherwise do I want my work to be handed down to posterity and I to be judged by it. I know that nobody can take away from me what I am, or give me what I am not, as the old saying of Duclos, that righteous connoisseur of the world and of human beings, goes: "One *makes* and *destroys* only one's *own* reputation."

As regards the specific criticism of the *Divine Things*, that it has maliciously deformed the doctrines of the philosophy of nature or philosophy of identity, has intentionally altered and apparently falsified them,[1] many experts have so satisfactorily justified my writing without my intervention that I have no worries about it. I am referring to *Göttingische gelehrte Anzeigen*, 1812 n72, to *Hallische allgemeine Literaturzeitung*, 1812 n56, to *Heidelbergische Jahrbücher*, 1812 n22, and to *Leipziger Literaturzeitung*, 1812 nn 90, 91, 92.

It would be easy to add more evidence to support those positive assessments, e.g., no one mentioned the review of Fichte's *On the Essence* [158] *of the Scholar*

---

1 [Friedrich Wilhelm Joseph Schelling, *Denkmal der Schrift von den göttlichen Dingen u. des Herrn Friedrich Heinrich Jacobi*, sw VIII, 34.]

and His Appearance in the Domain of Freedom signed F.W.J.S., published in *Jenaische Literaturzeitung*, 1806 nn 150–1. It is so pertinent as to be enough to prove what had to be shown.

An excerpt of the present text has been so misinterpreted by a group of highly respected readers, and read so counter to my intention, that I must indeed make room explaining my responsibility in this mistake.

It is a passage in which to the Messenger, full of enthusiasm for Christ's personality as portrayed in the Gospels, there is counterposed a **detached** philosopher who scorns allowing to get excited about any personality whatsoever; he is completely satisfied with the concept, the idea, and for that reason considers anything beyond it as ill or, to give it a better turn, as **idolatrous**. In his [ensuing] talk, the **detached** philosopher, who in all this comes out to be an idealist impervious to outside illumination, expected that the Messenger, challenged regarding a self-contradicting doctrine [alleged to him], would respond with a rebuttal raising the issue whether he alone was indeed the one in contradiction, or rather the same objection also applied, and with even greater force, to the one who made it against him, and would [thus] set the said philosopher against him.

This scheme fails. Instead of being drawn into it, the Messenger responds to the detached philosopher's bittersweet talk and [159] arrogant friendliness only with a tacit smile, a tacit head-bow.

At this point the author of the *Divine Things* steps in **in person** between the Messenger and the detached philosopher, and as I believe sufficiently brings to light the absurdity of the latter's allegation against the former. He cannot demonstrate that the objections against the Messenger stand for nothing though he finds himself siding with the latter, more so than with the idealist, as the following text – which here assumes a new tone – displays in a way that is clearer, more distinct, and comprehensive. Yet, the one who prays devoutly in front of an unrefined sacred image is still there presented as superior to the philosopher who wants to kneel only in front of his own vague idea of God but cannot do it.

But even abstracting from what follows immediately, and further follows up to the end of the first part of this work where the **integral** internalists (*ganz Inwendigen*) and the **integral** externalists (*ganz Auswendigen*) are pitted head-to-head in opposition, the author's attitude is revealed decisively enough from

FOREWORD TO THE PRESENT NEW EDITION

Epictetus' rude treatment of them that the author here equally reserves for the idealist in particular.

Epictetus dealt with a category of philosophers of whom he says in Discourse XXI that they proceed solemnly as if they had swallowed an obelisk, and would love that anybody who crosses their path formed a high opinion of them and declared: "what a great philosopher!" The rude words, quoted directly from discourse XXII, are: "What shall I say to this slave? If I am silent, he will burst. I must speak in this way: 'Excuse me as you would excuse lovers; I am not my own master; I am mad.'"[2]

The author could not imagine that any reader would be mistaken here and, instead of recollecting Plato's *mania*,[3] would assume the peculiar notion that [160] the author had made fun not of the detached and self-sufficient philosopher, but of the Messenger, the one truly inspired by divine feelings and ideas. The clear purpose of the author's work is to show, in the most evident way, that the **pure** religious idealist and the **pure** religious materialist oppose themselves only like the two valves of the oyster that holds the pearl of Christianity. Neither the Messenger nor his friend, the author of the *Divine Things*, want such a division; they want the pearl. They only diverge in opinion over the value of both the oyster and its valves, which means that the historical faith of the one is not the historical faith of the other. The author of the *Divine Things* believes that the history of Christianity involves the entire history of humankind which includes the former; the Messenger seems to have the opposite opinion. The author does not intend to start here a new debate on this subject matter: in his work he has already expressed his opinion with accuracy, frankness, and consideration for the numerous paths and means of divine revelation to human beings, while expressing the best of his knowledge. He regards as happy those [161] on whom a brighter light and more stable and happier certitude are bestowed. Those who want to challenge him are welcomed; he will not meet them head on, for he is convinced that anybody who picks up this book without prejudices and reads it in its entirety will do justice to the intention from which it springs. The author could just not tolerate, without responding out loud, the criticism that he had done injustice to a man that he himself highly esteemed, his old friend, the Messenger of Wandsbeck.

---

2 Epictetus, *Discourses of Epictetus*, tr. by G. Long (New York: Appleton, 1904).

3 [Plato, *Phaedrus*, 244a–9d.]

Necessary Foreword

[3] The following text took shape out of an announcement of Volume VI of the complete works of the Messenger of Wandsbeck intended for the *Impartial Correspondent of Hamburg* to which I had committed myself for my friend Perthes.

I knew that I was not cut out for this kind of work, but I was accommodating enough to promise to make at least an effort on condition that the whole space of the usual eight-column journal's supplement be devoted to my report. This was granted without any resistance. However, this was not enough. I was granted two, then three, then four times the initial space, and eventually as much as I would need.

To settle the issue and gain the necessary room for the advancement of my work, which had led me far beyond the limits of a review, I asked Herr Perthes to apologize once and for all on my behalf to the *Correspondent of Hamburg* and then to publish my essay on its own, which I wanted to hasten bringing to completion, under the title of:

A Failed Attempt at a Partial Review for the Impartial Correspondent of Hamburg of the Complete Works of the Messenger of Wandsbeck.

The suggestion was accepted and thereupon the printing of the *Failed Attempt* actually began.[1] The work was to be published at the 1798 Jubilee Fair, and indeed it was announced in the fair-catalogue among the books imprinted that very year.

---

1   [See Mues, "Editionspraxis," 161.]

NECESSARY FOREWORD

As it happened, the author, who was at the time wandering here and there, had to leave Hamburg and only by the end of the year [4] was he once again in a position that allowed him to devote himself to literary work.

He had just picked up his interrupted work, to which little was missing for completion, when he got involved in the famous event that led the philosopher Fichte to be expelled from Jena. To this incident others would be added; hence, the decision was eventually made to take the **failed attempt** in the literal sense and condemn it to extinction.

I had already made use of some excerpts from it for the *Letter to Fichte*.[2] I used even more excerpts from it at Reinhold's pressing request for an article for his *Contributions for an Easier Overview of the State of Philosophy at the Beginning of the Nineteenth Century*.[3]

The first theft was insignificant, and the stolen material could again be extracted with no harm from *Letter to Fichte* on the occasion of a new edition. On the other hand, the other theft for Reinhold's *Contribution* was so considerable, and the material so re-worked in the move from one place to the other,[4] that nothing would have helped the text that had suffered from it, suppose the author had again decided to bring it to completion, except, as things stood, a full rewrite of its second part which had been the one stolen.[5]

Repeated efforts to come to such a decision were not spared. As often as I had the occasion to read the first part of the work to some friends, or some excerpts from it, I was always exhorted not to leave it in such an unfinished state. But I was actually moved to the decision only by myself. Just how, let it for once be known for the future.[6] [5]

What so long made this decision difficult was less the necessity which had arisen to compose the second part anew than the impossibility to give to the first part a different form than the original. The text had to start most inappropriately with the words: **the reviewer, etc.**, otherwise the whole text could not be published.

---

2 *Letter to Fichte*, Hamburg 1799.

3 [Vol. 1, Hamburg, 1801.] See the third issue: *Über das Unternehmen des Kriticismus, die Vernunft zu Verstande zu bringen, und der Philosophie überhaupt eine neue Absicht zu geben.*

4 See the *Vorbericht* of the aforementioned essay, 1–5. [Jacobi, *Werke. Gesamtausgabe,* 2:261–3.]

5 [For a clear geography of this intersection between different contributions and editors, see Patrick Cerutti, "Notes et Commentaires," in *Des choses divines et de leur révélation*, edited by Patrick Cerutti (Paris: J. Vrin, 2008), 191.]

6 [Remark is not present in the first edition, added only in the second.] For the joy

Originally, the chosen title "**A Failed Attempt at a Partial Review etc.**" took care of the problem; but it was of no use after so many years.

At any rate, no sense fussing about an incidental puzzlement, for which there is in fact no reason since this foreword takes care of it.

The question is whether the author has **auspiciously** or **inauspiciously** strayed from a review of the sixth volume of the complete works of the Messenger of Wandsbeck into general considerations about **religious realism** and **idealism**, letter and spirit, revelation of reason (*Vernunftoffenbarung*) and positive doctrine, and whether the completed line of remarks can justifiably be given the heading under which they are now published.

The treatise about Lichtenberg's Prophecy, already published once in a *Taschenbuch für das Jahr 1802* [6], not in a place appropriate to it, now appears where I believe it belongs, as **Introduction**. I wish none of my readers would spurn being introduced by it.[7]

Munich, 5 October 1811

---

caused by the first part of *Ideen zur Geschichte der Entwickelung des religiöse Glaubens*, by **Kajetan Weiller**, published in May 1808, four years before the second and six years before the third part, I resolved and, so to speak [5], took the vow to bring to conclusion the text *On the Divine Things*, and to get started at once and not to give up no matter what happens. A series of bitter setbacks that started to develop in those very years made me defer the realization of the purpose; the will and hope to complete the work had never abandoned me, not even for a moment. May this reference to Weiller's text serve to draw more attention to it. As for its value, I only refer to the report written on it in the *Göttingische gelehrte Anzeigen* (n26, 1815), which anyone impartial, unbiased, and free from prejudice towards the person, will acknowledge. In a **serene spirit** I dedicated the first edition of *On the Divine Things* to **the author of the *Ideen*,** just as now I **publicly** dedicate them to him, since they belong, besides me, to nobody but him. I also know that he appreciates the text like I do. Thus, I raise this monument to the most pure and disinterested friendship. [Kajetan Weiller (1762–1826), was an author highly critical of Schelling's philosophy, as it is evident in his *Der Geist allerneuesten Philosophie der HH. Schelling, Hegel, und Kompagnie* (Munich, J. Lentner, 1803).]

7 [Reference to the discussion that followed Jacobi's speech *Ueber gelehrte Gesellschaften*. See Jaeschke, "Kommentar," 193.]

[7] On Lichtenberg's Prophecy

[9] **"Our world will become so refined (*fein*) that it will be as ridiculous to believe in God,** as it is today to believe in ghosts."[1]

That was the prophecy of a departed. From the grave this voice sounds in all our ears.

Oh, prophet! Did you only see this? Did you not also see what followed? Did you see nothing more, or did you simply not want to announce what comes next, its fulfillment?

The prophecy continues:

"and then, once again after a while, the world will become even more refined (*feiner*). And it will pursue, now hurriedly, the highest summit of refinement. Once the peak reached, the judgement of the wise men will turn once again; and knowledge will change for the last time. Thus – and this will be the end – we will again believe only in ghosts. We ourselves will be like God. We will know that being (Seyn) and essence are – and can only be – ghosts.

"At this time, the bitter sweat of seriousness will dry up from every forehead; from every eye the tears of longing will be wiped away, and laughter will sound out loud among men. Thus, since reason will have completed its work, humankind will have reached its destination: the same crown will adorn every transfigured head."

---

1 C.G. Lichtenberg, *Vermischte Schriften* (Göttingen: J.C. Dieterich, 1800) 1:166. [See Mues, "Editionspraxis," 170.]

ON THE DIVINE THINGS AND THEIR REVELATION

If I am raving, then the prophet raved before me: if he announced the truth, then with his words mine also will be fulfilled.

The truest can only be as true as that **God lives**, as true as that **a God** exists **in heaven**, i.e., independent, apart from, and above nature, of which He is the free creator, its most wise and benevolent ruler; father of all beings, with fatherly **sense** and **heart**. Should this living God become in the human being's view a mere rainbow, so that in the clouds of the human mind He shows Himself through **refraction** and **collection of rays** [10], should the human being learn to deem God a psychological deception akin to that optical deceit, then his entire cognition has already taken this very route and, in accordance with the same rainbow theory, must ever transfigure itself until, at the end, to the Epoptes[2] there remains as war-booty only a universal nothing of cognition – **but now manifest!**

It is not different: for such a human being the entire creation necessarily vanishes with the Creator. In his spirit these two destinies are inseparable. In his spirit, as soon as God becomes a ghost, so does nature also, as well as the spirit itself. For such is the human **spirit**: that he recognize **God**; that he perceive Him; that he have the **presentiment** of Him concealed in nature[3]; **learn** of God in his chest, worship Him in his heart. Such is his **reason** that a God's existence be more manifest to him and more certain than his own. There is no reason where this revelation is not. Or: can you call reason what brought to **knowledge** only non-thing (*Unding*) and mere delusion? Then reason would not be the faculty of truth and wisdom, but of ignorance: a knowing **non**-knowing, a knowing non-**being**; a faculty of desperation, the worst of the enemy's gifts.

The human being's privilege consists – says the wise man from Stagira – in being able to know something higher and better than himself.[4]

He finds himself as a being completely dependent, derived, concealed to himself: yet he is enlivened by a drive to inquire into his origin, to recognize himself in it, to experience by himself **the true through** this origin and **from** this origin [11]. He calls **reason** this drive that identifies his genus.

---

2 Contemplator: so were called those who had gone through all the degrees of initiation in the Eleusinian Mysteries, and were hence left to **contemplation** (*Anschauen*). Those still in the process of initiation were called **Mystai** (initiates). – Nowadays, the class of the **Mystai** is lost, made the object of ridicule, for there is no need to peer into the hidden in order to understand: all is in the open.

3 [Jacobi will implement this passage in his 1816 *Vorrede*. See Cerutti, "Notes et Commentaires," 192.]

4 [Apparently Jacobi refers to Aristotle, *The Nicomachean Ethics*, X, 6–9, 1176a–9a.]

ON LICHTENBERG'S PROPHECY

Each and every living being's drive is the being's **light**, its right and strength. Only in **this** light can it walk, and it can act (*wirken*) **only** out of this strength.

Every finite being owns within itself neither its life nor the flame of its **light** or the **force** of its heart. All beings are just brought to life and revived by something **beyond themselves**; they **receive** their existence (*Daseyn*); and not even for a moment do they hold their **living** existence in their own hands. As much as their existence was **received**, so much does it have to **continue** beyond them. They are altogether, generally speaking, **breathing** creatures, i.e., in need for their **preservation** of a constant flow from outside.

The gifts of life are as manifold as the ways to awaken it; manifold its conducts, and so its uses. Like an animal, the human being first awakens just like a sense-perceiving creature in a purely sensory nature. Like an animal, he first only recognizes the mother. Yet, for the animal, the mother is only the **breast**, not the **face**. Therefore, when it forgets the breast, it also forgets the mother. The animal has no heart and consequently it has no reason. The human being turns away from the breast that nourishes him, looks up face to face, he **feels** love, **learns** love, and attains cognition. He could only cry, now he can laugh – Behold, there does the mother lift the laughing, babbling infant, already capable of stretching out his hands and soon capable of the first kiss, from her **lap** into the father's **arm**.

Just as the concealed and invisible soul makes itself **visible** on the face of the human being, comes to light, communicates itself non-conceptually, and by means of this secret communication gives birth to language and the understanding of language; so too does **God** immediately express Himself through the face of nature; He communicates Himself non-conceptually to the human being through sensation (Empfindung) transformed into **devotion**; and teaches the spirit, **also** awakened **to the suprasensible and uncreated**, to stammer the delightful tones [12] of the beautiful and the good, and eventually to express that word of life: His name.

Nature has no face for those who do not see God; to them nature has no reason, it is a non-thing with no heart and will, an obscure shapeless being creating shapes without essence (*Wesenlos*) – one that in the absence of essence eternally builds images without any model, purely **out of other images**; a horrible mother-night breeding from eternity to eternity only appearance and shadowy life. And at the dawn of the day, only death and destruction, murder and lie.

ON THE DIVINE THINGS AND THEIR REVELATION

Our prophet knew all this well. He said – and no doubt he was **on his feet**[5] since he spoke this way – "believing in a God is an instinct. It is so natural to the human being as it is to walk on two legs. It can be altered in some, and wholly suppressed in others, **but as a rule** it is there, and it is indispensable to the inner good shape of the faculty of cognition"[6] [13].

Thus, faith in a God is instinct. It is as **natural** to human being as **standing upright**. It is unnatural to him not to have such a faith, just as unnatural is to him the bent position of those fumbling animals that rummage the ground, neither facing nor viewing the sky. He can suffocate this faith, but generally the faith is there, and where it is not present, the faculty of cognition is **deformed.**

I repeat: the noble man who said so, stood upright and felt that **this direction towards the sky was not a human invention! A God made the human being stand upright and put in his innermost sight the stimulus to look up to Him!**[7] In that moment he recognized his **better origin**, his higher vocation, more ardently and deeply than he recognizes his existence on earth.

---

5 "Certainly, says Lichtenberg, sometimes a thought can be pleasant when one lies in bed, yet the same thought is no longer pleasant when one stands." *Nachlass*, part II, 109. Moreover, part I, 33: "I noticed very clearly that I have often different opinions depending on whether I am lying down or standing" – see especially part I, 185–6. Lichtenberg's touching complaint (part I, 41) about the mutability of his mood is curious, as in the note on page 33: "he was almost afraid of the fact that in him everything would turn into **thought**, and **sentiment** would be lost." Further: "since the middle of the year 1791 something that I cannot yet describe has stirred in my entire economy of thought. I just want to sketch it out to get back to it more carefully in the future: namely, an extraordinary mistrust in any human knowledge, mathematics excepted, that nearly spills over into writing. What still ties me to study Physics is the hope to discover something useful for humanity."

6 See G.C. Lichtenberg, *Nachlass*, part II, 127 – "In general (see 88) our heart recognizes a God, but then it is difficult, or even impossible, to make it comprehensible to reason (or understanding). It might be asked whether mere reason (or mere understanding) without the heart would have reached God. After the heart had recognized him, did reason (or the understanding) also search for him."

On page 101: "should it be so evident that our reason cannot know anything of the suprasensible? Shouldn't the human being be able to spin his ideas of God as **efficiently** as the spider its web to catch the fly? Or in other words: shouldn't there exist beings (**higher**, undoubtedly) that admire us for our ideas of God as much as we admire spiders and silkworm?"

7 "<u>Cum ceteras animantes (natura) **abjecisset** ad pastum, solum hominem erexit, ad coelique quasi cognationis, domiciliique pristini conspectum EXCITAVIT</u>." Cicero, *De Legibus* I. c. 9. ["While (nature) has bent the other living beings down toward

ON LICHTENBERG'S PROPHECY

Yet within this faith, which is indispensable for the inner good shape of the faculty of cognition, what does the human being comprehend, and how is the comprehended grounded for him? How does the deep thinker, the wise person, explain and justify this faith? How does he represent the object attested to by his spirit?

He explains and justifies it to himself in the same way as he explains and justifies to himself faith in nature and existence, in internal and external consciousness. He shows to his spirit the object of this faith and tests it before it, just as he represents and tests the spirit itself, or the spirit of a friend, or that sublime spirit of a Socrates or Pythagoras, of a Timoleon or Cato. He does not explain or test, but rather, he feels, **sees**, and **knows**.[8] In the human being the understanding that explains [14] and **produces** proof has neither the **final** nor the **first** word. Even the sense that produces representations does not have them, not the one nor the other. Nothing inside of the human being has either. In general, there is no first or last say in him; neither Alpha nor Omega. He is addressed; as soon as he is addressed, he first replies with his feelings, with his prophesying longing, mixed with reluctance and desire, horror and joy; he expresses them with noisy gestures, and eventually with sensations, thoughts, and words. Only those who can interpret understand. There is always something between us and true essence: feeling, image, or word. Everywhere we see only what is hidden. Yet, we see and **perceive** it as something hidden. We label what is seen and perceived with the word, which is a living sign. This is the dignity of the word. It does not reveal itself by itself, but it gives proof of the revelation, it confirms it, and helps spread what has been confirmed.

---

their food, it has made the human being alone erect, urging him to look up toward heaven, as if it were akin to him and his first home." Translation by A. Ignesti and P. Livieri.]

8 "To those who inquire: "Where did you see the gods, from what do you deduce that they exist, that you worship them thus?" First, our eyes can in fact see them. Then, I have certainly not seen my soul either, but I prize it. So too with the gods whose power I experience on all occasions; it is from this that I deduce that they exist, and I revere them." Marcus Aurelius Antoninus, *The Meditations*, XII, 28, 128.

"There are propositions in current use at **every** level of knowledge that hover over the inconceivable on mere faith, with no further support. One upholds them, without knowing where that certainty on which they depend comes from. The philosopher possesses the certainty that the common man has when he believes that water always flows downwards, because it would be impossible for it to flow upwards." G.C. Lichtenberg, *Nachlass*, part II, 80.

ON THE DIVINE THINGS AND THEIR REVELATION

What is found everywhere of a genus is not invention, fabrication, or the **product** of the fabrication of one or more of its members. So, individual human beings have no more invented and fabricated religion and language than they have invented and fabricated sight and hearing. They have rather learned language and religion, just as they learned to see and hear. The individual would have never learned to see, if colours and contours had not come before his eyes independently of him; he would never have learned to see in a not already articulated and rhythmic nature, one with no tones, accents, and syllables. Nature had to be already prepared and organized for him, and he just as much for it, for a lead between the two to arise; **for him to be in conversation with it**, to feel, live, think, will and act, nature had to be already sorted out for him. Isolated, by himself, he is nothing: a completely impossible being. His pure consciousness is a mere empty space of thought that he is not himself able to fill; that therefore he also cannot **interrupt**, so that, by means of this [15] interruption, he might at least repeat himself in his nothingness, emit his own echo, an "**I am**" – an echo of **nothing**. I repeat: there is no faculty in him for any Alpha or Omega, no strength, that he might **determine** by himself alone and thus bring to light at origin even only a dream-creature of fantasy.

You are! – the One, the First! – not I, who am not able to posit anywhere a first beginning or a first end, neither in me nor outside of me, not even only in thought: no **first** measure, no **first** weight, no **first** number. It was of an **Other** to create, to invent all this **by virtue of the deed**; of that mysterious **word**, the **beginning** of all beings that was with God and God was it, which, **uttered**, became created light, created life – this wonderful creation of God.

On this point Plato and Job, who came before him, agree.

Do not call God the **infinite being**, says Plato, for existence stands opposed to the infinite. It is essentially without being, eternally only the in between of a more or less of the being-present of a **not-yet-present**, an existent non-being. Its image is the hallucination of the shapeless, of a pre-being non-thing that would be a First; First of all, yet not of any singly – it is the non-thing itself.

Call **Him** the one who **gives** measure, in whom the measure is **originally set** – it is said: He himself is measure! – by giving measure, the creator of every **actuality**, of every **existence**, worlds and beings; by **determining measure**, the creator in every being of its strength, of the relations proper to it, of its own living **soul** that **supports** and guides it. Call Him the one without an other, the **all** of wisdom and goodness, the **Creator-God** – the **Spirit**!

Before Plato, Job searched for the dwelling of the understanding, the place where wisdom comes from.

ON LICHTENBERG'S PROPHECY

"Wisdom is concealed, he said, from the eyes of any living being. God knows the way to it and its place. When God gave the wind its weight and provided the water with its distinct measure, when He decided the **direction** of rain, and the path [16] of lighting and thunder, then He also saw and defined wisdom; He **prepared** and **invented** it."[9]

He **invented it!** He invented the law and the **finite** being; manifoldness and unity in unexplorable connection; existence and nature; the **miracle** of the senses and the mystery of the understanding: **the human being.** And along with the human being, according in his likeness, He created **an intuition of Himself outside Him,** a mortal life with a seed of immortality: the rational soul, the spirit, the **creature.** With this spirit **in** him, He created the capacity for a higher love, a will that desires His own volition, the law of justice, and a wise rule; He created piety, defeat of death, divine blessedness.

Tell us, you men of wisdom, who secretly know the entire truth before the deed, know it from your own selves, yet are unable, from those selves alone, even only in thought, to fix a point in the void and create for it a **first** place where there is no place, and there to generate with it the beginning of a line. You cannot because it is not possible to draw even the **smallest** line, for the smallest line is a **non-thing.** Therefore, the line that in **thought** gets lengthened is **only** longer, but is still a non-thing. **Originally,** you are unable to produce any weight because here, as well as everywhere, a first and a last, a beginning, a middle, and an end – **the very fact of unity** – are missing. A first number, a first measure, a first being and a first word are all missing. Tell us, you, eternally in a **more and less** of **nothingness, only** freely spinning in a pre-existing infinite, still thoroughly indeterminate and universal; tell us, you, secret creators of creation: how could a human being create **thought** with word, and **word** with thought? How did he come about making his **voice distinct** by means of the movement of the tongue and his breath? How did he come about giving body to thought, wherein he transmitted it and, by communicating it, presented and preserved it? How did he invent making it spin in air so that it would last and outlast even the most stable?

You do not know! And you do not even know how breasts, mother, and father were created for the first infant who would be born; how a first love generated them, and how a second love supported and took care of them – Indeed! [17] The human being, before existing, has no more presupposed and prepared his existence than he has presupposed and prepared the first word pronounced

---

9 [Partially modified from Job 28:12–27.]

by his mouth before that word existed. He rather irradiated his innermost being through his eyes, portraying and painting it with colours on his forehead and cheek, just as he equally let it resound with distinct voice. In every living being, with the gift of sensation there comes the gift of expression; just as, in beings of the same constitution, with the gift of expression there comes the gift of empathy; the understanding. Without this gift of immediate revelation and interpretation the use of language among human beings would have never arisen. And **with** this gift, from the beginning, the whole genus at the same time invented language. Tell us, what can be truer than this: the invention of the genus coincides with the invention of the word. They have the same age. Any race creates its own tongue; not one understands the other, but all speak. All speak because all, not in the same fashion though still in a similar manner, **received together with reason the gift** to distinguish and recognize the internal from the external, that which is concealed from that which is revealed, the invisible from the visible. The expressive sound of sensation, of feeling, is, **as a sound**, not more similar to sensation and feeling than the word is to the thing, than the expression **lion** to the animal designated by this name. What has been said regarding sound applies also to the most vivid sight of the eye, to the most telling trait of the cheek, to any expressive wink of the face, and to any expressive gesture. All this needs interpretation. But such an interpretation develops immediately, it arises through instinct; it never fails to come, it is never missing.

"Through instinct?" you ask, "Through that **blind spirit, so foolish and so typical of beasts?**"

I answer: Yes, through it! It is the only one that truly sees, who knows from the source; it is the spirit of **providence**, the spirit of God.

There is prophetizing, fore-saying, also in the beast, and only a **higher** one in the human. The one knows what it internally desires, seeks and finds but does not have cognition of it: food not yet tasted, distant, not yet visible to it. The other equally seeks and finds an invisible that he does not have cognition of [18], yet which he knows in his need for it – the need of a spirit whose **being** is to have the knowledge that the life he has is not in himself; that he exists from an Other, without whom his life would vanish from him. As it happens to the newborn's lips that clutch to the mother's breast, sucking from it, so it happens to man's heart that, surrounded by nature, takes hold of God by worshipping him.

The rising spirit, says our Lichtenberg, throws the body to its knees.[10]

10   *Nachlass*, part I, 47.

ON LICHTENBERG'S PROPHECY

And Epictetus says: "If I were a nightingale, by singing I would want to do what the nightingale does. If a swan, what the swan does. But I am a rational being, so what I do by singing is to praise God. That is my vocation (*Beruf*), and I want to fulfill it."[11]

What would life mean to me, shouts Marcus Aurelius, in a world without God and providence![12]

If the nature of the human being, if the force and inspiration of the instinct that is proper to him separating him from animals, raising him above them, consists in so to sense and think; if he alone, as a **rational** being, can sense, judge, think, and desire in this fashion, then these sensations, impulses, and thoughts, this faith that governs and penetrates his whole being, cannot become for him foolishness without he too turning at the same time into foolishness and fable, **along with** his reason, his superiority over the animals, and his human nature. He is clearly deceived in his reason if he is deceived in this faith, because only reason has placed such a lie in him, deceiving him thereby and grounding his entire reputation on this illusion.

Its entire reputation! For reason has no other power than to concoct this deception and to give to it a force that oversteps all sensory or intellectual truth. As far as it is exclusively directed to the suprasensible and the supernatural, its proper and unique field is that of inconceivable effects and [19] inconceivable beings, the field of miracles. Should it lose this field, it is left with no permanent home. It now occurs to the [resulting] **fantasizer**, who presumes to rule with his high and eminent ideas over the faculty of cognition and to rank in it at the top, that that faculty cannot attain any cognition but can only **contrive** empty fantasies totally lacking in understanding.[13] They are delusions, in which the understanding is kept, prevented from truly achieving understanding. The understanding – corrupted and captured by them – believes in all seriousness that these empty pretences can make themselves true and hit upon something substantial. It occupies itself with them to this end, elaborates them, and in this elaboration it loses itself more and more, so that one could truly say: the understanding **loses** the understanding and is estranged from the senses – **solely and exclusively because of reason!** – At the heels of this insight and this cognition there then follows the conclusion, full

---

11 Epictetus, "Discourses," in *Discourses and Selected Writings*, ed. Robert Dobbin (London: Penguin, 2008), 42. [Translation modified to meet the excerpt quoted in Jacobi's text.]

12 Marcus Aurelius Antoninus, *The Meditations*, II, 11, 14.

13 [A reference to Kant, *Critique of Pure Reason*, B 269 and B 571.]

of light and concreteness, of **pure common sense**: reason, in so far as it is essentially **senseless** and thereby clearly unable to know the truth and – due to this lack – unable to reach the truth, has to renounce once and for all its ruinous claims to the highest rank in the faculty of cognition, and henceforth must content itself with working solely under the supervision of the understanding. Under this supervision and true guardianship, reason, as the original faculty of fiction-making, has to facilitate the conquests of the understanding by producing for the latter **drafts** that continually expand its limits. Nevertheless, reason should never hazard to undertake something on its own: it must always **wait** upon the understanding, serve it, and obey it.

But it is impossible to carry this conclusion through because reason, when contested in this manner, takes a stand against the understanding – this vain subverter – and shows up its nudity. Reason demonstrates to the understanding – only because, says reason, it cannot **show** it – that the understanding has only **hands**, no **eyes**. It demonstrates to the understanding that it can only either **nod** or **shake** its empty head to indicate whether what the senses bring to it to form a concept is, or is **not, one and the same thing**, a **full** or **empty** hand [20]. By itself, it cannot even count up to **three**, for it does not have in itself the "whereon" or the "why" for starting, restarting, or stopping: nothing to start with and **no reason** to start, nothing to continue from and **no reason** to continue, nothing to stop at and **no reason** to stop; it does not have an **end** from which to **begin anew**. In general, reason demonstrates to the understanding that by virtue of its essence (Wesen) it **cannot** posit in advance anything by itself, and, as a consequence, it **absolutely** cannot explain, synthetize and thus **compare** anything. In fact, to be able to add things up, it must first be able to **multiply** by itself, and in order to multiply by itself, it must first be able to subtract and divide by itself and in itself, without being taught anything of this sort. **In light of** its essential emptiness, all this is impossible. – And so on, in every way, does reason indisputably prove to the understanding that there is absolutely no cognition in the understanding **at origin**, neither of the untrue nor the true; nor, generally speaking, can the understanding **come to** any cognition of the **true**, and consequently of the untrue **through** the true. Reason proves to it that it goes about deceiving **in a twofold way**: it mints the impure and deceptive metal of sense perception with concepts through conceptualizations, and with this minting the understanding makes it look as if metal had been transformed into pure gold, and so it takes it itself. It oversees these treasures, and by dint of steady gathering, splitting, melting, and minting, it

ON LICHTENBERG'S PROPHECY

nourishes its own expectation with that; by working on this mass of unessential materials and forms, it would eventually bring forth something essential.

Reason finally becomes outraged by the human understanding rebelling against it and claiming superiority over it. And so it declares: "alienated from me, you are just an inverted animal; equipped with your sense perception, **without which you are nothing**, you are **blind** in your **intuitions**, but you want to **see** in your **representations** and **concepts**. You want to distill cognition from appearances in which nothing appears, foundational truths from unfounded experiences, an irrefutable story by gathering and assembling events that are merely invented [21].

"You call me senseless, and therefore you consider me a faculty of delusions. In line with your critical wisdom, you recognize – loudly proclaim – that by virtue of this very sense perception, about which you boast to me – **as if it alone would have at the end to confirm and prove everything through representation** – you are nevertheless utterly separated from everything true, from everything that stands by itself. You take pride in it, **such** a truth-giver that it is, and swell up with even more pride **because** of it, as if you were capable of turning what is acquired through it into anything true, **possessed by you**, while holding it only in worthless pennies – counting the counterfeit coins over and over again, **blindly** counting without anything that can be counted (since this always remains an inscrutable secret for you!). You do not even have in and by yourself the ability to **count**! For the latter came to you with those **pennies** also, is of one origin with them, at one with them and the same fiction. Look! You, above all and always, are answerable only to **sense perception**, for you the only creator and unalterable possessor of the **first** and **last**, consequently of **all true value**. You belong to it, share its bread, and cannot sing any song but its own. Its being (Seyn) is your knowledge, its drive your action.

"And I should bow before you, renounce my **worship of God**, give it up, disown it, to serve and sacrifice like a priestess at your idolatrous altar? – Even if I knew myself as a mere **phantasy**, I would consider myself too noble and sublime. Nevertheless, I am not a phantasy, I am an essence (Wesen) of **truth**, I am its immediate voice. Without me there would not even be a **murmur** of it on earth. The one who destroys my **first** word, destroys all my words: I speak **only** of God. I exist only as a **sign** of **Him**, as a mark that refers to **Him**: without Him I am a non-being, a non-thing"

✗

ON THE DIVINE THINGS AND THEIR REVELATION

[22] It can be rigorously and clearly demonstrated to the one who attentively and exclusively seeks the truth that, if the human being can only have a fabricated **God**, then he can also only have a fabricated **nature**. The sense-perceived objects would still have a primacy over the **suprasensible** ones; but they would prove to be **doubly** fabricated because of their double origin: one part from sense perception, the other part from the understanding that belongs to sense perception.[14] The senses present to us (this is generally presupposed when one philosophizes) only their own changes, but they represent nothing of **what** changed them: they present mere **sensations** as such. The understanding is simply the place where these sensations are assembled in heaps through the imagination, which gives them shape and direction, as if they were not mere sensations; and where, classified by species, they are arranged into rows, in order that they may harmoniously constitute a common mind in a common consciousness, **which is the non-sensing understanding.** The voices of sensation all flow into one another, calling and answering each other, dissolving, echoing in a loud resonance, and, with this **echo**, mind appears. In this mind, sound comes and goes, but nothing **resounds**. If the mind asks itself about its sound: **what** is it that makes that sound, and **where** does that sound come from? **In what** and **with what** does it resonate? If it asks what distinguishes the two, and which of the two comes first, it does not even know what the question is about. But the question is in the mind and lasts forever. Gladly did the understanding destroy this question, and to destroy it made its own echo so **independent** and **pure** that one could no longer perceive in it even the hollowest **sound** that would yet even **appear** as **wanting** to say something meaningful. To the understanding taken only for itself, both, riotous sound and question, are revolting: vipers in its bosom that do not die; flames that do not extinguish [23].

Without image or resemblance! – The manifold, changeable being of sense perception is opposed to the simple, unchangeable being of the understanding. In fact, the latter's relationship to sense perception is one that destroys and abolishes sense perception's variety and manifoldness; the striving of the understanding is in general a mere **opposition** with regard to everything **external to it.** Above all, the understanding seeks to bring to an end the trouble

---

14 Where there is sense (*Sinn*), there one finds beginning and end, separation and connection; there, one finds the one and the other, and the sense is the third. With sense there necessarily comes understanding: **consciousness of connection and separation.** A sense that is only sense would be a non-thing, as would be a thoroughly mediated cognition. [See Kant, *Critique of Pure Reason*, B 74.]

ON LICHTENBERG'S PROPHECY

that sensation produces against its will. Consequently, there develops that continuous process of **equating** that we call connection and which is a continuous lessening and simplification of manifoldness until – **if it were possible** – its complete removal and annihilation. It is only because such complete annihilation and simplification is impossible that the understanding stays active. While being inactive in and for itself, without pursuits or demands, desire or business, the understanding, in its **disturbed** calm, only wants to regain the **undisturbed**, idle, and empty calm that it painfully misses. Assailed by sense perception, the understanding is violently compelled **to be aware** of it. – I say, **violently!** In fact, since in the understanding there is no beginning of an action, no spontaneous outcome of it, only a perpetual going back and **withdrawing into itself**, there is also no spontaneous attentiveness in it, such as belongs rather to vigilant and easily excited senses. Should the understanding feel at any time, more or less with **fright**, the latter's **coming-out-of-itself**, it becomes anxious and makes the effort to **return to itself** as quickly as possible, striving, wherever it strives, to return to its own homogeneous essence: the **pure** – unconscious – consciousness. To that end, it also makes concepts. These come to it in this anxiety, from it and because of it, as instinctual defence mechanisms, the immediate expressions of its **simple** nature's antipathy for the manifoldness of sense perception. Of the many and manifolds forcing themselves into it, only so much does it in turn extract from itself, as need be, with the help of concepts, as these are able to grasp. Without this hostile relation and need, concepts would have in the understanding neither **ground** nor the least **possibility**. In no way out of good will does the understanding therefore concern itself with the sense-perceived. Would it do it, say, to order it, organize it? or [24] – **even determine it in the first place?** The latter would mean **to cause** the many and the manifold, to produce it **originally**: a total nonsense, since the manifold as such must already be determined in advance, and the understanding – for its part – only aims at **un**-determining, deconstructing individuality, being, and actuality.[15] It works out of malice to wear out these things artificially, progressively to destroy them. Continually drawing ever wider the circles of the concept that become for the manifold of sense perception ever narrower circles of **existence**, what it wants is to see before its eyes this existence finally totally submerged into the **widest** of all concepts – truly

15   It is said of the understanding that it **parses**. Yes, but: not what is already articulated? Original articulation is not within the understanding's capacity, nor, for the matter, are dividing and **multiplying**. The original articulation is the secret of creation.

the concept of a manifest nothing – and thus behold the being of hollow cognition fully realized.

And that would be the human being! A nothing more than a composite of sensory and rational illusions, of illusory **visions** and illusory **ideas**: artfully constructed visions and ideas, the human being himself the product of an empty fantasy without being. On the one side, a dreamt-up nature; on the other, a dreamt-up God; and in the middle an understanding that assiduously only translates for this non-being – that is, the **human being** – its own dream of truth **into** finally **the truth of a dream**, a necessary, eternal, and universal dream from which there is no awakening except in a universal nothing. And the only thing this understanding would clearly show to the human is that nothing is anywhere ever **truly** shown to him: not through the senses that only exhibit their own modifications; not through reason that, motionless, has not much to show anyway; not through fantasy, the deceiver, that fools him with pictures, **sense-perceived** pictures of a not-present sense perception and suprasensible; not through itself, the very understanding, that from one sense-perceivable thing only shows another *ad infinitum*, posits nothing original, in dispelling illusion brings experience to nothing.

If this is it: the whole of human being is in fact this tangle of fraud and deceit with no beginning or ending; a being afflicted with a sense perception that does not convey anything true, and with an understanding that does not countenance anything untrue yet does not produce anything true, but hovers instead over watery stretches of completely empty appearances only to brood over God knows what [25] – an understanding that, in order to dispose itself of an illusion that it would ground and turn into truth but which is neither to be grounded or turned into truth, must seek a mere nothing of cognition as its highest aim, only to realize that it is unattainable. If this is indeed how things stand, if the unification of such a sense perception with such an understanding on the basis of the mere blank soil of an empty imagination constitutes the whole essence (Wesen) of human being; if it is only by means of fantasy that this being secures **existence** inside and outside himself; if from reason he can only obtain his own **annihilation**, and if, nevertheless, the worst that can happen to him is to be deprived of reason, then is the thus revealed humankind's lot one of grimmest despair indeed.

You, intrepid ones! You, sublime ones, who reveal this lot rejoicing, drawing it a win, for it fully explains the long-hidden secret of your being and therewith of **all** beings. Allow us – O you blessed, transformed into pure light and no longer in need of deceiving eyes – allow us to glance at your heaven of cogni-

ON LICHTENBERG'S PROPHECY

tion, send us from above a comprehensible word that explains to us how a becoming through which nothing becomes and a nothing eternally rising from nothing can be understood. And explain to us how something – whatever it may be, whether a **dream** or an **illusion** – can all by itself come to be, as dream or as illusion, from a **pure** faculty of dreaming, **alone truly** a **nothing** of fiction-making and posturing! So be it! Let word be against word, challenge against challenge. Do vouchsafe us just one comprehensible word on how this great All that we both call **creation** would present itself and spring to existence from eternity to eternity as an appearance that comes only from fantasy, an appearance in which nothing true appears, and therefore as a something unreal produced only by fantasy, a being without permanence, a permanence without being. Do vouchsafe us just one **truly** comprehensible word on the subject, and **in return** we shall owe you regarding a creation that **a God** made out of nothing, not just one only comprehensible word, but a satisfactory answer to every question you ask us about this doctrine [26].

In this regard I offer the following for a start, in fragmentary remarks.

The human being has only one alternative: either he derives everything from **One** or he derives everything from **nothing**. We prefer the **One** over nothing, and we name it **God** because this **One** (*Ein*) must necessarily be a **personal one** (*Einer*), otherwise it would be the same universal nothing but differently named, essentially undetermined yet all-determining; the non-thing of the Platonic infinite, sheer otherness; a totality (*All*) but **not** a unity, a manifest impossibility, **even less** than nothing.

The **One** is therefore a **personal One**, and this personal One was and had to be before everything and anyone; a **One without another**: the **perfection** of being, the **perfection** of the true.

Human cognition is grounded on **imperfection**, as does its existence. Therefore there is in it that constant referring from a one to another without end. The human being sees and recognizes only through **resemblances**. He does not see, nor does he recognize the **incomparable**; not himself, his **own spirit**; and not God either, the Highest.

Incomparable is the human being, a one for himself without any other, himself a being by virtue of his spirit, the **defining property** by which he is **who** he is, **the personal one that is he and no other**. He finds himself to be this one who **alone is a personal one** and **remains the same** through every possible change, not *ex post facto* through a comparison with himself, as if he were a conceptual essence (*Wesen*), an essence of the **mere imagination**, but at origin. In fact, where would comparison and imagination take place? In what would the self be equal to itself? And what would a self that is not yet equal to itself be? A self still without its own being and **permanence**: one rather deriving its identity by equating, differentiating, and assembling itself, in fact by merely relating itself to a self with a being and permanence of its own, one with its **own proper being**? Finally, what was there to initiate all this? – This spirit finds itself as this being not as a result of **knowledge**, but through an **immediate sentiment of being**[16] independent from the memory of past conditions. It knows that it is this personal one [27], a one who remains the same and cannot become another, because **spirit's** immediate self-**certainty** as spirit is inseparable from its being **spirit**, from its personal identity (*Selbstheit*), from substantivity.

But the self-certain human spirit, a **vowel**, needs **consonants, nature** and **God,** to **give expression** to its existence; or more precisely: it is no **pure** vowel.

It cannot express itself without expressing God and nature at the same time, indeed, without **sounding** them **first:** thus does it know, with at least the same certitude with which it knows **that it is,** that it **is not the sole being** (*Alleinig*); thus does it attest to the existence of another being, similar and dissimilar to

16 [Note absent in *Werke.*] The manifoldness of sensation (Empfindung) already presupposes conjunction: the conjunction presupposes memory (*Gedächtniß*) and imagination (*Einbildung*). Memory and imagination [27], however, presuppose an absolute and original first principle of consciousness and activity, a **principle** of life and cognition, an originary **being in itself** that, as such, can be neither a **property** nor an **effect**; it cannot be in any way something **occurring in time**, but rather it must be **Self-Being, Self-Cause,** something **non-temporal** and, according to this property, also in possession of a **non-temporal** and merely **internal** consciousness. This non-temporal, merely internal consciousness, that distinguishes itself in the clearest way from the **external** and **temporal** one, is the consciousness of the person that **enters** time but absolutely does not **arise** in time as a **mere temporal being**. – **Understanding** belongs to the **temporal** being, **reason** to the **nontemporal.** The understanding, when **isolated,** is materialistic and deprived of reason: it denies spirit and God. Reason, when **isolated,** is idealistic and unintelligent (*unverständig*): it denies nature and makes itself into God. The integral, undivided, real and true man has reason (*vernünftig*) and understanding (*verständig*) all at once: with an undivided self and with equal confidence he believes in **God,** in **nature,** and in the **personal spirit.** This threefold – generally unphilosophical – faith must be able to turn into a faith that is in the strictest sense **philosophical** and confirmed by reflection. And I am audacious enough to say that I know that it can turn into it, that I see the way back on which a **speculation** (*Nach-Denken*) gone astray will return and consequently produce a first and true philosophy, which is a science and wisdom that enlightens the **whole** of man.

ON LICHTENBERG'S PROPHECY

it, standing outside, next to it and **before** it, with the same force with which it asserts its own existence. It feels, experiences originally, and can also recognize that its **autonomy** [28] is as limited as its **dependence**, that just as it can necessarily be a personal one **only among others**, [and hence] impossibly **first** and **unique**, so, in order to be a personal one among others, must he **necessarily** be one and **not** another, must be self-subsistent, an **actual**, a **personal** being.

God alone is the personal one that is only one, the **unique**; He is the **one without another** in the highest sense *par excellence*; in no way is He a one **only** in relation to another being, nor is He an individual being, conditioned by pre-existing and coexisting beings. He is the being that is absolutely sufficient to itself; **unconditionally** autonomous, He is the only **perfect** and completely **true** being.

How? And should this God, since He is necessarily **perfect** and **sufficient in himself**, and therefore not an individual being merely **derived from** and **belonging to** a genus, be necessarily deprived of self-consciousness, of personality, and therefore also of reason?[17] Should He necessarily [29] be a **non**-person, a **non**-intelligence, because He is not a limited, dependent, and

---

17 [Footnote is present in the second edition.] In Friedrich Schlegel's review of the text *On the Divine Things* – a review that is rightfully appreciated, insightful, and written in the most magnanimous tone (Deutsches Museum, Band I, Heft I, 79–98; [see *Religionsphilosophie und speculative Theologie. Quellenband*, 328–39]) (96) – there appears the following claim: "Anyone who speaks carefully will not make use of the expression **reason** with reference to God; but anyone who acknowledges God as a spirit, speaks of the divine **understanding**." It is true that, **more generally**, we only speak of divine **understanding**, but it is wrong to say that one who carefully speaks of God will never make use of the term **reason**. When we speak of God we make use of this expression anytime we address Him as a personal being acting in freedom and with providence, and especially when we consider Him under **these** characteristics. We do not translate νοῦς κόσμῶν as the organizing **understanding** but as the organizing **reason** (Plato, *Werke*, ed. F. Schleiermacher, part 2, vol. 3, 89). [See Plato, *Phaedo*, 97c.] How would we have it otherwise, since we ourselves possess personality, freedom, and creative power only because we are **rational** beings? – In the human being we call **reason** that by virtue of which he not only recognizes a nature **under** him – which he rules over – but he also recognizes and – especially – obeys a God **over** him. Mind you, it can also be said that, to the highest being, one should no more attribute **reason** than one should attribute **sense perception**, considering that, unlike the human being, He is not conditioned by a twofold externality, which means, that He does not hover between an "above Him" and an "**under** Him" (Cf. Part 2, 10). It can also be said with truth, however, **only** within the limited relation of a "**no more … than**." We know that God does

not see with eyes, and yet we speak, unreproached, of His eyes, of the all-seeing. We know that God, unlike the human being, does not think by forming concepts, and yet we speak, unreproached, of His understanding. Why then should we not be allowed also to speak, unreproached, of a divine reason, considering that reason is the highest element in a human being created in the image of God, and that it is precisely [29] this element that makes man the image of God? I ask: if there is not a divine **reason** but only a divine **understanding**, why would we call **divine**, incomprehensibly mixing up the terms, that which would be absent in God yet is so crucial and distinctive in the human being? And what would raise the divine understanding above the merely human? – We know what raises the human understanding above that of animals: it is the enlightenment by means of reason or, what is the same, by means of the spirit that dwells in man and comes from God and makes him participate in God and his cognition. To be sure, God cannot be the **mere recipient** of Himself, the way human beings are of Him by virtue of a finite and incomplete reason received from Him. But even less (allow me this expression that comes out of necessity!) – **even less can** God, who is a spirit, exclude Himself from Himself and become, following his true nature, **deprived of reason**, an infinite animal, or perhaps not even this, but instead a mere living whole. Many thinkers from the old, middle, and modern age, have denied that in the depth of His being God has self-consciousness, personality, freedom, and providence along with it. Fr. Schlegel resolutely opposes such thinkers in the aforementioned text, and does so in an even more detailed way in the Lectures of some years later about the history of old and modern literature. Schlegel thus allows us to speak, as was long normal among those **who recognized God as spirit**, not only of a divine **understanding**, but also and **eminently** of a divine **reason**.

It is evident here, as elsewhere, that an unsolvable problem presents itself with the use of the words reason and understanding. It is a problem that has its roots in the fact that human reason and human understanding mutually condition each other, so that in the reflective consciousness now the one concept, now the other, predominates. As a consequence, a linguistic usage has arisen that philosophical judgement in many ways opposes but the philosophical writer nevertheless must abide by, and can even follow without the risk of being misunderstood, provided he has first adequately discussed those concepts and thoroughly determined their reciprocal relation. This is not the place for a deeper analysis of this most important question. But allow me to conclude this remark with just a couple of hints about human reason and its difference from the divine one.

Human reason has to be seen, on the one hand, as the faculty of perceiving the divine which is **outside** and **above** the human being; on the other hand, as the faculty of perceiving something divine **inside** the human being, and – as being itself this divine element. If the rational being were not originally of divine nature, it could never have then reached either a true cognition or a true love of God.

If the eye were not sun-like
How would we be able to see the light?
God's power did not live in us,
How would God's work be able to enrapture us?
(Goethe, Vorwort, in *Zur Farbenlehre*, XXXVIII, Tübingen 1810)

ON LICHTENBERG'S PROPHECY

imperfect being? Precisely because He alone has life in Himself and needs neither nature nor sense perception [30]; precisely because He does not **receive** existence, cognition, and truth in any sense, but rather **gives** them always and everywhere; for these reasons should He – and He **alone** – be the one that **is not**, the not-living?

Indeed, the one who is not, neither for himself nor anywhere! For a being without self-being is absolutely and universally impossible. But a being-oneself without consciousness and, conversely, a consciousness without self-consciousness, without substantiality and at least an attributed personality, is wholly impossible: the one as well as the other are nothing but empty words. Therefore God is not, is the non-being in the highest sense, if He is not a **spirit**. And He is not a spirit if He lacks the fundamental feature of spirit: self-consciousness, substantiality, and personality. But were He not spirit, He would not be the beginning of things inasmuch as they have **actuality** and **real** being. In fact, wherever there is something **real**, namely **spirit**, there necessarily lies the beginning of things. Any real being or existence is impossible if it is not in the spirit and through a spirit.

The healthy and non-artificial reason has never questioned the truth of this principle. You understand by yourselves that non-being cannot produce being; that the ground of unreason cannot produce reason and the rational; that a blind chance cannot produce wisdom and understanding; that what causes death and what is dead cannot produce the living; that insensitive matter cannot produce the sensitive soul, love, compassion, self-sacrifice, justice; that what destroys cannot produce what creates and orders. Above all, you understand by yourselves that the lower cannot by itself produce the higher and the better; nor can it by itself transfigure itself, turning itself into it; or do it **gradually**, with the **mere** empty help of a mere empty time, or **immediately**, with no time lapse but in a trice suddenly.

But a spirit! You wonder – how can a spirit produce something outside itself, something real: more spirits? How can it produce something that is completely opposed to it: a sense-perceivable, material world? How can a **beginning** come from the Eternal?

Who told you that what **you** call "a beginning" has come from it? And what do you mean when you speak about what is first and [31] what is not first? Can you say that you see something **really** coming into being and **really** ceasing to exist before your eyes? Or would you **prefer** to say that it is neither a beginning nor an end, that nothing really changes, that nothing is born and nothing dies, that everything remains unchanged? **Reason** forbids the former; the latter, a

126 ON THE DIVINE THINGS AND THEIR REVELATION

feeling that with respect to reason is at least just as **irresistible.** – It all comes down to this: that at the start you would marvel that there be **anything which is and acts,** or deny that there anywhere be anything which is and endures. Here, at the heart of the incomprehensible that completely surrounds you, do reflect on, and choose whether you should behave toward this incomprehensible as a friend or as an enemy.

Don't you look everywhere for a First? But can a First ever be comprehended? And what would the First be for you if not a **cause?** And what would a cause be for you if it were **that which never is?**

Pause here and ponder, ever deeper! The more completely, silently, and purely you concentrate in your innermost self, the more clearly you will discover that **He is!** – He who made the eye: He sees! He who made the ear: He hears![18] He who prepared this heart: He lives! He who gave birth to this spirit: He wills, and knows, and **is!**

18 [Ps. 94:9.]

[33] On the Divine Things and Their Revelation

[35] The author of this review is among those who cannot forget how much gratitude of every sort **Asmus, Messenger of Wandsbeck,** has won from them in the past twenty-five years. During all this time, he has made his way, staff in hand, through the vast expanse of Germany: he passed on what had been entrusted to him not only to the wealthy in big cities or the sumptuous in their palaces, but also, with equal diligence and fidelity, and, indeed, with even greater friendliness and willingness, in remote villages, in solitary huts, to the poor, the afflicted, and the oppressed. A good, upright soul! And because of this I think that if even a small a tax were levied on every big or small window on which he knocked and across it delivered something dear to its occupant, the sum would be considerable enough to elicit even Mr Pitt's attention.[1]

Actually, these considerations do not pertain to my task; they really are an impertinence since they make me suspect as a reviewer. Anyone who knows of gratitude, his own or a relative's, and fails, as I have admitted to have done, to keep it in abeyance, is rightly considered corrupt. Fortunately, it is the public's stated intention by having me step in as reviewer of this writing that I carry this taint and make a display of it. For the author himself lets others know, in the provisional announcement of the sixth part and now once again in the preface, that he imagined that we all – [the reviewers] who have to deputize for the public when it comes to judgment; have to prepare the public's

---

1   [William Pitt (1759–1806), prime minister of Great Britain during the French Revolutionary and Napoleonic wars, in the years 1783–1801 and 1804–06.]

opinions, suggesting them and getting him to understand them – that we would be hard on him. He imagined that we would serve him in the manner the chamberlain Albiboghoi did during the audience at Jeddo in Japan, when he asked the emperor permission to cut open his abdomen "so that he might be brought to think otherwise."[2] [So did the author imagine. But] a magnanimous public wants in no uncertain terms that the opposite be shown, and, to that end, the **impartial Correspondent** of Hamburg itself had to agree for once to allow something corrupt and biased. But let us get on with it!

All good things truly come only in three, said the author in the aforementioned report [36]. And yet he could not help it and had to experiment whether they could be brought up to **six.**

We have them all before us and, after scrupulous examination, must remark that the author, considering that he spent **twenty-five years** developing his *Opera Omnia*, never intended making his rule the motto "*Nulla dies sine linea.*"[3] Taking this under consideration, albeit against our will, we must still judge him with some severity.

Credit can and should be given to him for consistency: his sixth part is of no less value than the preceding. He owes this to his **serious style:** it is not one of those styles of art that one adopts, chooses, or makes for oneself. Quite the opposite, this style creates its art. It is an art which, one has to admit, is not the kind that is the prerogative of **exclusive eminent people,** the great virtuosos who pass themselves off as such with no respect for anyone else: it does, however, have the good side that it never profits from what it does, even less could it die of it.[4] "The man" – said our author in a little treatise about music in his first fascicule (87) – "who was the first to have music play during a divine service, had no intention to recommend himself to the audience as a composer; nor did the prophet Nathan, when narrating the story of the poor man's only sheep, want to gain the title of a good storyteller, etc." – He goes on to say: "the first poets of every nation must have been its priests; perhaps these were also the first to come up with the idea of giving more incisiveness and strength to their chants by means of stringed instruments. Music might have been born inside the altar or might have been introduced into the temples; we have to admit here that there was a time where music lacked **any proper justification and made wonders while having the form of a servant.**" – Later, in Greece,

2 The Messenger's *Sämmtliche Werke*, part III, 114.

3 ["no day without a line."]

4 [The German reads: "die aber dagegen auch das Gute mit sich bringt, daß sie nie etwas vom Handwerke annehmen, noch weniger am Handwerke sterben kann."]

ON THE DIVINE THINGS AND THEIR REVELATION

where in the beginning music had only been used for the celebration of gods and heroes and for the education of the youth [37], it was so long refined and polished to the point of being made into a **fine art.**

With no self-justification and in role of servant: these two features strikingly qualify the style and the art of our freemaster (*Freymeister*) in all his works.

When some new and profound sentiment or some great and excellent thought has taken shape in his imagination, and wants consequently to emerge in its innate shine, he holds it back so that he can first douse its rays. He blushes, squirms, and hides – **he does not want to have done it.** That is the reason for his peculiar way of dressing up an idea, the comical expressions, the jokes he inserts, the smile he brings to the lips of the reader while at the same time moving him often to the core of his being. One should recall the dedication to his friend Hain, with the explanation of the memorials engraved on copper in background: if one were to reread those pages, one would understand what I mean.

Good Asmus! You do not desire any of such stars – whether those of literature or those of politics – as "**shine on the front flap**"; you do not aspire to them because of the other star, the one "**on the naked breast.**" It suffices for you. You can contemplate that shining star, any star indeed that your wide-open eye encounters in the blue sky, "can thus contemplate it for an entire half hour as if it were an open or delicately concealed spot above the world, where the soul shines brighter, and over that you can rejoice within ... What the Herr Magister and Professor Ahrens – who otherwise knows everything like the back of his hand – could never do!" – Therefore we, as your cousin, want to love you more than we love any Magister and Professor Ahrens, and won't let your plain hair and large shoes with thick soles bother us, because we like you much more like this: it suits you.

With his fifth part our author has nevertheless begun to set himself somewhat more at the same level of the **honoratioribus**, and has also signed the first treatise in it, **On Immortality**, with his scholarly name, **Matthias Claudius,** for all to see. Actually, he has silently moved along with the times [38], albeit not at the same pace that required too much of a back and forth for which he might not have been either capable or agile enough. – Moreover, he kept himself at a distance from those whose banner displays Minerva with a **cuckoo** instead of an **owl** on her helmet. – However, generally speaking, he marched on with the rest. As evidence, we would like to quote an excerpt from the recently published sixth part.

There, in the fourth letter to Andres, page 183, it reads: "The human being is in himself richer than the heaven and earth, and possesses what they cannot give ... The wisdom and order that he finds in the visible nature, he gives to it more than he derives them from it, for he would indeed not be able to become aware of them if he were unable to relate them to something he has in himself, just as one cannot measure without a meter. The heaven and earth are for him only the confirmation of a knowledge of which he is conscious and that gives him the audacity and courage to master and rectify everything by himself. And in the middle of the glory of creation, he is and feels bigger than everything around him, and longs for something else."

However, having read this beautiful passage, the reviewer would like to ask the author a question, namely: could it be that what we **read in books**, or what is **recounted** to us orally, or we experience **historically**, differs from that of which we have an immediate intuition? Could the dead letter perhaps have more power than the living nature? What if the letter indeed contains and alone gives the measure of measure, so that the spirit would be worthless or almost worthless without it?

Many of our author's statements allow us to answer **positively** to this question. Now, since times immemorial, there have been many learned and ingenious men, among them even deep thinkers, who have held that view. But I cannot think of anyone having **at the same time** allowed that deeper philosophical insight that the above passage shows to be disclosed. It is only such a juxtaposition and combination [of the insight expressed in the passage and other author's statements] that is disconcerting. But were that the only passage! Rather, in each part, we can find many passages [39] of a similar or even more remarkable nature.

For example, in the fifth part of the aforementioned work **On Immortality**, so deeply written and outstandingly conceived as brilliantly developed, it is most diligently shown that those views and concepts that are unanimously recognized as **superior**, and whose possession constitutes humankind's essence and privilege, are neither given to us from the outside world, nor artificially produced in our innermost part by means of analysis and synthesis. On the contrary, we find them in us without having **sought** and **craved** them, like something that we cannot resist.

Without having sought and craved them, because no one can seek and crave something without already having some knowledge of it: "One must already know where one wants to climb before placing a ladder."

ON THE DIVINE THINGS AND THEIR REVELATION

The external world, or **nature**, does not produce those superior views, concepts, **ideas** (which, according to the author's correct remark, will ultimately reduce to one), nor can they be deduced from it either. And yet they ineradicably cling to the innermost part of the human being, proving "that in the human being there is not only something **other** than in all the rest of nature, but also that this other is **more** than nature and **above** it."

With the help of stirring examples, he shows how this **other** undeniably makes itself known in a twofold way: as something **higher**, as well as something **extrasensory** and **supernatural**.

For one thing, thanks to the power of this **other**, the human being forces the **outer** nature to change its effects in a large variety of different ways, to accept its influences over it, to submit to its intentions and thoughts, and to do and produce what nature, by itself, would not and could not produce.

But this other and higher then reveals itself even more decisively through the dominion it exerts over the nature **within the human being himself**. Here, working against the power of the spirit, there stand blind powers of nature, i.e., such as act merely according to the law of the stronger, yet living and sentient: they rebel against that power, and a battle ensues in which victory [40] appears to shift back and forth. Nonetheless, the power of the spirit, rising up over and over again with immortal strength, affirms the rights of its crown, of its scepter.

As indestructible as the **Ideas**, there rules within the human being the consciousness of a faculty and an impulse rising with the spirit, with intention, resolution, and thought over everything that is **merely nature**. Aware of its own superiority, this consciousness stands against the latter (against what is merely nature) and seizes hold of it to impose on it, from outside it, the laws of justice and wisdom, of the beautiful and the good, which are foreign to it: arousing and controlling those blind powers through blind powers in order to make room for light and justice.

Within the human being, this consciousness is inseparable from the sight of a being **above** him: a being which is not only a **Most High** (*Allerhöchst*), but who is God, the **Unique** (Alleinig). This sight points to an **omnipotence** (*Allmacht*) which is not merely the **overpowering-force** (*Allgewalt*) of a blind world, of the soul of nature that obeys necessity (in fact, its imaginary ghost), but is rather the **will** of a **being that wills** (*Wollend*); of a being that **out of love** consciously and freely allows everything that enjoys existence to exist. Freedom without love would only be a blind chance, and reason without freedom would merely be a blind necessity that becomes aware of itself. It is only for the sake of the beautiful and good, out of love for them, that a world exists.

The being (Seyn) of a rational and **finite** entity, its consciousness and acting, are conditioned by two elements **external** to it: a nature **below** it and a God **above** it.

Only God can be in and through himself alone; he is the **absolutely perfect being.** The human soul distinguishes itself from nature inasmuch as it rises above nature by virtue of its freedom. It distinguishes itself from nature: it receives God's judgment by virtue of the consciousness of its spirit.

For all these reasons – says our author – the recognition of all this should come to human beings either immediately from God or immediately from the soul itself. – "For the sake of modesty (he says), I will only assume the latter hypothesis."[5]

This claim is crucial and grants more than we ask. Besides, we wholly agree with what has so far been claimed [41]. Clearly, eyes and sight do not come from the objects that are seen, nor appetite from food, nor the heart from the tendencies it manifests. Every sensation and every longing comes from **selfhood**, from **being in itself**, from **life**: every perception (*Vernehmen*) comes from something that senses itself immediately and essentially, and which, at the same time and just as immediately and essentially, perceives in the same indivisible instant **nature and God**, the finite and the infinite, eternity and time. That which, by sensing itself, is aware of **freedom** and of **God** as the highest good; that which, by producing morality reveals religion, and by revealing religion, produces morality, both inseparably: that is the *spirit*, and there is no truth outside of it.

Therefore, as sufficiently proven by the aforementioned excerpts, the **Complete Works** do not only admit but also prove, that in order to seek God and what pleases Him, one must already have in one's heart and spirit both God and that which pleases God, because we cannot seek or investigate what is not already somehow known to us. Yet, we know about God and His will because we were born from God and are created in His image, we are of His species and of His race.[6] God lives in us, and our life is **hidden** in God.[7] If God were

---

5   Part V, 22.
6   [Gen. 1:27.]
7   [John 4:16.]

ON THE DIVINE THINGS AND THEIR REVELATION

not present in us in this way, i.e., **immediately** present through His image in our innermost **self**, then what – outside of Him – would make Him known to us? Images, sounds, signs which only impart what is already understood? Spirit to spirit: what?

Thus, **Simplicius**, in his interpretation of Epictetus, had the following to say against those who expressed themselves regarding the human being's turn toward God as though God, for having turned away from the human being, had to be first to turn toward him: "they are, in this matter, similar to those who throw a rope around a rock on the shore, and while pulling their boat and themselves ashore, [42] are foolish enough to believe that it is not they who are approaching the rock, but rather that it is the rock that is gradually coming towards them."[8]

Created in the image of God, God is **in** us and **above** us: model and likeness; separated and yet indivisibly connected: such is the notion we have of Him, and it is the only one possible, for by it does God reveal himself to man as living, never ending, for all times. A revelation through external phenomena – call it as you wish – can have in relation to the inner **original** revelation at best the same relation that language has to reason. I said "at best" and I add: no more can a **false** God exist by Himself outside the human soul than the **true** be a **phenomenon** outside of it. Just as the human being feels and imagines himself, so does he represent God for himself, only **mightier**. For this reason has the religion of humans always conformed to their virtue and moral condition. A famous commander under the government of the French King Jean wrote as motto on his flag: L'Ami de Dieu, et l'ennemi de tous les hommes.[9] In his heart that meant: **For me, against all.** Only moral elevation raises us to a worthy concept of the highest being. There is no other way. Not all piety excludes malice and vice. That it be worthy, it must itself be a virtue: one, then, that presupposes all other virtues; the noblest and most beautiful [among them], **like the blossom of all their impulses put together, of their combined strength.** Thus, we have in us the God who became man; it is not possible to know another one, not even through a better doctrine. In fact, how should we even understand such a doctrine? Wisdom, righteousness, goodwill, and free love are not **images**, but **powers** whose representation is acquired only with use, **by acting autonomously.** The human being must already have

8 *Commentar*, In *Epictecti enchiridion*, 397, ed. Schweighaeuser (250, ed. Heusii).

9 ["The friend of God, and the enemy of all men." King Jean II le Bon (1319–1364). The commander was probably Seguin de Badefol. See Cerutti, "Notes et Commentaires," 198.]

accomplished actions involving these powers and already have acquired those virtues and their concept before a doctrine of the **true** God can reach him. Thus, I repeat, God must be born in the human being himself, if man must have a **living** God and not just an **idol**. He (God) must be born in the human [43] being humanly, or otherwise the human being would not have any sense of Him. The objection that in this case God would be a pure **invention** would be more than just wrong. And how would then a God that **is not invented** be made, how can he be **recognized** as the **only true** God?

"I would surrender – says our author in this work on immortality – I would despair before the excessive power of the earthly shadow in our hearts, if there had not been humans of virtue. But these great human beings taught me that the soul is immortal and invincible if it so wants to be and has the courage to defend the fact."

Splendid! Nevertheless (if we may ask the author again): how can admiration for those great human beings – Confucius, Socrates, even **Christ** himself – come to the admirer's heart, to his senses and spirit? Can they be anywhere else, in anyone, except in the representation that one has made of them and that dwells inside him? Doesn't the author's remark also apply here, that "in sight, it is the eye and the one who sees that matter. And each person sees not only his **own** rainbow, but also his **own** sun and moon"? – And how imperfect and weak [is] this comparison when at issue is the acceptance of moral examples into one's heart and spirit?

An example cannot impose itself as example, cannot give anything at all: it must be **accepted**, and as accepted, so it **is**. – Ultimately, if those great men enchant us, is it not just because of what is splendid and good in them, and of what is splendid and good **in and for itself**? It is because they represented the splendid and good, because what is splendid and good dwelt in them, that we call them great, sublime, worthy of imitation; it is not the other way around. It is impossible that something becomes a virtue for the mere reason that one imitates it. On the contrary, something is imitated only because it is **for itself** a virtue. Great men do not give me the measure whereby to measure them and the good. I am the one who possesses that measure: it is in me like an original and independent principle whereby I know the good. If that were not the case, it would be impossible to **experience** anything about the good.

ON THE DIVINE THINGS AND THEIR REVELATION

[44] Asmus, the Messenger, together with his **cousin** and his learned friend and benefactor, Herr **Matthias Claudius**, <u>homme de lettres à Wandsbeck</u>, basically do not think, sense, and believe otherwise, and it is only on occasion – a circumstance that does not in truth make them lesser human beings, whether in heart or spirit – that they, the **Messenger** particularly, seem here and there to be of different opinion. This recently became very clear to this reviewer when, in order to review the sixth part of the Letters to Andres, he reread those of the fourth part. In the very first letter he found this description of **Christ**:

"A saviour from all need and ill (*Uebel*); a deliverer from evil (*Böse*); a helper who did good wherever he went and **did not himself have a place to rest!** One before whom the paralytics walk, the lepers heal, the deaf hear, the dead are resurrected, and **the Gospel is preached to the poor**; one whom the wind and sea obey; **who let the children come to him, pressed them to his heart and blessed them** ... He who did not care for exhaustion or offence but was meek unto his death on the cross so that his purpose be fulfilled – one who came to the world to bless it but **was beaten and martyred there and left it crowned in thorns.**"

What a portrait! What sublime and touching contrasts! What power of beauty, grace, and majesty gathered in the traits of this perfect ideal of divinity and humanity combined! The author adds: "**Andres!** Have you ever heard anything like it and have not recoiled in awe? For the **mere idea**, one would be ready to be branded with iron and broken on the wheel. And would it occur to anyone to laugh or mock it, that one must then be mad. One who **has** the heart in the right **place** prostrates himself in the dust, rejoices, and worships."

Here does the soul of a man rich in sentiment disclose itself. It makes itself be known in its faith, such as it is, at origin, the fruit of the most elated emotion, of nothing but superior love, pure awe and sublime joy – light, spirit, and life –: the reflection of divinity itself in the human breast. His heart overflows and is shaken by one idea: Is it possible, can it ever occur to anyone here [45] to mock, to laugh? And, with noble indignation, he cries out: whoever who would, must be mad. – How is it possible to laugh and mock when the actual truth was not even necessary, when a simple idea, a merely **invented** representation could seize the human being to the point where – completely absorbed in it – one forgets everything else for it, one gives everything to it, to the point of being branded with iron and broken on the wheel? **Invented**? These words echo again inside him. Oh, how much higher than all human fiction is it, this representation! Anyone capable of such fictions would also be capable of creating worlds, calling spirits into existence, giving rise to life

136 ON THE DIVINE THINGS AND THEIR REVELATION

and the highest beatitude by the mere strength of one's breath. One thus needs only the idea to know that here one possesses **more** than just an idea, that one has actuality and truth in profusion. If **such** signs of truth deceive, if what imposes itself to us as the innermost feeling of truth lies to us about its being, then falsehood is superior to truth; it is more powerful and sublime, and it is also holier and better; then is the whole human soul just a fraud. – Absurd blasphemy! Anyone whose heart is in the right place will not imagine such things: such a one does not waver, does not doubt; he prostrates himself in the dust, rejoices, and worships.

Condemn those who embrace such enthusiasm and the confidence that comes with it. As for me, I do not condemn these things; I respect them, despite the innocent mistakes or illusions that may accidentally attach themselves to them yet without corrupting their pure ground.

But we cannot get away with just this witness. Rather, we earlier called merely **circumstantial**, without further explanation, the reason why we do not want to consider this man, whom we are investigating because of the contradictions in his teachings, nonetheless less worthy than us, despite the contradictions and their consequent errors or illusions. We owe a stricter account of this reason, for, after all, we give witness to the truth alone and not, like him, to truth mixed with error. We must be clear on this score, lest we be suspected to be in worse contradiction with ourselves than the Messenger is with himself, and even to be secretly conscious of it. To this end, it is perhaps best to instigate the Messenger to a rebuttal that would display him in full force. This is what we shall attempt. [46] We shall address him with philosophical sobriety, firmly indeed yet most friendly, as follows.

"It is clear to us, upright man!, that to you all that the human being can see of the divine, and all that which, in such a vision, can awaken him to virtue and to a divine life, takes the form and the name of **Christ**. Your soul remains honest, since it **only** venerates in him what is divine **in itself**. And, in yourself, you do not degrade reason and morality through **idolatry**. That which Christ was for himself and outside you – whether or not he corresponded in reality to the concept you have of him, whether or not he even existed in reality – is irrelevant both to the **essential** truth of your representation and to the quality of the attitudes that follow from this representation. What he is **in you** is all that matters; in you he **really** is **a divine being**. Through him you perceive the divinity as much as you can. **With** him you soar up to the highest ideas and – harmless mistake – imagine that you are soaring to them only **in** him.

ON THE DIVINE THINGS AND THEIR REVELATION

"All this is evident to us, and so we are not scandalized when occasionally you further misplace the essential, which is the idea, after the unessential, which is its semblance; that you let the matter escape its form, and [thus] lapse into a sort of **religious materialism**. At bottom you believe just as we do that the spirit alone enlivens. But if the spirit alone enlivens, then its essence must be of one who **has life in itself**. This you equally understand, and yet this proposition is just the one that sets us apart. We claim that true religion cannot be given an external shape that would be unique and necessary to it. On the contrary, it belongs to its essence not to have such a shape. "God – the *Timaeus* states beautifully – **is what everywhere yields the best**"[10]: the spirit and the power of the good. The one who is driven by this spirit walks the way of divine beatitude, and it is indifferent which means of the imagination sustain him along it – perhaps the ones that were the first to awaken him and lead him, and continue helping him. As far as these means are concerned, however, it is important that they never be raised above the rank of mere servants; for the moment they otherwise [47] claim sovereignty, they oppress and drive out the spirit. For that reason, what was borne out in the eighth and ninth centuries in the famous **dispute over the legitimacy of** [sacred] **images** is of great import and universal relevance. Theologians of profound mind stumbled over the question whether the **divinity** of Christ and his **bodily shape** would not be equally worthy of veneration and respect? They thought that the two are inseparably unified in the person of the human-God. The cult of images won accordingly; it became **orthodoxy**, and an annual celebration by that name was established to ensure its perpetual confirmation. Now, we want only one thing from you: that you exempt us from the cult of images, just as we allow it for you without hesitation, on the condition previously mentioned which you in fact fulfill. Here is our hand. Give us yours."

Contrary to our expectations, the Messenger does not reply; he however declines to shake our hand. While we were speaking to him, we could read on his face that he did not want to follow us.

In all fairness, we must forgive him. For how could his heart not revolt in indignation at the demand that he consider his highest object of admiration and love only a thought he has himself produced? At bottom Christ would indeed owe everything just to him and he, on the contrary, nothing to him. It would then indeed be of indifference to him whether the object of his imagination actually be in reality or not; the object's **being on its own**, its **actuality**, would be of no concern to him, for on the other side of his own representation,

10   [Plato, *Timaeus*, 30a–b.]

the object, Christ, would in all cases be but **nothing**. He realized that the **true** would lie in the **idea alone**; he grasped that this true would by nature be above all a fiction, something produced by his sole activity; that never would it be something **perceived**, the kind called **true** being or such as could have its ground on such a being. Thus [, thought the Messenger,] would one have the **spirit** that one must then gift, in its entirety, to oneself. Anything else would be just as good as a lie. – That story so dear to him, for instance, even if it were completely true [48], even if it were true down to the last detail, would not in itself have more value or influence than a similar story without any foundation or one completely made-up.

I say that our account, as so understood by the Messenger, could not and **cannot** in any way allow him a reply, not even one word. None was possible and none can be, for not even for the blink of an eye could he have considered the being (Dasein) that had become so inner certain to him as no present experience [could be], since it was not such as came to him (*ihm erwachten*) in an experience, as possibly a creation issuing at source from his imagination's vivid (*klaren*) nothingness. That being had [rather] instilled in him a **faith** that imposed itself on him, not just in the manner of a self-witnessing truth, as does one's own life, as common self-consciousness does, but with yet greater truth, greater pervasive force of feeling – a faith towering far above any **knowledge** in him obviously empty of being (*wesenlos*). Indeed, he turns away from us with only a silent bow, and smiling. – And if we attempted to hold him back, he would reply with an answer that, though not exactly the same, is similar to that of **Epictetus**: "Forgive me as lovers are forgiven. I am out of my mind. I am mad."[11]

It is easy to miss the point we wanted to mediate. To the charge of **religious materialism**, of an implicit cult of images and idols that we make against the Messenger, he responds by accusing us of **religious chimerism**, of reverie, self-divinization, and nihilism. And enough can each charge adduce to its justification that two practised advocates, in strict philosophical arbitration, could go on with the pros and cons of each charge to the extinction of both, with no right left to find. But we do not want to come to such a process. We rather come to an agreement, and, to this end, gladly wager all possible efforts.

---

11 Σύγγνωθι μοι, ὡς τοῖς ἐρῶσιν· οὐκ εἰμὶ ἐμαυτοῦ, μαίνομαι. Epictetus' dissertatio, Lib. I, cap. XXII.

[49] Accordingly, going back to what we previously said, we only have to add to it that, regardless of how much we must insist on what we have already affirmed – namely, that sight does not originate from what is seen, sensation from what is sensed, perception from what is perceived, the **self** from the **other** – we nonetheless equally acknowledge and affirm as being just as true and certain that, each by itself alone, sight sees **nothing**; sensation likewise senses **nothing**; perception perceives **nothing**; and, finally, that the **self does not come to itself** by itself. Truly, we must first experience our existence from the other.

It further follows that there is no **inner** for us without **outer**; that no **I** is either actually or potentially present without **You**: hence, that we are as certain of the other as of **ourselves**, and that we love the other in the way we love the life that we partake with it. The existence of each finite nature is therefore made of being and non-being, enjoyment and need, love and nostalgia: each is made and acts according to the love and nostalgia that constitute its distinct nature.

Two species part and combine in the human being: he knows a superior and an inferior love, a superior and an inferior existence. In appearance, the more noble, like its opposite, assume the most different shapes. None of these different shapes shows the thing itself: spirit – not unmistakably – prophesizes only on their basis. Should the **nobler** spirit err prophesizing, no harmful deception thereby results in him: what we call "his illusion" are higher visions of the true, the beautiful, and the good. Surely did the object of Heloise's sublime love deserve this great love that cultivated her gentle soul, beautified it, gave it wings – but it was not **Abelard**!

One who cannot err like this, cannot take possession of higher truths either; these are not **acquired** through the understanding, i.e., in the manner of legal entitlements: they must be **conquered** by reason soaring **prophetically** above the horizon of the understanding. Yes, reason makes fictions (*dichtet*) – if you want to call that the fact of seeing in the spirit alone – but what reason makes is the truth (*dichtet Wahrheit*)! Akin to the divinity from which such a truth comes, and drawing inspiration (*nachdichten*) from it, reason discovers that which is. Conceiving of spirit's feeling, radiating it, enthusiasm comes upon it. And in its grip [50] reason comes to know itself fully: finds and experiences its origin – it becomes certain within. In this state, inspiration is the **essence** of its knowledge; the source of its trust. At a loss of it, reason does not understand itself, does not believe its own words; imagines but illusions; mistakes truth for dream, and dream for truth. Lost in itself, reason finally warns the understanding against its own deceit, its own madness.

Salvation renders us alive with spirit, with reason, and wise, and certain within! Let us worship that spirit, because without it there would not be any worship on Earth: nor beauty, nor love, nor faith, nor virtue – nor stars in this night of existence, in this darkness of a life surrounded by death.

Let us now turn to our writer, to his ideal, and to his uncompromising attachment to the letter of this ideal or spirit, to its **body**, its **clothes**!

Some years ago, a wonderful man wrote to the reviewer the following: "What Homer was for the ancient Sophists, the **sacred texts** were for me. I inebriated myself at their spring, perhaps to the point of abuse: εὔκαιρως ἄκαιρως. Still today, when my heart has become dull, cold, and lukewarm, it is always with the deepest emotion that I read chapter XXXVIII of Jeremiah, his rescue from the depth of the pit with the aid of **worn-out torn rags**. My superstitious faith in these relics is actually a heartfelt thanks for the services they have provided and still provide to me, despite any reason [that holds court] criticizing from the stage, and not out of the hole, of the pit."[12]

Everybody knows what happened to so many old and modern admirers of the Homeric poems: they read their poet so persistently, with ever more eagerness, reverence, rapture, and eventually with so awakened a spirit that they found everything in his works. Homer became for them the Book of Books; it included the sum of truth and wisdom; it determined and established what constituted the good and beauty with the prestige of a positive revelation. Of him it was said, as the saying goes: **He is it.**

Now, if this can understandably be excused because of Homer's merits, and because of human nature, with no offence to either [51], how much more is a similar reverence for the Holy Books, not only to excuse, to understand, but eminently to justify, in **one** who was educated by them to all that is good; to whose sense of morality they stand as language stands everywhere to reason, the body to the soul – the visible world to the one understood?

Can any cognition, any virtue or beauty come to us shapeless, revealing itself to us without something that reveals it? – And suppose the impossible: we acquired their concept. Could we instill and hold this concept in us, by itself, separated from shape – a concept void of intuition, representing nothing? Would it be in us something that gave us life and connected us with the living?

12 J.G. Hamann. [See Hamman's letter to Jacobi, 6 January 1785.]

ON THE DIVINE THINGS AND THEIR REVELATION

However, these considerations remain far from the matter at hand. To move closer on the issue and press ahead, I ask: who has ever had a friend of whom he can say that he loved only his **concept** and not the man with a given name; that the man with the name was not the object [of the love]: that it was rather he that detracted from the object because of its defects?[13] If there ever were such a person, however true and selfless his love for the friend, yet greater would be the indifference with which he would see him at rest in a grave. He would indeed hold on to the concept of his love for the dead friend but could just as well think of another in his place with greater accomplishments and not the least defect: for his love, this friend would be immortal!

Not for us, ordinary humans. In friendship we love the man with a given name, exactly as he is, with his virtues and his flaws, without close reckoning of **just how many and just how few** of them. A love according to qualities is just a love deadened by the letter – not the living, **genuine** love that comes from the heart. The genuine, true, sincere love – grown to perfection in a noble soul – resembles the **unconditioned**, necessary, and eternal love with which we love ourselves, and because of which we cannot renounce ourselves. In the living being this love represents a second life, **higher** and better than the first; and it is the love that first gives spirit to life. One who has received [52] the divine gift of loving **outside of oneself,** with unconditioned, necessary, and eternal love – just as life loves itself in itself – such is the one who loves sublimely. He has given birth, as Plato says, to something immortal from a divine seed[14]: he has become capable of the purest virtue, of overabundant hope, trust, and beatitude – in a word: he has become capable of **God.**

Surely, much can seriously be brought to bear against this path of personal, individual, **positive** love or friendship, a path that in lack of better counsel we defend for such beings "who are not pure personalities but just **real persons**; not pure **faculties** but just real **beings**" – indeed, as much can be brought to bear against it as the spirit can against the body, reason against language, virtue and freedom against constitutions that are a state's prerogative. In such a personal friendship, it can be said, must not the substance be contaminated, even essentially corrupted by the person, the unconditional by the conditioned? Is not such a friendship necessarily tainted by blind faith and confidence? Does not opinion stubbornly rise in it above the understanding; biased judgment above sound and impartial judgment; appearance above reason; love above

13   [See Jacobi's letter to Roth, 8 July 1817. See Cerutti, "Notes et Commentaires," 200.]
14   [Plato, *Phaedrus*, 276a–7a.]

justice? – Did not **Caius Blossius** acknowledge before the Roman Senate that, if his friend **Tiberius Gracchus** had commanded it, he would have set fire to the Capitolium – but protesting, of course, that **Tiberius** would never have commanded such a thing?[15] – Therefore, does not every absolute personal friendship, like every absolute patriotism, carry the risk of perpetrating crimes?

All this might be true. Yet the fact remains that from time immemorial, and wherever there has been talk of love and friendship among human beings, only such a positive, personal and consequently exclusive, partisan – even blind and superstitious – or, in a word, **absurd** friendship or love has ever been taken as the authentic and only true friendship. Further, never and nowhere has a human being been less respected because he, out of devotion to friendship – **true** friendship – had tried to reach perfection in it, as if it were a virtue. That man [53] was not less esteemed even when he was incomprehensibly mistaken about the object. Unanimously do we overlook this mistake because we know that love cancels it. Here, **in love itself**, there is nothing but truth: love sees only what is good and beautiful, just as the good and the beautiful, together with the **essential** truth, are seen only with and through love. Truth without being is a non-thing. And so is error without being, for, to be truly error, it must refer to **being** – that is to say, to what constitutes the content of truth – as **abolishing** it. Even insanity does not make it possible to love an unworthy object that is **recognized** and viewed as such. As the old saying goes, repeated in all languages and confirmed by the experience of all ages: "among wicked people only corruption and conspiracy are possible; friendship and love are only possible among good people." – The elements of love are pure pleasure, respect, and admiration. Love is the very perception of the good and the beautiful with which the latter enters the human being, becomes part of him, thus making him good and beautiful. Therefore, wherever **true** love comes into being, therein is the good and beautiful necessarily intuited and does truth come to the soul. And since in this intuition – **in it alone** – does love inhabit, the latter cannot either gain or lose in inner virtue because of what the object that perhaps only accidentally awakened it might be in itself, independently of the representation of it. **Beautiful** and **true** love is entirely **inside** the human being, it has taken possession of him. The mistake regarding the object is completely **outside** of him and leaves his soul unblemished. It is not the **idol** that makes the **idolater**, nor the **true** God that makes the **true worshiper**: for the presence of the true God is only **one and universal**.

15 Cicero, *De Amicitia*, c. XI.

ON THE DIVINE THINGS AND THEIR REVELATION

Our unusual Messenger says: "**Only philosophy** is supposed to **teach** (as he heard from a Master in the Academy – where he has not studied yet has frequented) whether God exists and what God is, and without philosophy there is no thought of God, etc." And he continues: "But that's only what the Master **said**. For my part, nobody can reasonably accuse me of being a philosopher. And yet, never do I cross the forest without happening to wonder who might ever make the trees grow, and the intimation then occurs to me, distant and faint, of an invisible being; and **I would want to wager that,** [54] **at that moment, I am thinking of God, so much do I shudder with respect and joy at that intimation** (part I, 20)."

On another occasion, he speaks of a European who "was in America and wanted to see the waterfalls of a certain river. To this end, he struck a deal with a savage to walk him there ...

Once the two had made their way and had reached the waterfall, the European looked on wide-eyed and **began taking in the sight**: the savage prostrated himself to the ground full length and stayed in that position for some time. His travel companion asked him why and for whom he was acting in such a manner; and the savage answered: **for the Great Spirit**" (part IV, 135).

On this, our opinion is as follows: in the forest the Messenger really thought of God, and the savage who fell upon his face in front of the waterfall had the true God before his eyes and in his heart. It is my opinion that even in the presence of a crude sacred image, a devout soul can be pervaded by the highest thoughts and sensations, by the **essential** truth, and can eventually go his way sanctified, but only on condition that his heart be rightly elevated in his chest. Certainly, the sight of someone kneeling in front of such an image is disgusting if one does not understand what is going through the person kneeling, or if one abstracts from it and only considers the image. But to the devout soul kneeling before the crude image I juxtapose the philosopher with his merely pure concept of God. The latter does not wager on his concept because he knows that it is overabundant, and he knows that it is impossible philosophically to bet on its conformity to an object. The philosopher does not prostrate himself before this ambiguous object which he recognizes only on the basis of causes without really and seriously admitting its existence – not indeed before this, his own uncertain thought. – It would be too laughable. Nor, before his thought, does he piously even bend the knee: the sensation and posture would offend his dignity. The philosopher keeps his calm, knowing full well what he has to do. Full upright, he positions himself in front of his God, so that, facing him, with perfect presence of spirit, he pays respect only to himself.

And what to call what we are made to feel at this sight? Are not both, the idol and the human being, just as off-putting in one prayer as in the other? And both are here integrally internal (ganz inwendig) [55].

"Cousin – the Messenger writes to his friend Andres – if you meet a human being who thinks highly of himself and who is full of himself, then stay away from him and have pity on him. We are not great, and our happiness lies in the possibility to believe in something greater and better ... Those who do not think so, and believe they are better than they are, fill their purse with lies, which does not make it any less empty (part IV, 215)."

He also says: "It seems to me that the one who knows **a right thing** must ... If I could only see such a one just once, I would really like to know him. I would also really like to make a portrait of him: with bright, cheerful, calm eyes; with a great, peaceful consciousness ... Such a human being cannot be full of himself; even less can he despise or scold others. Oh! Arrogance and pride are wicked passions: grass and flowers cannot grow in their proximity (part I, 21)."

It might well be impossible to find among human beings one who **knows a right thing**. We know what is hardly worth knowing; we know completely and with sufficient insight only those truths and beings which, like those of mathematics, have more being and truth in their image than in the thing itself. More precisely, they are actually true **only** in image, and have nothing but relations and forms of such relations as their **content**. We profit from these cognitions and gain inestimable instruments to give our ignorance a number of new forms for changing, increasing, organizing it, and thus making it the most agreeable companion of life. In this, we pay no attention to the fact that we are in fact only playing a game with empty numbers, formulating new principles only to formulate ever more, without getting **even a hair-breadth** closer to a true result, to a meaning for those numbers, the **real truth**. This game with our ignorance is surely the noblest among games. Yet, on closer look, it is nonetheless a **game** by which time is **spent** without really being **filled**, is not **held still** to secure a real, substantial existence. The laws of its varied usage, sorted out and brought to system, constitute our sciences. We are powerless with these laws against [56] our radical ignorance but are rather distracted from it by them. For the cognitions that science **properly understood** affords are **in their way perfect**. We possess them in a true sense, have them totally in control, whether for passing them on or using them ourselves – and when we do use

ON THE DIVINE THINGS AND THEIR REVELATION

them, we do it with the greatest reliability. Thanks to them, we become ever greater masters, not only in our own game, but of the game itself.

It is a completely different matter with those among us who only strive for those cognitions that are – according to the **Kantian** expression – "**merely foreseen and fervently desired by reason**." These cognitions do not have as their object what **whiles away** the time, but rather what **brings it to a standstill** and **resolves** it; the object's **intention, fulfillment,** and **explanation**, the purpose of nature and ultimate human goals, the sense of God and the essence (Wesen) of truth. Whenever we possess such cognitions, have them in control for actual use, we do it each time only to the extent that the spirit in each of us is capable of bringing it to life in us. Such cognitions cannot be distinguished from the actual power of the spirit, cannot be **produced from outside** nor confirmed from outside, not for us or for others. All the means aimed at this goal are like the knot in a handkerchief: one sees the knot, and it triggers the memory, but one cannot tell what one should remember. It is in life that those cognitions must be grasped, that they must constantly be held. To be capable of this is the noblest and highest power of the soul – a power not to be found in any sort of Solomon's ring of ancient or modern philosophy that one need only purchase and put on, or in any talisman of some so-called religion that one puts on while performing prescribed rites. It is a power that the human being must invoke and awaken in himself. "All ceremonies," Friedrich Richter said, "tend to go mad with age, as dogs do." But what are our letter-bound systems of cognition of the spirit, be they philosophical or religious, **once life is gone** from the truth, but the sediment, the *caput mortuum,* of reason? What, but at best **formalities** and **ceremonies** of the latter's appearance that **legal mimics** with no spiritual [57] investiture conceive, bringing forth a new spirit that indeed makes one madder than any dog can become.

If we sufficiently kept this in mind, we would not get as worked up as it happens over incidental differences in representation, fashion, and figurative, symbolic, or abstract presentation. We would not grant to one form of opinion an advantage over other forms, as if truth and reason dwelled exclusively in the one while the others contained nothing but irrationality and lies. One would think that at least we, **Philosophers,** do not make that mistake, since we well know, and therefore always remember, that truth and reason are not to be validated by opinion, but opinion by reason and truth. Reason demonstrates its power precisely by rising freely with its judgement above every particular point of view, bringing at play an insight that overtakes or destroys the illusion attaching to a limited individuality. Unfortunately, the prerogative of infalli-

ON THE DIVINE THINGS AND THEIR REVELATION

bility, of being independent of the prejudices of the sense-imagination (*sinnlicher Einbildung*), is in practice encumbered by so many stipulations that the philosopher, not to judge except infallibly, would in conscience have to abide by their limitations – would indeed have a say **just** about everything, without however saying much or for long about any.[16] Should he not abide by such limitations [58], that would happen to him as we see every day occurring: he would every time take his deceiving conviction for the inspiration of a being who is non-deceiving; and, as for those who contradict him, he would not be able to think of them except as contradicting in his own person **reason in person** – consequently, **truth itself**. The obvious exception: when one knows that what one holds is only an **opinion**, without pretending that one's conviction were anything more than that, that it rather was certainty. Where no such exception occurs, the mentioned confusion of deceiving with non-deceiving

---

16 In the *Philebus*, Plato speaks of two different kinds of cognition: "one turning its eyes towards things which come into being and pass away, the other towards things which neither come into being nor pass away, but are the same and immutable forever" (61d–e). There is no question that the latter, with regard to the true, has to be taken as truer than the first.

On that subject, Socrates asks whether that person has sufficient knowledge, who "knows the definition of the circle and of the divine sphere itself, but is ignorant of this human sphere here and these circles, even when he uses other kinds of rules and circles in building houses."

Protarchus: "We would find ourselves in a rather ridiculous position if we were concerned **only** with divine knowledge, Socrates!"

Socrates: "What are you saying? Should we put into our mixture the **uncertain** and **impure** art of the false (or incomplete) rule and circle?"

Protarchus: "Yes, that is inevitable, if any one of us is ever to find his own way home."

Socrates: "But we must also add music, which we said a little while ago was full of guesswork and imitation and lacks purity?"

Protarchus: "That seems necessary to me, if in fact our life is to be, in some sense, a life."

Socrates: "Do you want me, then, like a doorkeeper who is pushed and hustled by the crowd, to give in, open the doors, and let all the kinds of knowledge stream in, the inferior kind mingling with the pure?"

Protarchus: "I for my part can't see what damage you would do to accept all the other kinds of knowledge,"

(N.B.!) "**as long as we have those of the highest kind.**" Plato, *Werke*, ed. Schleiermacher, Th. II, Bd. 3, 232–3. [English translation has been taken from Plato, *Philebus*, ed. D. Frede (Indianapolis: Hackett, 1993). In Jacobi's text Socrates speaks to Protagoras and not Protarchus like in the original Greek.]

ON THE DIVINE THINGS AND THEIR REVELATION 147

reason necessarily occurs. In this situation, if we call upon reason, we understand by that name a certain something that by right would have to inspire our convictions in all human beings, indeed, would do it unfailingly if these just had sufficient reason or duly used whatever they have of it. Accordingly, by the nature of the issue – with more or less zeal, indignation, and outrage – we then also assume responsibility for a reason and a truth that have been challenged, wounded, persecuted, in danger of being suppressed. And since reason and truth indisputably are the main and closest concern of the **philosopher**, seeing that the latter "is **ideally the very legislator of reason and consequently of truth**,"[17] he must naturally feel the insults directed at them more vividly than any other class of human beings, and must also outdo this in zeal to protect and defend them, to make them more universal and authoritative. Hardly is there an indignation [59] that would surpass the **righteous** wrath of the philosopher – the related wrath of the theologian possibly excepted.[18]

The writer of this is no mere **free thinker** but a philosopher **of profession** so ensconced in it that he has never either practiced or understood any other.[19] Already somewhat advanced in age, might he be as self-pleased for it, and do himself as much good by it, as possible. However, because of the above considerations for which he had the most favourable conditions to develop, working them out in his mind, already for quite some time he has come to know himself more, **pleasingly** more, by [adopting] a fairer way of thinking based on this conviction: namely, that we are all necessarily subjected, with no exception although by **accident** not in **equal measure**, to the irresistible force of

17 Kant, *Critique of Pure Reason*, B 867. [Quotation is not accurate. Bold by Jacobi.]
18 "Senses do not mistake, nor does the immediate cognition of reason; only the arbitrary second-hand reflection does, by wrongfully assuming that what does not appear as perceived in the object is also not present in the object.

"Neither intuition that lies on the ground of **demonstration**, nor the immediate cognition of reason that lies on the ground of **deduction**, can be wrong; only mediated judgments of the understanding can be wrong.

"In the realm of immediate cognition of our reason, different kinds of conviction of equal validity can stand next to one another: knowledge, faith, and premonition. The whole debate about truth and validity of cognition does not touch at all the intimate being of reason: within reason there is nothing but the pure truth, in the one form or the other, of the finite or the eternal, the forever enduring in nature or the forever changing of beauty." J.F. *Neue Kritik der Vernunft*, vol. I, 339. [Reference to *Neue oder anthropologische Krtik der Vernunft*, Heidelberg 1807.]
19 [Possible reference to the dispute with Schlegel on the *Woldemar*. See Jaeschke, *Kommentar*, 207.]

misleading opinions, and should we want to escape from this domination, we would first have to cease being human – not thus to become **more** than human, but just **nothing**.[20]

Forcefully does the author tear himself away from this theme, his favourite one, to link a **second** claim to the first, namely, that he, despite his fairness of thought, is in no way **tolerant**, and absolutely does not want to be seen as such [60].

In his estimate, it is only vain boasting and hypocritical **foolishness** to assure that one is tolerant of every opinion except for those that would **lead to intolerance**.[21] This would imply either that one is completely indifferent to all truth, finding intolerable only the idea of its high value and of the greater merit of one conviction over another, or that one speaks utter nonsense. What does not **withstand** does not stand: but each withstanding is at the same time an assault. What stands while withstanding excludes. Every life, every individual existence, every property is exclusive; and, for any of these, one has the right and the duty to fight against the aggressor because each, by nature, can be one's own only by exclusion and **war**. With right we however maintain an innermost conviction more enthusiastically and emphatically than we do for our blood and property: we cannot give it up without giving up our reason and personal existence along with it. Indeed, we all call reason that which makes us certain within, **what says yes or no in us with supreme authority**. Without certainty, there is no reason; without reason, there is no certainty. Whoever, acknowledging this, grants his fellow humans **the right to be intolerant** he grants himself, is alone **truly** tolerant. And in no other way **should** one be intolerant, for a real indifference towards every opinion can arise only from a thorough lack of faith, the utmost dreadful degeneration of human nature. Only in complete and firm confidence do noble efforts flourish, do hearts and souls rise. To those who have lost this confidence, nothing can appear important and venerable: their soul has lost the noble strength, the power, of **seriousness**. A trivial ghost. – I shudder ... Look! It roams about and **laughs – and laughs!**

---

20 See Plato, abovementioned passages of *Philebus*.
21 [Cerutti notes that this is likely a reference to Schleiermacher's *Über die Religion. Reden an die Gebildeten unter ihren Verächtern*. Berlin: J.F. Unger, 1799, 63.]

ON THE DIVINE THINGS AND THEIR REVELATION

But how – one could ask – can firm confidence be reconciled with **that fair way of thinking**, based as this is on the conviction that there is no rule unfailingly applied in the cognition of truth? with the conviction that the most erroneous principle might seem to us as certain [61] as the truest? with the clear insight that, suppose a knot tied in our understanding, for us simply undoable, between an inconsistent proposition and another that we know with certainty, reason itself would then force us **either** to give up the certain proposition as untrue, or, for the sake of the latter, no longer consider the other as inconsistent – to find, in effect, that the **impossible** is **thinkable**? This is an insight that excuses too easily. It makes it easy to understand what already was at the time of Marcus Tullius **common experience**: nothing is too absurd not to become the well-intentioned doctrine of a philosopher.[22]

However, that combination would be impossible, if there were not original, simple, **immediately** certain, and absolutely **positive** truths imposing their validity in our mind as highest truths, derived without proofs from other cognitions, without **testimonies** of any kind. On these alone is based that ennobling confidence of the heart and the spirit that could not be what it is if its light were only a reflection and its power were only derivative.

This immediate, **positive** truth unveils itself to us in, and with, the feeling of a drive that rises above every sense-perceivable, changeable, and accidental interest, and irresistibly manifests itself as the **basic drive** of human nature.

From time immemorial, humans have called **Divine Things above all** what that drive strives for as objects of cognition or of will, and have called **virtuous** the sensations, inclinations, dispositions, and actions that are their first apparent effects. For this reason, that feeling is sometimes also called **moral feeling**, other times **feeling of truth**. The true, good, and beautiful in itself is revealed in it without intuition or concept, inscrutable and unutterable.

Just as the beautiful is known in the pure feeling of admiration and love that it inspires, without characteristic features – **the beautiful only by its beauty, immediately** – so is also the good only known by its goodness, immediately, in the pure feeling of respect, high esteem, and reverence. But both, the good and the beautiful, presuppose the true on which reason is [62] grounded. The faculty of presupposing the true, together with the good and the beautiful that come with it and are in it, is called reason.

For the human being, the truth above all truth is thus the knowledge residing in the innermost of his consciousness **that he has the vocation and**

---

22 Marcus Tullius Cicero, *De Divinatione*, Lib. II, cap. 58.

ON THE DIVINE THINGS AND THEIR REVELATION

possesses the power to rise with the spirit above the animal element added to his being.

The human being rises above the animal element through wisdom, goodness, and willpower. All other virtues develop from those **primary** and **fundamental virtues**: justice, moderation, resolution, self-control, loyalty, truthfulness, benevolence, magnanimity: every noble and loving attitude, like twigs from the main branch.

These features, whose combination determines the **virtuous character**, are for their own sake, not desirable in view of other ends from which their rule would have to be taken and their need derived. They originate in absolutely no need but from a **source** rather which is just as independent of the **concept of duty** as of the desire for **happiness**. They are independent of the concept of duty because this concept is either based on the feeling of what is **worthy of unconditional respect** or does not belong at all to the sphere of what is **properly** moral.

They are independent of the desire for happiness because – as Plato claimed and Cicero repeated – the **gods are not called good because they are blessed, but rather are called blessed because they are good.**[23] It is inconsistent to want to value happiness merely for its **usefulness**, and even more inconsistent to value virtue merely for that reason. Virtue cannot derive its value from another good to which it is related as if it were the means to an end – nor from any intention **distinct from itself**, nor yet from any **reward**, even if **divine**. Indeed, why should God reward virtue if it **were not** good and desirable **in itself**, if it were **not rewarding** in itself? – **God** Himself would have to find satisfaction in it only because He rewards it! And we, in turn, would have to find **Him** worthy of worship only because He could connect reward and punishment to **arbitrary** commandments, and could thus **establish** good and evil, **create** them out of nothing.

Epictetus thought differently. The most benevolent effect of virtue, he claimed, is the partaking of itself: no good deed can earn you greater merit [63] from your neighbour than to edify his soul through moderation, justice, resolution, and goodness.[24]

For all that, one should not say, speaking of virtue, that it is the **highest good**, because this expression seems to refer to a previous comparison that

23 [Plato, *Laws*, X, 899b. Cicero, *Tusculan Disputations*, V, 15–16. See Cerutti, "Notes et Commentaires," 203.]

24 [Epictetus, *Philosophiae Monumenta* (Leipzig: Weidman, 1799), Bd. III, 116, fr. 169.]

ON THE DIVINE THINGS AND THEIR REVELATION

does not take place here. A comparison is possible only between [two] **different** things, and then only by virtue of a third with reference to which they are made **similar**. Now, virtue and that sum total of goodness that we usually call **happiness** are either one and the same – which is the case if the former is conceptually related to the latter like ground to consequence – or are opposed. They are clearly opposed if one conceives happiness as that ideal of the imagination that includes the satisfaction of all inclinations, the fulfilment of every purpose that sense perception lays out.[25] For the vocation of virtue is not to **be at the service** of inclinations, desires, and passions – i.e., of sense perception in general – but rather to **rule** over them and to **put them at its service**. If virtue had no other vocation but to provide the human being with the highest degree of well-being and comfort in enjoyment by moderating his desires and making him skillful in all ways at stimulating them and pacifying them harmoniously – even if for all eternity – we would not be able to call this virtue **holy** and **sublime**.

Happiness, as we have defined it here, has nothing in common with virtuous character **except** that **both** are the very sum total or perfection of something desirable **in itself** and are therefore sought **for their own sake**. This is a quality that, like **sheer** existence, does not admit of a "more" or "less," hence of differentiating determination[26] [64].

---

25 [Jacobi is referring to *Grundlegung zur Metaphysik der Sitten*, in Kant, *Gesammelte Schriften*, 4:418.]

26 An important remark: every immediate object of a natural instinct, like life – which in rational and non-rational beings alike has the prerogative either to posit itself as **an end in itself** (*Selbstzweck*), or **to be for itself** – shall be desired for its own sake, and not for its effects (could we say **unselfishly, categorically?**). The representation of the appetite cannot originally precede the desire, the craving, nor can it **ground** the instinct, since appetite springs from the relation between object and instinct. Therefore, representation can no more **produce** desire than reward produce virtue. The mind's movement (*Gemüthsbewegung*) that drive elicits, and we call desire, is a movement whose sole aim is to arrive at, and unite with, the object. This remark has universal application. At first, we desire and want an object not because it is pleasant or good, but rather we name it pleasant or good because we desire and want it; and we desire and want it, because our sense-perceivable or suprasensible nature so brings it with it. Therefore, there is no principle for knowing the desirable and the good except the faculty of desire, the original desire and willing themselves. **In our innermost selves**, we recognize and **call** pleasant, good, and beautiful, those objects we desire, want, and love. As Pascal said, so profoundly and sublimely: *L'intelligence du bien est dans le cœur*. [Pascal, *Pensée sur la religion, et sur quelques autres sujets* (Amsterdam: 1758), Bd. 2, 205. See JWA 3, 208.]

ON THE DIVINE THINGS AND THEIR REVELATION

Thus, on the basis of this quality or characteristic feature, **however desirable in and of itself**, virtue can as little be recognized as compared. There is no **third term** with reference to which virtue and happiness, its opposite, might be compared; no third term that we might use to determine their relative value, measure and weigh them against each other. Virtue's **highest and incomparable** value can be acknowledged only **voluntarily**: I find in my consciousness that I want above all either **virtue** or happiness – mere **pleasant existence**.

If I want happiness over anything else, my concept of it will determine what is **good** and **worthy of respect**, and the worst of crimes may become a duty for me. Only virtue is then what makes me competent, skilled, and fit to lead an enduring, and, if possible, uninterrupted good life; there is no other virtue.

On the other hand, if I do not will happiness at all costs, nor invest it with the highest value; if I will **virtue** above everything else – i.e., absolutely – by this willing I become conscious of a higher drive, the source of that will, and by virtue of it of a higher object compared with which that other ideal of the imagination, called happiness, vanishes like a shadow. I feel this drive as my essential, true, and highest power, and on account of this feeling, I necessarily ascribe to myself the faculty to determine all my desires based on sense perception, all inclinations and passions, in accordance with virtue's [65] demands. This faculty has always been called **moral freedom**; it can so little be equated with the unfortunate ability to will opposite things – good as well as evil – that, on the contrary, we are **not free** precisely to the extent that this unfortunate ability dwells in us. We can ascribe freedom to ourselves only insofar as we are aware that there is in us a power aimed at the good, able to confront all resistance. Why does this power, which is the very spirit of human being – the faculty in him by which he has **his life in himself** – not overcome that opposition? Why does it only allow us to strive for that freedom, to approximate it, and does not really make us **be** free? That is an impenetrable mystery. That is the mystery of creation, of the union of the finite and the infinite, and of the existence of individual personal beings. For that reason, it reigns through all of nature, which, everywhere, as within our chest, simultaneously announces and hides a God. It hides Him in such a way – according to the words of an inspired poet – that "one might become an animal and, in conscience, deny God who has been reduced to nothing in the visible world; yet on the other hand, it announce Him so vividly, filling all in all, that nobody would know how to save oneself before **the inner reach of His activity**."[27]

---

27   Johann Georg Hamann, *Kreuzzüge des Philologen*, 1762, 184.

ON THE DIVINE THINGS AND THEIR REVELATION

Only the highest essence **in** the human being bears witness to a **Most High outside** of him; only the **spirit** in him bears witness to a **God**. For that reason, his faith sinks or rises according as his spirit sinks or rises. Necessarily, just as we find and feel ourselves in the most intimate part of our consciousness, so do we determine our origin and present it to ourselves and to others. Either we recognize ourselves as born of the spirit, or we imagine ourselves as a living belonging to the dead, a light kindled by darkness, a non-thing hatched out at the dumb night of necessity and chance. Insanely stretching our wit, we fancy that life has come from death, that the latter gradually alighted to life – so did unreason gradually alight to reason, nonsense to the intentional, chaos to a world. On the **core** of this All, this **perfect non-thing**, are formed, but only as [66] a skin or a peel – better still, as only moulds or pustules on the peel – what we, fools that we are, call order, beauty, harmony – in the human being, call his spirit: the desire of the true and good, of freedom and virtue.

Thus does the fool say in his heart: "There is no God!"[28] For the intelligent human being God is as present [to him] as his own soul. In his spirit, God is present as the one who began and determined everything: the **first** and the **last**.[29] In his heart, God is present as the one who omnipotently wills and produces the best everywhere: the author and the **power** of the good.

Says the abovementioned author: "Try to read the *Iliad* after having removed by means of abstraction the two vowels Alpha and Omega and tell me then your opinion about the poet's **intelligence** and **melodiousness!**"[30]

Exactly the same applies to nature: it gives only silent letters. The sacred vowels – without which nature's writing cannot be read, nor the word which brings a world out of its chaos spoken – **are inside the human being**.

And this – finally to come back to you! – this, **my friend Asmus,** applies to every external revelation of God, with no distinction, and speaks **against** you just as **for** you.

It speaks **against** you every time you elevate the silent letter above the vowel, as though it were the former that produces the latter – which is impossible, even with the aid of a miracle.

It speaks **for you** as often as you have an objector who does the same but differently, and with **his** silent letter challenges **yours**. But yours assuredly has more breath.

28   [Ps. 14:1 and 53:1.]
29   [Ap. 1:17 and 21:6.]
30   [Johann Georg Hamann, *Kreuzzüge des Philologen* (Königsberg: Kanter, 1762) in *Hamann's Schriften.* Berlin: Reimer, 1821–43, NII, 207, 16–19.]

ON THE DIVINE THINGS AND THEIR REVELATION

You may perhaps object: in the end, with only vowels, one would not achieve much, since with only vowels, no intelligible word, let alone human language, would appear. Bearing this in mind, esteemed [67] grammarians named consonants **main sounds** and vowels **auxiliary sounds**. Different peoples of the East, notably the Hebrews, consider the vowels to be such an inessential part of words that they adopt only a couple of ambiguous symbols in their stead, and write only the **consonants**. Consequently, you should be given superiority, **since you know better what is right**, all the more so in comparison with those who praise themselves for managing with only vowels, and who barely tolerate consonants as something that [only] *de facto* exists.

I am willing to grant you this superiority that you claim: incidentally, I would only reproach you for the hastiness with which you foist the **written** word on the **spoken**. You say: did the Hebrews not leave out vowels and make do with a couple of ambiguous sounds in their place? Surely not **when speaking**. – However, it is hardly worth the effort to reproach you for this, since consonants and vowels are both indispensable in audible **speech**. Articulate sounds, the syllable, and the word, come into being only by virtue of consonants. From the perspective of a well-formed speech in a given language, the grammarian therefore can with reason name the consonants the main sounds and the vowels auxiliary.

Nevertheless, your remark is most welcome to me, since I have the right for my part to point out to you by way of contrast that the **main consonants** and the **main vowels** are the same in every human language: there is but **one** and the same **alphabet** at their root. The great diversity of languages comes into being only from the different combinations of consonants and vowels within words, and the different combinations of words – as parts of speech – within the frame of speech. Inasmuch as they can all be related back to a universal grammar, they are equally able to serve as instruments of reason, given that no one is necessarily more sensible, more spiritual, more moral, just because French, English, Italian, or German is his mother tongue. Barbarian or semi-educated people speak barbarian and semi-educated languages. However, originally, it is never language that gives a people their culture, but rather it is always the culture of a people that passes into their language – either by improving it or by worsening it, as many examples show. The same happens with [68] habits, customs, laws, ethics, and **religion**. It is the spirit, the **living**, that everywhere creates, shapes, and improves everything.

If, after considering everything I said, you nevertheless once more challenge me **as philosopher**, as you did in the fourth part, on page 211, with these words:

"Ride to me, you courier, on a painted horse, and would the horse be flawlessly portrayed," I will not tarry, then, to show you that your threats work more for me than against me but would rather only ask you in return: Would I do it better with a **stuffed** horse? So it might seem at first look: the stuffed horse is more physical; one can mount it and suitably adjust one's position. Yet, the painted horse – if a Raphael sketched and completed it – is closer to the real horse, for there is a life in it that the other lacks. I refrain from pursuing the comparison.

Let no one believe that I am accusing the Messenger himself of riding a stuffed horse. He apparently rides a very living one that carries him onward splendidly, a horse that has wings. For this reason I have often envied him, and others who like him enjoy the same advantage. I have myself wished to make a try at it and would have made it had my winged steed stopped so that I may mount it. But it never wanted to stop that long, and so I have nothing to say about that condition except that it must be very pleasant to be carried across hills and valleys, over swamps and marshes, without jolts or worries. Besides, I cannot imagine how a human being should gain **worth** that way and become better in **himself**. I believe that **this** advantage should instead be found on the other side, benefitting in their efforts those who, left to their inner impetus, steadfastly inch themselves forward to destination. After all, one must use one's own inner impetus also to mount a winged steed and **hang on** to it, or otherwise the steed could not be said to be **ridden**. Only children and fools say that they are **riding a horse** when in fact **straddling** a stuffed horse or running around with a stick between their legs. Even less does a dead weight merely loaded on a horse ride the horse. At the end, therefore, upon honest and careful examination, all comes down to just one's own inner impetus, to standing firm by wisdom, courage, [69] and good inclinations – and, in the same vein, that it is irrelevant whether one rides a winged steed or does without it. The horse does not make the man any more than the cowl makes the monk.

I can assure the **inattentive** reader that if after every kind of turns, parables, and images I always go back to the same point, that I interrupt myself and struggle only to end up repeating myself, this does not happen due to thoughtlessness and negligence, but out of the utmost prudence and greatest diligence.

I see two parties: the supporters and the adversaries of the positive, or **realists** and **idealists** – in both the broadest and the most exclusive sense of the

156   ON THE DIVINE THINGS AND THEIR REVELATION

terms. On both sides I also see much wrong side by side to much right, and on this I rest my hope for a possible agreement between the two. I mean: if I succeeded to bring out what is wrong on each side and gradually bring both closer together, to such an extent that it would no longer be possible to see one without simultaneously seeing the other, then, perhaps, the conditions might be found for an amicable agreement.

Among the adversaries of the positive or **real-objective,** there is a class that especially stands out. I will call them philosophers in the **most extreme** (though not the highest) **sense of the term.** They have gone so far in purifying their love for truth that they no longer even concern themselves with the true. They have persuaded themselves, and are able to demonstrate, that in the most proper and literal sense of the term, **the true is not,** or that only what is not is the true. They teach that this cognition and this unique truth is the pure essence of all cognition and knowledge. Whoever has extracted it in its purity and has fully feasted on it, finds himself transformed into none other than the science that does not require any true outside itself – transformed, namely, into the absolute **IS** that is not a **something** in any form or shape. He is thereby safe from all error, self-deception, and fanaticism; he has gone from the **illusion of the true** to the essential and pure [70] **truth of the illusion.** He no longer sees in the light, but rather, having become light, he no longer even sees the light.

Now, such a wisdom, in order to deliver man from the illness of **error** and forever reconcile him with himself, nails him on the cross of the most despairing **ignorance;** by sheer martyrdom drives all **natural** life out of him – the life of faith, love, and hope – so that he may come to life again, undaunted, with a transfigured body made of **pure logical enthusiasm** that would at the same time be his soul. That wisdom sets over the soulless sensation a repulsive ghost incapable of anything but nod with its empty skull as if to say: **nothing, and again nothing.** Such a wisdom wants to be **all in all,** would pass off its skeleton for the father of spirits, for the creator of all things; its **Dii monogrammi**[31] for heavenly powers leading us with mighty hand out Egyptian slavery, away from the blind paganism of all earlier doctrines and into the integrity and brightness – which alone secures our beatitude – of its own doctrine, to a promised land where only the cognition of cognition flows, with no milk and honey or similar

---

31   Marcus Tullius Cicero, *De Natura Deorum,* L. II, c. 23. "Epicurus monogrammos deos et nihil agentes commentus est." ["Epicurus invented gods who existed only in outline and did nothing." English translation has been modified from the original to meet Jacobi's quotation.]

ON THE DIVINE THINGS AND THEIR REVELATION

impurities. And we should take possession of these powers without at the end running the risk of meeting the same destiny as the Hebrews who, because of their superstition and their absurdly extravagant tales, despite their horror of superstition became proverbial for their credulity, and the laughingstock of the world. The one who here bears witness cannot let this wisdom pass for true wisdom: he must speak out loudly and clearly against its doctrine.

But he must speak out just as loudly and clearly against a doctrine directly opposed to it.

As already said, to the just described class of integral **internalists in whom nothing external can penetrate** there stands opposed the class of **integral externalists** who claim that there is nothing in them that has not come from outside. These trust their senses only [71], i.e., they deny the supreme authority of reason and conscience as allegedly **the highest**. Neither their demands nor the **inner** word, but only a word coming rather from outside must absolutely decide what is true and good. Human beings, so they claim, would have known nothing at all of God had He not announced to them His existence by means of extraordinary emissaries. These emissaries were then also the first to teach human beings about the divine qualities. They taught them that the supreme being is wise, just, good, and truthful, but displayed God's **omnipotence** to them immediately, by means of miracles which they performed as extraordinary emissaries.[32] For the externalists, with respect to all the teachings proclaimed by God's emissaries, this material proof by means of miracles is not just the highest, but basically also **the only valid**. They allow only the actuality of miracles to be tested, i.e., **the truth of the mission.** If the latter is proven, then the content of the doctrine taught should not further be examined through reason and conscience: **power** has decided, absolute blind submission is duty. If one were to grant reason and conscience the right to make valid counterarguments, they say, the whole system would be then shaken to its ground.

---

32   It is remarkable that F. Socini, who had such a valid idea of man's moral nature, had the same theory. Indeed, he stated that the external revelation is the source of religion, and that without it man would not have reached the cognition of God. See F. Socini proelection. Theol., chapter 2, 3. See answer 40 in Rakau's Catechism and Osterod's teaching on the highest truths of religion, chapter 1, 9ff. (Marginal note of my friend Martini). [Socini were sixteenth century Italian theologians – Lelio and Fausto – who gave the name to a theological-moral doctrine which is still present in some interpretations of humanitarianism. Stemming from Protestant theology, it gave further impulse against both Catholic and Protestant dogmas in view of a mystical insight for a moral life.]

That is what the consistent partisans of a thoroughly and absolutely positive doctrine of religion have for a long time believed they had to affirm. There would be no end to heresy, they submitted, if reason and conscience had a valid say, or even the last word; faith's unity and firmness would never have been formed. They asked, and still ask, whether it is worth possessing the true faith, i.e., being enlightened by God through his emissaries. They say: "You would not want to say that it is not. So, also [72] then admit that there can be no greater crime than to prevent human beings from being equally blessed by the true faith. The way of inquiry would never lead to any such universal acceptance of the true faith and the admission to a necessary order of salvation conditioned by it. To hope for this would be madness. What remains then is only the way of authority: the coercion of faith by present or sufficiently authenticated miracles. And whoever refuses to comply by this authority, for he imagines, claims, and teaches, that there is in the human being a higher authority – the authority of human conscience and reason – such as one believes and trusts in himself more than in God; he is cursed."

Here, finally, I have wanted to contrast and oppose, sharply and clearly, the most extreme positions of both schools of thought, after having allowed them up to this point in the text, in more moderate shape and in a variety of ways, to bend this way or that, to waver, and even to mingle.

It now behoves me to explain, more incisively than has been done so far, how I approach these schools of thought; to which I am more inclined, the integral internalist or the integral externalist; or how I stand between the two with a conviction typically my own. I shall now present my position, no longer in the character of a reviewer but in first person.

X

My convictions are still exactly the same as the ones I presented more than twenty-five years ago in my book on the doctrine of Spinoza and in the dialogue on Idealism and Realism published shortly after.[33] At that time, we generally agreed on the intention of philosophy, on its ultimate purpose [73], and we only disagreed on the best and fastest way to reach that set goal.

That is no longer the case: rather, nowadays, we are unanimous in affirming and believing that to reach the wreath of truth, science, and wisdom, one need take a direction totally opposite the previous.

33   [Footnote present in the second edition.] See the *Vorrede* in vol. 2.

ON THE DIVINE THINGS AND THEIR REVELATION 159

How fast the systems of philosophy have changed in the last twenty-five years in Germany is well-known. Many thinkers have changed skin more than once. I too have let my soul wander, yet only with the option of turning back at exploration completed. Moreover, I did everything in my power to let the wandering each time run its course as fully as possible under the given conditions, so that, more instructive than even a Pythagoras, could report on what I experienced along the way.

Remember how Kant exhaustively exposed in his *Critique of Pure Reason*, at the same time as I did but with different goals and different means, the vanity of all speculative pretensions to demonstrate suprasensible truths, i.e., to be able to ground them objectively and impose them on the understanding like mathematical truths, by means of a logical mechanism. Remember how, despite this, he retained the general conviction, expressing it most explicitly at the opening of the *Critique*, that philosophy only has suprasensible concepts for objects; three ideas, namely, *freedom*, *immortality*, and *God*. He taught and repeated in all his works that everything that philosophy deals with serves only as means to arrive at these ideas and confirm their reality.

It follows from this assertion that if philosophy were to lose its unique goal, it would at the same time lose itself, and together with its purpose it would also have to forgo its entire essence (Wesen) and everything that pertains to its mission (*Geschäft*). With philosophy, however, also reason would be forgone (thus Kant again), and humanity itself, for the cognition of God and religion are, as Kant clearly affirms, the highest purposes of reason and human existence. – And especially to be noted here, vividly to be kept in mind, is that the words **God, freedom, immortality**, and **religion** had the exact [74] same meaning and value for our deep and honest philosopher as they have had for human common sense from time immemorial. Kant did not trade in fraud, or play games, with them.

Already in his earlier work *The Only Possible Argument in Support of a Demonstration of the Existence of God*, Kant expresses himself decisively as follows: "According to the proposition, 'All reality must either be given as a **determination** in the necessary being, or it must be given through the necessary being as through a **ground**' the question is left undecided whether the properties of understanding and will are to be found in the Supreme Being as **determination inheriting** in it, or whether they are to be regarded merely as **consequences** produced **by** it **in other things**. If the latter alternative were the case, it would then follow that despite all excellencies of this original being that spring to mind because of the sufficiency, unity and independence of the existence it has as a great ground, **its nature would nonetheless be far inferior to what one must need think when one thinks of God.** Possessing neither cognition nor choice, this original being would be a **blindly necessary** ground of other things and of other **minds** as well, and it would differ from the eternal fate postulated by some ancient philosophers in nothing except for being more conceptually described."[34]

The *Critique of Pure Reason* reads: "Since one is accustomed to understanding by the concept of God not some blindly working eternal **nature** as the **root** of things, but rather a highest being which is supposed to be the author of things **through** understanding and freedom – **and since this concept alone interests us** – one could, strictly speaking, refuse all faith in God to the **deist**, and leave him solely with the assertion of an original being or a highest cause. However, since no one should be charged with wanting to deny something just because he does not have the confidence to assert it, it is gentler and fairer to say that the **deist** believes in a **God**, but the theist in a **living God** (*summa intelligentia*)"[35] [75].

I have quoted these passages in order thereby to stress that nobody at the time was scandalized by the philosopher of Königsberg, thought less of him, or disregarded him as a man of mediocre understanding, because he taught that the true God is a living God who wills and knows, and says to himself: "I **am** WHO I **am**" – who is not merely an "is," nor an absolute Not-I. On the contrary, he provoked scandal only because he not clearly exposed the inadequacy of all proofs hitherto advanced by speculative philosophy for the existence of a living God, for the personal survival of the human soul in a future world and its capacity, already in the present, of absolute self-determination, but also because he irrefutably demonstrated the impossibility of even carrying on such proofs in the way they did, i.e., theoretically.

To meet this scandal and help philosophy not to lose itself along with its purpose, Kant compensated for the loss of theoretical proofs with necessary postulates of a **pure practical** reason. He gave the latter primacy over the theoretical, i.e., he explained how all the propositions that are indissolubly attached to an **a priori** absolute practical law are to be accepted by the theoretical reason as demonstrated; he called this acceptance pure rational faith (*Vernunftglauben*). With this, on Kant's assurance, philosophy would be fully safe-

---

34 Why in a more comprehensible way? (I. Kant, *The Only Possible Argument*, 133.) [Translation modified to meet Jacobi's quotation.]

35 [Kant, *Critique of Pure Reason*, B 661. Bold by Jacobi.]

ON THE DIVINE THINGS AND THEIR REVELATION

guarded and would finally reach the goal it otherwise always missed. By taking this step, philosophy moved beyond childhood and adolescence (Dogmatism and Skepticism), and entered its mature, virile age (Criticism).[36]

But already the natural daughter of critical philosophy, the Doctrine of Science, spurned the safeguards devised by her father. Without the Kantian postulates, she created a system of ethics that was purer and more succinct than the one provided by the founder of critical philosophy, and in so doing she deprived the reinvented moral theology of its ground and basis. "**The living and actual moral order became God himself**": a God expressly devoid of consciousness and [76] selfhood; a God that is neither a particular being distinct from the world and from human beings, nor the **cause** of the moral world order. This God is rather itself this world order, whose existence is purely and simply necessary, and whose efficacy does not possess any kind of ground or condition outside itself. To attribute consciousness to God, and what is only a higher degree of the latter, namely what we call personality (**being in itself and knowing of itself**) or **reason**: in a word, to attribute to him a separate existence or selfhood, knowledge and will, implies, according to the Doctrine of Science, turning God into a finite being, because consciousness and personality are tied to limitation and finitude. The concept of God as a particular being, or – to use Kant's expression – a **living** God to whom **perfection** of self-consciousness and thus personality of the highest degree must belong, is impossible and contradictory. This is now permitted to be said in all sincerity putting an end to the incessant chatter of the schools, so that the true religion of the happy Kingdom [of the moral law] blossom.[37]

These honest words caused quite a stir twelve years ago by being spoken publicly and openly, yet still on their merit. Already at the time, however, it was the loud proclamation more than the matter proclaimed that on the spur of the moment frightened a world already made ready for the latter by fifteen years of study of critical philosophy. The terror quickly subsided, and it might well be that hardly has there been an occasion in which the truth of the Italian proverb "una meraviglia dura tre giorni,"[38] was more strikingly verified. Shortly after, when the **second** daughter of critical philosophy abolished completely, i.e., also by name, the distinction that the first daughter had allowed to remain

---

36 See Kant, *Critique of Pure Reason*, B 789; Kant, *Critique of Practical Reason*, 215 and 225. [See Kant, *Critique of Practical Reason*, 96–8 and 101–2. See JWA 3, 211.]

37 See *Philosophisches Journal* by Fichte and Niethammer, vol. 8, fasc. 1, 1798.

38 [A wonder lasts three days.]

ON THE DIVINE THINGS AND THEIR REVELATION

between philosophy of nature and moral philosophy, necessity and freedom; when it declared that **there is nothing above nature, that only nature exists,** this no longer triggered any astonishment.

In reality, this **second daughter** had earlier, before its elder sister, already challenged the reinvented moral theology, mocking its inventor, not without sarcasm, because of his opening and closing point. To her, both were equally [77] scandalous: the God that this philosophy strove to make true, and the philosophy itself that wished to make it its **purpose.**[39]

Everything already sufficiently in place, she advanced her **diametrically opposed concept of philosophy.** She claimed that philosophy had to begin with the presupposition that only One is, and outside it nothing. If this philosophy cannot prove the truth of this presupposition and thus eradicate all dualism (of whatever name) at its ground, it must renounce itself. The liberation of nature from the supernatural, of the world from a cause outside and above it; in a word, the **autonomy of nature,** became the password of this new wisdom.

Not without reason does the new system of **Unitotality** or absolute Identity proudly claim to be returning to the oldest philosophy (which, however, is not to be held as the oldest **doctrine**).[40] The naturalistic systems are certainly the oldest speculative systems known to us: speculative physics under this or that form, poems about the creation of the world that both **anticipate** natural sciences and **go beyond** all experience: **Cosmogonies – Mythologies.**[41]

It must have been necessary for the human understanding to take this path when it started to philosophize; it had no other way to develop itself or to come to itself: its birth was the birth of a world, and the birth of a world was its birth. Only gradually does the human being emerge, determined on all sides, out of an obscure and confused chaos of sensations and representations. He emerges with a mutually conditioning **Outside and Inside of him,** with an I and a Not-I inseparable from each other. Remember in Herder's *The Oldest Document* (*Die älteste Urkunde*) the sublime **lesson of Dawn** (*Morgenröte*). Read in it the symbolic description of the history of the creation of the world and of the human beings in six steps or days: what here can only be indicated, will emerge there in stirring clarity. [78]

---

39 See *Philosophisches Journal einer Gesellschaft teutscher Gelehrter*, ed. F.I. Niethammer. Fasc. 7, 1795.

40 [For the doctrine of the Unitotality, Jaeschke refers to Schelling's *Bruno* in Schelling, *Sämtliche Werke*, 1, 4:312.]

41 [See JWA 3, 216 where W. Jaeschke finds a clear statement in Schelling's *Bruno* in Schelling, *Sämtliche Werke*, 1, 4:309.]

ON THE DIVINE THINGS AND THEIR REVELATION 163

But despite the inseparability of the internal and external in human consciousness, the two speculative systems of **materialism** and **idealism** – **seemingly** so opposed – are concocted in the human understanding in twin birth. If the **one** is the first to appear, the **other** already holds him by the heel, like Jacob did to Esau, and is pulled out as good as at the same time. Indeed, he had also stuck out his hand **first**, like **Zerah** the son of Tamar, demonstrably well ahead of the other.[42] Throughout the history of philosophy we see these twins arguing and quarrelling with each other over the right of primogeniture, by virtue of which the one would rule and the other submit. It is not possible to bring this quarrel and argument to an end through compromise and reconciliation; it has to be demolished by equally demolishing the mutual claims. This is the work that **Kant** sought to undertake.

This eminent man thereby initiated in speculative philosophy a revolution truly comparable in significance and weighty consequences to the one Copernicus had caused in astronomy three centuries earlier, most directly in astronomy but indirectly in all other sciences of nature.[43]

The indisputably proven core of Kantian philosophy is that we conceive an object only inasmuch as we can let it arise before us in thought, can create it in the understanding. We are however utterly unable to create **substances**, either in thought or truly outside us. **Outside us**, we can only produce movements, combinations of movements, and out of these shapes; **in us**, concepts and combinations of concepts that refer to perceptions by way of either the outer or the inner sense. Consequently, there can be only two sciences in the strict and real sense of the word: mathematics and general logic. All other disciplines earn the title of science only insofar as they turn their objects – through a sort of transubstantiation process – into mathematical and logical beings.

Clearly, such transformation and transubstantiation cannot be accomplished with the objects specific to [79] metaphysics: **God, freedom,** and **immortality**. These three ideas lie completely outside the circle of those two sciences and cannot possibly be **realized** by the means at their disposal. This means that it is just as impossible to demonstrate through the principles of mathematics and of general logic that a reality corresponds to those three ideas, as it is to place this reality before our eyes and experience it with our outer senses. Therefore, with regard to the three ideas, **science** remains completely neutral, and has to accept that it no longer has the right either to affirm

---

42 [Gen. 25:26 and Gen. 38:27.]
43 [Kant, *Critique of Pure Reason*, B XVI and B XXII.]

or to refute their reality. Kant rightly claims as his greatest merit that he has in fact broadened the use of reason by apparently limiting it; and, as a consequence, that he has abolished **knowledge** in the domain of the suprasensible; thus, to have made room for a **faith** immune to metaphysical dogmatism.[44]

Long before Kant, at the beginning of the eighteenth century, **G.B. Vico** wrote in **Naples:** "we demonstrate geometrical objects because we make them; if we could demonstrate physical objects, it would mean that we made them. Therefore, those who try to prove a priori the existence of God must be blamed for impious curiosity. The clarity of metaphysical truth is the same as the light that we can only know through opaque objects. In fact, we do not see the light, but we see bright objects. Physical objects are opaque, that is, they have form and are finite; in them we see the light of metaphysical truth."[45]

Even older than Vico's words are those of the profound Pascal: "Ce qui passe la Géométrie nous surpasse."[46]

That such insights were already at hand strewn here and there does not diminish the merit of the great author of the *Critique of Pure Reason*, just as Copernicus' merit is not diminished because the old [80] Italian school had taught before him that the Earth together with the other planets orbit around the sun, or that a similar cosmological system, known as the Egyptian system, was known even before Philolaus.[47] Actually, this juxtaposition is not quite the point, for it is likely that Kant never read Vico's above-mentioned passage,

---

44 [Kant, *Critique of Pure Reason*, B XXX.]

45 Giovan Battista Vico, from Naples, royal professor of rhetoric, *De Antiquissima Italorum Sapientia ex Linguae Latinae Originibus Eruenda Libri Tres*, Naples 1710.

   Kästner in the "Philosophisches Magazin" edited by Eberhard, vol. 2, 4, 402, asked the following question: "What does **possible** mean in geometry?" and he answers as follows: Euclid would require Wolff (who presumed to demonstrate the possibility of the most perfect being) to **make a most perfect being**, that is, in the same sense Euclid made the icosahedron, i.e., in the understanding. It would not be a question of **producing** a most perfect being **outside him**, since the icosahedron too does not need to be outside the understanding.

46 Pascal, *Pensées*, P. I Art. 2: *Reflexions sur la Geometrie en général*, ed. 1779. [English: "what goes beyond geometry transcends us." Translation is mine.]

47 Ahead of Philolaus, one could also cite Nicetas (or Iceta, as Ernesti would rather read) of Syracuse, since he had already asserted: *cum terra circum axem se summa celeritate convertat et torqueat, eadem effici omnia, quasi stante terra coelum moveretur*: ["Because the earth turns and rotates on its axis at an extremely high speed, exactly the same effect is produced as if the heavens were moving while the earth was at rest." *Early Greek Philosophy*, volume IV, *Western Greek Thinkers*, Part 1, ed. by A. Laks and G.W. Most, Loeb Classical Library 527. Cambridge: Harvard Univer-

ON THE DIVINE THINGS AND THEIR REVELATION

whereas we know of Copernicus that he was first enlightened by what is said in Plutarch of the theories of the Pythagoreans, but especially by the report of the Egyptian cosmological system that he had drawn from Martianus Capella.[48]

It is only one step from Kant's discovery that we only comprehend and perfectly conceive what we can construct to the system of identity. Kantian criticism, rigorously carried through to its consequences, had to have the **Doctrine of Science** for result, and this science, in turn rigorously carried through, had to result in the doctrine of the **Unitotality**, an inverted or transfigured Spinozism, an **ideal-materialism**.

How is it possible, will the attentive thinker now ask, that a man of the acumen and mental strength of a Kant would not be himself aware of results only barely at a remove from his philosophical course? And, if aware of them, did not fully push through with them and himself give to his system the perfection necessary to its survival? It is not admissible that while working at his critique he distantly saw, here and there, where the *summum jus* of his doctrine would have had to lead, but, frightened by the *summa injuria* entailed by it, attempted a way out, a gentler, conciliatory but still legitimate way. Kant was too honest a man to deceive himself and others in this way; also much too wise and prudent not to know what could not last. The enigma therefore demands a more satisfying resolution [81].

I have already given a few hints towards one in the *Letter to Fichte* (preface, vi–x) and in the treatise *On Criticism's Attempt to Reduce Reason to the Understanding* (Reinholds Beytr. Heft III., 11–13). Since then, two excellent men have discussed this subject in detail: **Bouterwek** in his **memorial** dedicated to the philosopher of Köningsberg (Hamburg 1805)[49] and **Fries** in his *New Critique of Reason* (in three parts, Heidelberg 1807).[50] These two men have discussed the issue so thoroughly, and have presented the question so learnedly, doing

---

    sity Press, 2016, 267.] Marcus Tullius Cicero, *Academia, Quaestio* L. IV, c. 39. Marginal note by Martini.

48 [A jurist and writer, he lived in Carthage between the 4th and the 5th century CE. He is the author of *De nuptiis Mercurii et Philologiae*, an encyclopedic work that provides one of the earliest systems of liberal arts: Grammar, Dialectic, Rhetoric, Geometry, Arithmetic, Astronomy, Music (or Harmony).]

49 [Friedrich Bouterwek, *Immanuel Kant, Ein Denkmal* (Hamburg: B.G. Hoffman, 1805).]

50 [Jakob Friedrich Fries, *Neue oder anthropologische Kritik der Vernunft* (Heidelberg: Mohr und Zimmer, 1807).]

166 ON THE DIVINE THINGS AND THEIR REVELATION

justice to it in view of the whole of philosophy, that it would have been sufficient for me just to refer here to them, had not the distinctive goal of the present work also required something more.

I will begin with a passage of Bouterwek's *Memorial to Kant*. On page 85, one reads: "The new idealism (which is an **ideal-materialism** and has therefore given itself the name of **System of Identity**) can indeed be rigorously deduced from the Kantian system by logical extension. However, this extension of the Kantian philosophy is as foreign to its **spirit** as are **Quietism** and spirit-seeing."

In my opinion, **what is meant here** can be said more broadly, unambiguously, and incisively, as follows: just as Plato's doctrine is opposed to Spinoza's doctrine, so too the **spirit** of the Kantian philosophy is opposed to the spirit of the doctrine of Unitotality.

Justification for this strikingly sharp opposition is that Kant, at the beginning of his doctrine of ideas, explicitly and repeatedly refers to Plato as his **forerunner**, just as the author of the newest doctrine of Unitotality explicitly and repeatedly refers to Spinoza as **his**.[51]

"Plato," Kant states "made use of the expression **idea** in such a way that we can readily see that he understood [82] by it something that not only could never be borrowed from the senses, but that even goes far beyond the concepts of the understanding (with which Aristotle occupied himself), since nothing encountered in experience could ever be congruent to it. Ideas for him are archetypes of things themselves, and not, like the categories, merely the key to possible experiences. In his opinion they flowed from the highest reason, through which human reason partakes in them; our reason, however, now no longer finds itself in its original state, but must call back with toil the old, now very obscure ideas through a recollection (which is called philosophy). I do not wish to go into any literary investigation here, in order to make out the sense which the sublime philosopher combined with his word. I note only that when we compare the thoughts that an author expresses about a subject, in ordinary speech as well as in writings, it is not at all unusual to find that we understand him even better than he understood himself, since he may not have determined his concept sufficiently and hence sometimes spoke, or even thought, contrary to his own intention" (B 370).

"Plato – he adds – noted very well that our power of cognition feels a far higher need than that of merely spelling out appearances according to a synthetic unity in order to be able to read them as experience, and that our reason

51 See supplement A.

ON THE DIVINE THINGS AND THEIR REVELATION 167

naturally exalts itself to cognitions that go much too far for any object that experience can give ever to be congruent, but that nonetheless have reality and are by no means merely figments of the brain."

Kant therefore followed Plato and believed he understood him better than Plato had understood himself. Already in the introduction to his *Critique of Pure Reason* (B 8–9), he showed us clearly what led Plato, in his opinion, to misunderstand himself: "the light dove – we read there – in free flight cutting through the air the resistance of which it feels, could get the idea that it could do even better in airless space. **Likewise, Plato abandoned the world of the senses because it set such narrow limits for the understanding, and dared to go beyond it on the wings of the ideas, in the empty space of pure understanding** [83]. He did not notice that he made no headway by his efforts, for he had no resistance, no support, as it were, by which he could stiffen himself, and to which he could apply his powers in order to put his understanding into motion" (B 8–9).

Unshakeable in his conviction that reason, as a **faculty of cognition**, relates to nothing but the understanding and can only **lose itself in fantasy** when it exceeds sense experience, Kant could not but see and judge this way. Curiously, it remained hidden from him that, in his system, the understanding is also not able to obtain true knowledge, because all the concepts of the understanding receive their validity only from intuition; yet intuition does not represent anything real, but only offers representations of phenomena, i.e., **mere** representations, pure or empirical, which "**include or present in themselves absolutely nothing of what concerns a thing (*Sache*) in itself**," nothing that belongs to a thing (*Ding*) itself.[52] Regarding such representations, it must remain eternally problematic whether there exists an object for them **independent and external to them**. Under such circumstances, this question becomes entirely futile and really foolish, because resolving it does not bring any objective cognition.

Thus it so happened that Kant, as Bouterwek aptly put it, "ended up suspended between the absolute reality from which in his opinion the human understanding had to be absolutely severed, and the sense perception, above which he nevertheless had to rise; so much that, floating between heaven and earth, he lost the one and the other"[53] [84].

---

52 [Kant, *Critique of Pure Reason*, B 62.]

53 Here is the pertinent passage: "The real poet, according to Shakespeare, turns his gaze from earth to heaven and from heaven to earth; **then** he brings down into real existence the forms of unknown things, which his imagination produces, and gives

168 ON THE DIVINE THINGS AND THEIR REVELATION

But that that was the case, Kant himself firmly denied it; and he denied it not just verbally, but in the innermost part of his mind, where the firm convictions from which he started remained for him unshakeable: on the one hand, the conviction that to accept **appearances independently from what they show** (*Critique of Pure Reason*, B XXVII) was inconsistent; and, on the other, the conviction that reason would be but a nothing, its name reduced to a mere sound, if the highest ideas it produces (God, freedom, and immortality), whose production earns it that name of **reason** – the **highest** faculty of cognition, the **spirit** of the human being – were merely illusions with no objective content, untenable mere pretences only made to lure and mislead, lacking any demonstration whatsoever. Yet, he went on to speak in full confidence, the science that deals with the demonstration of those ideas that are in essence the products of reason, is the oldest of all the science and, presumably, would be the last left standing even though the rest were all engulfed in the jaws of an all-devouring barbarism (B XIV, XV) [85].

---

a place and a name to the airy nothing. In the same way, Kant, the cold thinker who disdained all poetry in philosophy, turned his gaze from the boundaries of objectivity surrounding our senses up to the unconditioned, infinite, and eternal, and from there down again to those boundaries. There, he believed to have discovered the impossibility of bringing the infinite and the eternal – which hover before pure reason as what is absolute, necessary, and self-standing – down to the sphere of the knowable. For lack of an absolute reality, the goal of his [84] intellectual aspiration was to comprehend under the form a **scientific** system the sum of all **conditions of the possibility** of human knowledge given within those boundaries. According to some perceptive anti-Kantians, he did not obtain anything more than Shakespeare did. Also Kant, it is said, while between heaven and earth, lost both. And when he proved – or believed he had proved – the impossibility of a knowledge of the absolute reality and posited merely the **appearance** of the real at the basis of a system of **pure forms** of cognoscibility, at that point, it is said, the poet who did not want to be a poet also gave only to the air-like nothing a home and many school-legitimate names. However, even assuming, which is not here the place to examine, that by the enormous work of his intelligence Kant has only systematized the human forms of representation, contributing little, or nothing at all, to the clarification of the **ultimate grounds** of human knowledge, the fact remains that no speculative mind before Kant had ever thought of such a system of all human knowledge. This system, so audaciously designed and ingeniously executed, could be achieved only with the help of an imagination that allows the understanding **to hover between** absolute reality – from which it must absolutely be cut off – and sense perception – beyond which it must rise. Thus, this great theoretical work could only be built on concepts." See Friedrich Bouterwek, *Immanuel Kant. Ein Denkmal* (Hamburg: Hoffmann, 1805), 25–9.

ON THE DIVINE THINGS AND THEIR REVELATION   169

In fact, therefore, Kant did assume that there is in human reason – **as the law of its truth immune to all error** – an immediate cognition of both reality in general and of its supreme ground, of a nature **below** that cognition and of a God **above** it.[54] But since an immediate cognition, an original and absolute first knowledge, excludes all proofs (for such proofs would otherwise be the foremost and very first in cognition, its origin), it was only by a detour that Kant managed to import into philosophical **science** those **basic truths** that determine reason itself. For philosophical science demands proofs; it demands **external sanctioning** that a truth be not admitted which is not confirmed by the testimony of **at least** two witnesses.[55] The detour consisted in turning the truths from immediate cognition to mediated cognition by granting practical reason supremacy over the theoretical. The illusion could thus be at least intimated that those truths were discovered by science, whereas in reality, by the introduction of the said supremacy, only the immediate feeling of the true and the good, the positive revelations of reason, were being duly elevated above every scientific proof, for or against them, over every approval or objection coming from the ratiocinative understanding.

In the **theoretical** part of his philosophy, Kant thus subjected reason to the understanding, making it the latter's mere servant; indeed, even reducing it as a faculty of cognition to less than nothing, for he left it with only the ability to **concoct** deceptive **phantasies** over and above the sensory experience which is the object of the understanding. But then, in the practical part of his philosophy, he elevated reason above the understanding. There, the latter no longer had a say wherever reason made its decision, which it did in complete autonomy by a *sic volo, sic jubeo, sic est*.[56]

Kant was right **twice** and therefore he was wrong. The fact that he did not transform his double right into a single yet **complete** right, but rather remained divided and equivocal, full of ambiguities, till the end of his days, belongs to the most instructive events in the history of philosophy [86].

On the clear insight that this perceptive man was the first to attain regarding the conditions as well as the traits and firm limits of a **scientific** cognition possible to the human being, one might well believe that he would have had kept steadfast in mind what scientific proofs can and cannot do – that by them one can indeed elucidate cognition, but not increase it in content or

54 See Jakob Friedrich Fries, *Neue Kritik der Vernunft* (Heidelberg: Mohr und Zimmer, 1807), 1:199–207.

55 [Dt. 19:15 and Matt. 18:16.]

56 See Kant, *Critique of Practical Reason* (Riga: Hartknoch, 1788), 258. [Kant, *Critique of Practical Reason*, 114–15].

ever secure a **ground** for it. If that had really been the case, it would have never crossed his mind either to refute Idealism, or to denounce the hitherto absence of such a refutation as a scandal for philosophy,[57] or also to voice repeated sad complaints about the fact that human reason, indeed fortunate to presuppose God, immortality, and freedom as ideas inherent to it, is nonetheless **unfortunately** unable to demonstrate theoretically the reality or the objectivity of such ideas, or truly **prove** their validity. Rationally considered, the search for a **proof** of the existence of a real world outside our representations and matching them, and of a creator of this world superior to it, just as the search for the immortality and freedom of the human spirit, would have had to be foolishness to him and to anyone truly taught by him. Even the desire for such demonstrations or proofs would have had to vanish as pure inconsistencies. It had become apparent, and anyone of even only mediocre yet unprejudiced spirit would now find clear, that these truths must either be accepted as originating from the immediate authority of reason whose knowledge needs no proofs, for it is supreme and underived, a **cognition independent of criteria**, or rejected as empty deceits. It could indeed be shown, in more ways and more strikingly – and this was already brought to light also independently of the Kantian discovery – **how** and **why** any effort to **demonstrate** the supreme cognition as true cognition – i.e., to want to **deduce** it or to lead it back to something truer and more valid – is in itself absurd and only means being bent on its destruction [87].

The ground of every proof is always and necessarily **above** that which should be proven through it: the former includes the latter under itself, truth and certainty flow out of it over what is to be proven; the latter acquires its reality from it.

For instance, to prove **actual existence**, something must be found outside it that would support it, just as mediated cognition would be supported by the immediate, the concept by the thing; alternatively, something that would **cover** it, as when in geometry a figure is made to cover another in order to arrive at the first demonstration of equality and similarity. In the same vein, regarding existence, **a that** is to be found that would be one and the same with **this**, and also not one and the same; an actual outside the actual that would be more actual than the actual yet at the same time also – the actual.

Likewise, if it must be possible to prove the existence of a living God, then God Himself must be demonstrated and deduced from something which we

---

57 [Kant, *Critique of Pure Reason*, B XXXIXn.]

ON THE DIVINE THINGS AND THEIR REVELATION

can acknowledge as its ground, something that would be before and above Him, as if God should evolve from His principle. For the mere **deduction** of the **idea** of a living God from the nature of the faculty of human cognition leads so little to a demonstration of His actual existence that, on the contrary, it necessarily destroys (assuming that the demonstration succeeds) the natural faith in a living God that one sought to increase and strengthen with a philosophical proof. Indeed, this shows us with great clarity how this idea is an absolutely subjective product of human spirit, a pure **poetical invention**: by nature, the human spirit necessarily invents it and, for that reason, such an idea is **perhaps** – but **at most** only perhaps – a fiction of the true and, consequently, **not** a mere chimera; but it can just as well be, and perhaps even more so, a mere poetic invention, and therefore really **only** a chimera.

I say: **just as well, and perhaps even more so**, a mere **poetic invention,** and **therefore really a mere chimera,** because, that there be even only one possible case where the ideas or the pure concepts of reason have an objective meaning, one would first have to reject the objective meaning of the original concepts of the understanding, the categories, and therefore also the reality of nature [88] and its laws, thus deny that the understanding is somehow a faculty of the cognition of the **true.**

Here is where Kant is in conflict with himself, and where the **spirit** of his doctrine diverges from its **letter**: that as a **human being** he had unconditional trust in the immediate positive revelations of reason and its fundamental judgments, and never lost this trust, at least not wholly or definitely; yet, as a teacher of philosophy, he considered it necessary to transform this purely revealed and independent knowledge into one dependent on demonstrating, and the immediately known into one mediated. He wanted to build the understanding under reason as foundation and then elevate reason above it.[58] The supremacy of reason, its eminent dignity as the unique and sole universal ground and source of all principles, thus came to the fore only afterwards, and then only validated on condition that it reach a settlement with the understanding. But such a settlement could not be reached. Based as it would have been, **not** on **reserving** space reciprocally, but on reciprocal **surrender – on one side simply denying, the other simply affirming** – it amounted to the neutralization and dispossession of [any] supremacy. And since the

---

58 [Footnote is present in the second edition.] Or also: He wanted to build the understanding under reason as foundation and then elevate the understanding above reason.

understanding, **with its veto-power to which it claimed in advance to be entitled,** simply stood up against the unreasonable demands of reason, there was no way out. Practical reason could not make good on behalf of faith, outside the domain of science and cognition, what the theoretical (the understanding) had destroyed on behalf of science and cognition. The doctrines of God, immortality, and freedom had to be straight out abandoned. There remained **only a doctrine of nature, a philosophy of nature.**

And not even that remained. For to grant validity to the ideas of reason, even if only **problematically**, the understanding had indeed to recognize beforehand the **absolute invalidity** of the cognition specific to itself, its complete emptiness and nullity [89] as cognition of the real, that is, of anything **really objective** that exists by itself outside mere representation. This is an insight that the understanding had come to by simple self-investigation. As it truly and exhaustively investigated itself for the first time, it had discovered that what until then was generally called **nature** and its necessary laws was nothing but the human mind together with its entirely subjective representations, concepts, and associations of ideas. That nature, which up to that time was **conceived** as objective, vanished for good with its essence and all its works; once it was separated from external sense perception, it became nothing for the philosophizing understanding. In the face of the faculty of cognition, everything, the knower and the known, dissolved into an empty activity which imagined imaginary things: **objectively**, into a pure nothing. There remained only a bewildering intellectual reign of bewildering intellectual dreams, lacking explanation and meaning.[59]

And so close would our great critic have come to the insight and the result that **actually bring to fruition** the purpose of philosophy – the **decisive** judgment.

---

59 "If we do not assume that throughout the whole universe there prevails an original type of sense perception tied to the original conditions of all possible organic forms, then we would also have reason to be skeptical when considering the laws according to which our reason unites itself to our sense perception to give rise to an experience and to regard them as nothing but subjective laws of our representations. In other words, we are allowed to assume that all that, according to these laws, appears to us as true, could appear as false to other creatures that are differently structured although rational in their own way. But once this is admitted, the foundations of our faith in truth are shaken." Friedrich Bouterwek. *Ideen zur Metaphysik des Schoenen* (Martini: Leipzig, 1807), 110.

ON THE DIVINE THINGS AND THEIR REVELATION 173

There is but one choice for the human being: to accept **either** a nothing everywhere manifest, **or** a God who above everything alone makes the truth of all. – So close to this insight and yet not taking hold of it; so close to that decisive resulting judgement and yet not comprehending it, appropriating it, and revealing it as the sum of his teaching [90]!

What prevented him from actually taking hold of that insight, from comprehending the result, and made him prefer, in a highly artificial fashion, the key of transcendental idealism that, in truth, locks things tighter instead of opening any door, is found tellingly explained in the passage of his *Critique* where he opposes the interest of **reason** to the interest of **science** (of the understanding), **Platonism** to **Epicureanism**; and where, as **advocate of science**, he sides with the latter against the former, **Naturalism** against **Theism**.

"When being dogmatic, each of the two ways says more than it knows, but in such a way that the first (Epicureanism or Naturalism) encourages and furthers **knowledge**, though to the disadvantage of the practical, the second (Platonism or Theism) provides principles which are indeed excellent for the practical, but in so doing **allows** reason, in regard to that of which only a speculative (true, positive) knowledge is granted us, to indulge in ideal explanations of natural appearances, and to neglect the physical investigation of them."[60]

Kant was rightly opposed to a Theism that allows such explanations to reason, and which, as he mentioned elsewhere, perverts reason and makes it lazy. But the real Theism, **Plato's Theism**, is not such a seducer. On the contrary, it alone gives, in strict sense and with no damage, to **science what belongs to science** and to **God or the spirit what belongs to God or the spirit**[61] [91].

If reason truly refers **only** to the understanding and the understanding only to sense perception (K.r.V, B 671, 692), if reason only **gradually soars** to ideas starting from natural phenomena (K.r.V. B 491), then Kant is perfectly right,

---

60   [Kant, *Critique of Pure Reason*, B 500. Partly modified by Jacobi. See Kant, *Critique of Pure Reason*, B 490.]

61   "The science **of the ideas** is the highest in our spirit, and yet a **science on the basis of ideas** as its principles is not possible; only a faith is possible (a firm conviction transcending any science. Cf. J.F. Fries, *Neu Kritik der reinen Vernunft*, 2:324). All science belongs to nature, i.e., the phenomena, etc." Fries, in *Ueber die neuesten Lehre von Gott und der Welt* (Heidelberg: Mohr und Zimmer, 1807), 64. [Jakob Friedrich Fries, *Fichte's und Schelling's Neueste Lehren von Gott und der Welt* (Heidelberg: Mohr und Zimmer, 1807).] Cf. *Neu Kritik der reinen Vernunft*, vol. 2, § 101, 82ff, where three kinds of conviction are elucidated: 1) the conviction of the understanding through intuition; 2) the conviction of reason on the basis of itself alone by means of a completely reflected holding-to-be-true without intuition, which is the holding-to-be-true of **pure rational faith**; 3) the conviction typical of

ON THE DIVINE THINGS AND THEIR REVELATION

even against Plato. The ideas are then merely expanded concepts of the understanding without demonstrable objective validity, and science cannot warn us with sufficient seriousness against the deception in which such ideas are so skilled. In fact, if the Kantian deduction of the ideas is right, then nothing could be more absurd than to wish to start from those ideas, placing them at the top of [92] science.[62] But if, in keeping with the Kantian argument, we reject ideas **as objectively valid original cognition**, then the aforementioned **alternative** is necessarily reversed: the manifest nothing takes up place on the side of God and all that is suprasensible or **supernatural**; what alone is true and actual takes it on the side of the sense-intuitable, of the **nature that alone presents itself as objective.** Consequential thinker that Kant was, in keeping with his fundamental presupposition that we have called his insuperable prejudice, he should have caught this last consequence, and, by the same token, he would have then become the father of ideal-materialism, that doctrine of

---

the transcendental faculty of judgment, a conviction called presentiment, conscious of its distinctive and complete certainty only by virtue of feeling, without any defined concept (Cf. Bd. I s. 341ff, chapter: *Theorie des Gefuhls*).

At the end of the paragraph, Fries writes: "In our spirit, these three ways of conviction have the same degree of necessary certainty ... The prejudice in favour of knowledge is due to the aesthetic clarity, illuminating power, and commonality of sense-intuition, which does not really make any difference. Far from pure rational faith being a less sure holding-to-be-true than knowledge, it is rather the most solid we have, since it emerges straight out of the essence of reason. We would not have any knowledge if there were not already with it an element of rational faith, a conviction from mere reason beyond the senses. The same degree of certainty in conviction belongs to presentiment, although that must forego completeness as regards the determination of its object. It is only a relative holding-to-be-true, of faith deferring to knowledge, one that cannot count as complete, since it arises from the consciousness of the boundaries of our own being. We know, however, that no human reason shall accomplish the **salto mortale** outside itself to resolve the mysteries of the presentiment. The height of human wisdom is to know what we do not know, and cannot know without first having changed our own being." See also § 131, 195–9; further, 222, 223.

As I have explained in my *Letter to Fichte*, in my personal and rather different opinion, knowledge, faith, and presentiment differ from one another and act both in relation to each other and to the cognition of the true. See especially pages 27–32 of the letter and viii–x of the preface. See also supplement A at the end of this work.

62 Even if ideas are considered as original concepts, objectively valid and innate in man, they cannot produce any **science**. For science is always a copy of nature, even in its highest perfection, and cannot be drawn from other sources but nature itself, i.e., the sense-intuition – pure or empiric – of it, mediated by completed reflection.

absolute identity or Unitotality that appeared with much *éclat* only two generations after him.

It all depends on what reveals itself to us with unsurpassable clarity as the **first,** and what as only the **consequent,** a second: nature or intelligence? Either "reason itself has come forth from the womb of nature and is nothing in itself but the completed development of sense perception," **or** it came immediately forth from God and stands between him and his visible work – nature – perceiving both and vouching for both on the certainty of their very existence[63] [93].

Plato states that the denial of God spread among the human beings because they had been deceptively persuaded that the first is not the first, the consequent not the consequent. They were persuaded that they had been wrong to consider nature – which is the only **productive power** – as a product and, on the other hand, to take the product – the understanding that **merely reflects** and **imitates** nature, the **intelligence** – for what produces and is the first creator.[64]

Aristotle notes: up until Anaxagoras, all the ancient Greek philosophers, especially the **Pythagoreans,** had considered as the most perfect not the principle **from which** something comes into being, but **that which** comes into being from it, like plants, animals etc. Everyone had posited as ground a matter that moves irregularly, a chaos, and from it a **world,** a **cosmos** (*Geordnetes*) was allowed gradually to emerge. Different schools had different systems or **theories of creation;** but all had in common the fact **that they placed the principle of every formation in the original matter. Anaxagoras was the first to place this principle outside of matter.**[65]

"Neither Fire nor Earth nor any other such can cause things to be – says Aristotle – or become good; and those philosophers (who consider the All as One) could not have thought it either. It would likewise be absurd to entrust

---

63 "We have an idea of both God and the world before any scientific education and we do not dismiss the idea that God is the highest and absolute autonomous being, **superior to the world.** We therefore know in advance that any doctrine of God that submits God's existence to law or fate is wrong, just as any doctrine that involves a total or partial deification of the world is false." J.F. Fries, *Ueber die neuesten lehre von Gott und die Welt*, 35.

64 Plato, *De Legibus*, L. X. 891e.

65 [Aristotle, *Metaphysics*, A, 3, 984b, 11–19.]

176 ON THE DIVINE THINGS AND THEIR REVELATION

such a matter to chance or to luck. When one man said that a rational being was present – as in animals, so throughout nature – as the cause of the world and all order, he seemed to me like a sober man in contrast with the **random talk** of his predecessors. Such a man was **Anaxagoras,** as far as we know."[66]

In the fourteenth book of the same work (chapter 4), Aristotle claims: "there is a difficulty, even for the expert researcher, how the original elements and principles are related [94] to the good and the beautiful; and the difficulty is this: whether there is in the principles and elements something like what we mean by the good itself and the best itself, or whether this is not so, but these are later in generation. The modern theologians[67] seem to consider this issue decisive: they answer the question in the negative as regards the first hypothesis and say that both **the good and the beautiful appear only when the nature of things grow.** And they say this to avoid a real difficulty that confronts those who say, as some do, that the One is the original principle. The difficulty arises not because they posit the good as belonging to the original principle, but because it is the One that they posit as original principle, and the original principle as original element, and the many as products of the One.

"In this respect, the early poets agree in saying that the original beings, like the Night, Uranos, Chaos, or Ocean do not show as the highest and the supreme, while Zeus does. These representations have their reason only in the confusion concerning the supreme beings. These poets speak in a mixed and not mythical fashion and posit the first generator as the highest and best, as Pherecydes and some others do, and also as the Magi."

The distinction expressed here by Aristotle is of the greatest relevance and settles the issue. There can only be two classes of philosophers: those who regard the more perfect as emerging and gradually developing from the imperfect, and those who assert that the most perfect comes first and that all starts with it and from it. In other words, the latter claim that what comes first, the beginning, is not **some nature of things**; instead, what comes first and is the

---

66 Aristotle, *Metaphysics*, ed. Hippocrates G. Apostle (Bloomington: Indiana University Press, 1966) Book I, 3. Cf. G.G. Fülleborn, *Beiträge*, fasc. II, 160–1, and W.G. Tennemann, *Geschichte der Philosophie*, I, 117–19 along with the aforementioned Aristotelian remarks. Cf. W.G. Tennemann, *Geschichte der Philosophie*, 298ff, the section of Anaxagoras' philosophy. [Translation modified. See Aristotle, *Metaphysics*, N, 4, 1091b 4–10.]

67 These philosophers are called **theologians** by Aristotle because their research has the first cause as subject matter. Plato deals with them in the tenth book of the Laws mentioned above. [Translation modified to match Jacobi's quotation. See Aristotle, *Metaphysics*, Book 14, 4.]

ON THE DIVINE THINGS AND THEIR REVELATION

beginning of all is rather a moral principle, an intelligence that wills and acts wisely – a Creator-God[68] [95].

The doctrine of either of these two classes is opposed to the other in such a way that the two cannot be reconciled, even less united, in a third in which they might reach a point of equality or indifference.

The crucial issue is this: whether in the beginning was the **act** and not the will, or in the beginning was the **will**, and then, as its consequence, came the act.

To free this opposition from the time determination clinging to it, let us ask the same question in a different way, namely: should we assume, as Spinoza did, that the will only **accompanies** the act, so that the former is caused, led, and governed by the latter, or should we claim, with Plato, the exact opposite?[69]

The will presupposes understanding, insight, and intention. **A non-voluntary and unpremeditated action is a blind action, whether or not accompanied by consciousness.**

With reference to the universe (*Weltall*), our question must be presented in the following terms: does the universe exist by virtue of an inner self-enclosed independent mechanism that has neither cause nor purpose outside of itself; or does it exist like the work of **Providence,** the creation of a **God,** for the sake of the Good and the Beautiful?

Healthy reason, still unconditionally trusting itself, answers the latter question in the affirmative. For this reason has this opinion been the older and theism, as **faith,** preceded naturalism as **philosophy.** The latter, naturalism, arose at the same time as **science**; it started just as science began to develop and, as we have already mentioned many times in this essay, it became the **first philosophy.**

But were science ever to become perfect, a system deduced from one principle, complete, encompassing all that is knowable, then, equally naturalism would have to attain perfection with it. All would have to be found to be just [96] **One,** and we would then be able to conceive and understand everything on the basis of that **One.**

Accordingly, it is in the interest of **science** that there not be any God, nor any supernatural, extramundane, and supramundane being. Only under that condition – that **nature** alone is, that it be autonomous, all-in-all – can science

---

68 See Plato's already mentioned the tenth book of the Law, from the beginning to the end.

69 See Plato, *Timaeus*, 30b, and *Laws*, 897a.

178 ON THE DIVINE THINGS AND THEIR REVELATION

reach its goal of perfection and flatter itself for becoming equal to its own object and being **all-in-all**.

Even the **theist when studying nature scientifically** presupposes the autonomy of nature to the extent that he strictly forbids himself wanting to understand and explain anything **in** nature other than through it. He additionally recognizes as a **law of science** that it should not want to know anything about God; generally about anything supernatural, for science, like nature **of which it is the reflection** [*Reflex*], necessarily ceases where the supernatural begins.[70] Quite rightly, however, he demands the same of the naturalist who instead dogmatically claims that **everything is nature, nothing is outside or above it.** He specifically demands of him that he conscientiously abstain from using expressions borrowed from theism while presenting his doctrine, from thus distorting them and in fact making a **false doctrine** of them. None of this would happen if the language were unadulterated since nobody would be deceived by it[71] [97].

A **naturalism** that neither falsifies nor deceives; one that undisguised admits what it is to itself, **sincere, clear, and pure**; such a naturalism stands as a **speculative doctrine** side by side with theism, equally untouched by any criticism. With pride and even bitter scorn, it may well distance itself from theism, explaining that it is a mere spectre, nothing truly **scientific** with which it would work or be part of. For this, the wise man would not be angry with it. However, if naturalism is to remain beyond reproach, it must stick to its boldly sincere

70 To be sure, there is a knowledge of the supernatural, of God, and of divine things, and this knowledge is what is most certain in the human spirit; it is a knowledge which is absolute and immediately arises from human reason. And yet this knowledge cannot take the form of a science. [Remark present only in the second edition.] On this text see 340 [see JWA 3, 73], and also *Critique of Pure Reason*, A 828–31; B 856–9.

71 "A sober atheism is perfectly in line with the understanding when it is the result of an intellectual striving for a complete insight. But a poetic and mystic atheism which calls itself religion is unworthy of a philosopher; it is a dangerous seducer because it denies the human being the need for pure truth in order to delight him with intuitions, with which an inventive mind can do whatever it wants. Such an atheism not only favours every chimera of faith (*GlaubensWahn*) with the least poetic side, but it knows also how to fraternize with it according to time and circumstances in poetic phrases, whose prosaic meaning remains unexplained. The modest religion of faith and hope, which emerges from **moral** confidence, is intolerable to these religious people ... But as long as humankind does not perish, **the** religion that consists in sincere and genuine **faith in God** will not perish." F. Bouterwek, *Immanuel Kant. Ein Denkmal*, 124. [Text with major changes by Jacobi.]

language. It must never want to talk about God or divine things, about freedom or moral good and evil, or about true morality, for according to its innermost conviction all such things are nothing.[72] By talking about them, it would be saying what it truly does not mean. But whoever does this is a liar.[73]

[98] Concerning the **fundamental claim** of naturalism, there is no room for double meaning or ambiguity. This fundamental claim has already been mentioned and is universally known: nature is autonomous and self-sufficient; it **is one and all, and nothing exists outside of it.**

With this, however, the concept of nature – what it includes or **necessarily excludes** – is not yet given or in any way defined. For to say that this concept includes absolutely **all things** except the absolute nothing, or to explain that nature **is** the sum total of all being,[74] of every activity and becoming, of all that comes into being and passes away – neither of these explanations satisfies a real thinker. Such a thinker knows that Aristotle was right in demanding that every explanation should indicate both the **genus** and the **differentia** of an object.[75] Here, however, both are absent, since anything objective is missing. What we have is a bare **not**-nothing as the **positive** content of the concept of nature; as for its **negative** content, we have the **absolute** nothing without any characteristic feature to distinguish it from the other. Nonetheless, according to the

---

72 "The system that teaches that all is one (whether it calls itself Naturalism, Pantheism, Spinozism, or whatever name it wants) inevitably cancels the difference between good and evil, although it verbally denies doing so. In fact, if all is simply one, then all is good and any appearance of what we call wrong or bad is just an empty illusion. Hence the destructive influence which this system has on life: one can turn one's expressions as one wishes, one can adhere as much as one wants to the faith everywhere elicited by the voice of conscience, but ultimately, if we remain loyal to that ruinous principle, the actions of human beings are considered indifferently, and the eternal difference between good and evil, right and wrong must be abolished and declared invalid." Friedrich von Schlegel, *Ueber die Sprache und Weisheit der Indier* (Heidelberg: Mohr und Zimmer, 1808), 127, 97, 98, 114. [*Kritische Friedrich-Schlegel-Ausgabe*, 8:229–31, 199–201, and 217.]

73 [Footnote is present in the second edition.] See 48 of the second volume of this collection, the two places mentioned from Schulze's *Enzyklopadie der Philosophischen Wissenschaften* (61, 62).

74 [See Schelling's *Entwurf eines Systems der Naturphilosophie* in Schelling, *Sämtliche Werke*, 3:13.]

75 [Aristotle, *Topics*, vi–vii, 139a, 28–31.]

180 ON THE DIVINE THINGS AND THEIR REVELATION

opening statement, the two should determine each other within the concept and together realize its possibility.

To remedy this defect, the above definition might be rejected and the following affirmed instead. Nature is by no means the sum total of all being because such a sum total would be impossible; it would have a motionless non-thing for object. Moreover, nature is not even the eternal activity and becoming of things, as if it had this or that existence as its goal. On the contrary, nature abhors all existence and therefore any intention: nature is solely **production as such, pure** production without intention, the **absolute productivity**. A true **being** can be attributed only to this **absolute productivity** without object or subject, unconditioned <u>a parte ante</u> as well as <u>a parte post</u>. As to its products, the infinity of individual beings: they have no being at all; as such, they **do not** actually exist. It follows that there cannot be a **sum total** of all beings, but rather that there can only be a unique, eternal and immutable **being; the being of the absolute productivity.** – I say: trying to help oneself out of the original quandary in this way would amount to moving from one embarrassment to another possibly even worse [99].

For if an absolute productivity is one and all, but the infinity of what it has produced from eternity to eternity **is, as such, nothing**, then one should ask: what is in truth the **act** of this absolute productivity, the worth and object of its infinite activity? Epithets and circumlocutions will not eliminate these and similar questions but on the contrary only increase them. So, if one announces to us, like a higher and deeper doctrinal revelation, that nature, or the absolute productivity, **is the elemental cosmic power, holy, and eternally creative, that creates and actively produces all things from itself, and that it is the only true God, the living one,**[76] while the God of theism is just a fatuous idol, a fantasy that dishonours reason, then, after listening to these words, we should not remain silent. On the contrary, we would find a reason to ask even more urgent questions about the **works** of such a God: whether they should now be **one and the same** with Him, whether they should be only **in** Him or also **outside of** Him.

If they are only **in** Him, then they are simply variations or modifications of Himself, and nothing is really created except **time!**

One should consider that the only **true** and living God (Nature) can neither increase nor decrease Himself, neither improve nor deteriorate. Rather, with

---

76 [Schelling's *Über das Verhältnis der bildenden Künste zu der Natur*, in his *Sämtliche Werke*, 7:293.]

ON THE DIVINE THINGS AND THEIR REVELATION 181

regard to quality and quantity, this God which is **equal** to Nature or the Universe remains always one and the same, from eternity to eternity. It would therefore be impossible for God to effect any change whatsoever in Himself – for God to manifest Himself as a **transformative power** – if he were not Himself variability, **temporality**, and change. This variability is itself – so we were told – at **root** something **invariable**, i.e., the holy and eternally productive primal cosmic power. On the other hand, in its **outcome**, in the explicit and actual world, it is an absolute **variable**, so that at any particular moment the totality of being is nothing. Accordingly, one cannot dispute the naturalist God's creative Word that proclaims [100] from eternity to eternity: **let there be nothing**! He generates **non-being from being** in the same way as the God of theism **generates being from non-being**.

And so we would find ourselves in the situation of simply having to decide either to assume the revealed nothing as the only true in itself, or to declare totally unacceptable the opinion that nature is everything and that there is nothing above or outside it. For so much is clear to anyone of impartial mind: if nature is nothing except the holy and eternally productive primal cosmic power that creates and actively produces all things out of itself, yet its product – the world with everything in it at each moment of its **actual and explicit** existence – is **not**, then the **productive cause** of this world that moves from eternity to eternity from one form of nothing to another would have itself to be, like the effect, nothingness. The whole being of this cause is nothing but its activity, and at every moment it carries out absolutely everything that it is able to carry out. Its present is no more perfect than its past, and its future will not be any more perfect than its present. In fact, it does not produce anything but rather modifies itself eternally; that means, as already stated: **it eternally gives birth to time only**. Its production in an unbroken mutation is its only life and the only content of its life; it lives and does all that it does only through this; it has no higher purpose; its life has no **content**.

We have reached this result by seeking to determine at its very ground the concept of nature as one of an **autonomous** being that does not presuppose anything outside itself as its cause and does not produce anything outside itself as its effect, but is rather itself every cause and effect, the world and the creator of the world, the perfect equivalence of these two. We made our finding on the basis of the non-thought of an identity (an *idem esse*) of being and non-being, an identity that however had to be the identity of the unconditioned and the conditioned, of necessity and freedom – not, however, the identity of the revealed nothing: **in truth**, the identity of reason and un-reason, good and evil, thing and non-thing.

[101] **Indeed!** Let us repeat it more emphatically and incisively: "**the identity of reason and un-reason, good and evil, thing and non-thing**," for on this opposition alone, the inextricable **dualism of supernatural and natural, freedom and necessity, providence and blind destiny or chance**, does the human reason rest.[77] It arises out of these oppositions **that together form just one and the same opposition**; so that as the **reality, objectivity** and perfect truthfulness of the original contrast between the natural and supernatural, **or** between necessity and freedom, **or** between providence and blind destiny, are lost, the reality of reason itself, its truthfulness and dignity, are lost too. Consequently, with reason and through reason the human being would have nothing over animals without reason except the advantage of errors and lies.

To shed light on the truth of this claim, we want to take a somewhat closer look at the general division of the living beings of our earth: those endowed with reason and those deprived of it.

We unanimously call **rational** only that being in whose consciousness we find clearly expressed the aforementioned opposition – presented in many ways, but always one and the same – of natural and supernatural; by contrast, all those beings in whom the faculty of such a distinction, such a twofold consciousness, **does not** appear, are no less unanimously called **non-rational** or **deprived of reason** [102].

In our understanding, we attribute a specific kingdom to the countless genera and species of the latter beings and call it the **animal kingdom**. In that

---

77 Chance is the opposite of **intention**; it is not the opposite of **necessity**. It is synonymous with blind fate. We say that we succeed in doing something by chance or by blind fate when we do something unintentionally or unaware, when something springs up from us but unintended and unforeseen. To cause unintentionally is a blind doing, not an action. We do not say that nature **acts**, but only that it **operates**. This explains the opposition between the products of nature according to the laws of necessity, without freedom, and the works of **art** or **providence**, through and with free will. In every epoch where there has been philosophy, there have been philosophers who held the unconscious and involuntary activity higher than the conscious and intentional one, because the first appeared to them as the original activity. See supplement B. [Cerutti duly notes that here Jacobi refers to Schelling's *System des transzendentalen Idealismus*.]

ON THE DIVINE THINGS AND THEIR REVELATION

kingdom, as well as in the rest of nature, the **entire kingdom** of living and life-less beings, there rules only the law of strength. Overwhelming corporal pleasure and overwhelming corporal pain, the greater sensory desire and the greater sensory disgust, which are even greater, unstoppably and irresistibly exert supreme power across the immense animal kingdom. **Unstoppably and irresistibly** because in no living being lacking reason do we find anything that invites or drives it toward something that exceeds the life of its own body or species; the animal is absolutely one and the same with its body so that **being** (Sein) **and consciousness** coincide in it perfectly and one should rather say of it that its body governs the soul instead of the soul governing the body. Thus, the animal possesses neither knowledge nor conscience; it does not possess any cognition of the true and the good, nor does it possess **resolution** or self-determination: the animal is entirely driven by instinct. And since it knows nothing about itself, it knows no **purpose**. Like every being that belongs to the natural kingdom only, it is subjected and completely abandoned to an unavoidable destiny.

Above the animal kingdom, as above the entire kingdom of nature that includes both animate and inanimate beings, rises the **kingdom of spirits**. In this kingdom rules the love of the beautiful and the good, intention and cognition – wisdom, **providence**. The highest attribute of the spirit is that destiny does not prevail over it but rather it, **the spirit**, prevails over destiny. By virtue of this attribute, the spirit is creative and its creative power matches its freedom; in every being the degree of the former is exactly equal to the degree of the latter.

It is undeniable that the **human being** belongs to the natural, animal kingdom; but it is equally undeniable that he **also** belongs to the kingdom of spirits and, as a well-known and accurate saying goes, he is a citizen of two different worlds marvellously related to each other: a visible world and an invisible one, a sensory world and a suprasensible one. He is greatly conscious of this double belonging. He knowingly hovers between the sensory and natural on the one hand, and the suprasensible and supernatural on the other. The human being senses and knows that he is at the same time subjected to [103] nature and raised over it; and he calls what, in him, rises above nature his noblest and best part, his reason and freedom.

That being said, the spirit that inside the human being rises above nature is by no means a spirit contrary or hostile to nature, it does not want to tear the man from the man: such a division would mean annihilation. Everything that exists, except God, belongs to nature, and cannot stand but in connection with it. Hence, everything outside God is **finite**, and nature is the **sum total of what is finite**. Annihilating nature would entail the annihilation of creation: a foolish wish, but one that the sages of this world have expressed in the most different ways. Even recently the advice rang loudly: human being, make up your mind, cease to be yourself and let God alone exist, only then will you be helped and blessed.

Nature is the beginning of all things. In the beginning, says the oldest and most venerable tradition, in the beginning God created heavens and earth, light burst out, elements moved and split up: a universe appeared.

And God spoke to the earth: **Let the earth** bring forth grass and herbs yielding seed; and fertile trees, so that each would bear fruit according to its species and have its seed in it on the earth. And so it was.

And God spoke to the waters: **Let water be enlivened** with living beasts moving back and forth under it and over [its] vast expanse, and with fowls that fly above lands under the vastness of the sky.

And again God spoke to the earth: **Let the earth bring forth** living beasts, each after its species; cattle, creeping thing, and beast, over lands, each after its species: and it was so.

At the end God spoke neither to the earth, nor to the waters, nor to the whole of nature, but **to Himself** did He speak: let us create man, in **Our image**, after Our likeness.

And **God Himself** created man and immediately gave him the **spirit** from His spirit. Such is the human being, that in him there be the breath of God the **almighty**, the **creator** of nature, the **origin**, the absolutely **independent** and **free** [104].

The **consciousness** of the spirit is called **reason**. But **spirit** can only be immediately from God. Therefore, having reason and knowing God is one and the same; just like not knowing God and being an animal is one and the same.

There can never be in the human being an ignorance of God as there is in animals that lack reason. He **must** think God and he can only **deny** Him, just as he can deny his freedom and the spirit within him. He can deny Him indeed, but never totally destroy the knowledge of Him deep in his **conscience**.

Hence, the moment the human being recognizes himself as one who is free, which means, as a being raised above nature by virtue of reason, a being that has been commanded to create the good and the beautiful according to a model that is innate in him; the moment he so recognizes himself, he also recognizes that there must be a supreme being above nature and above himself: **God!** And to the extent that he **does not** so recognize himself as a free being

– independent of nature in virtue of his spirit – he also does not recognize God but sees **only nature** everywhere.

Nature is the power that in the universe keeps all its parts apart and at the same time in connection. In nature separation and connection presuppose each other; **to abide halfway constitutes the being of all natural beings**. From this come space and time, as well as that indivisible concatenation of everything with everything, the ground and abyss of human science and cognition with their infinite wealth and infinite emptiness. What occurs in nature occurs according to the law of the interrelation of all its reciprocally presupposing parts, which means, in an absolutely necessary and purely mechanical way.[78] By itself nature exerts neither wisdom nor goodness; only violence everywhere. It is what operates without freedom, knowledge, or will; only the law of strength rules in it. As the old saying goes, wherever goodness and wisdom are missing and only the law of strength prevails, there is no sublimity, hence no majesty: "Sine bonitate nulla majestas!"[79]

[105] Since nature, which is identical with the universe and manifests itself in it, is pure beginning and end without beginning nor end, and, in this sense, is therefore clearly a **negative** infinity, it is impossible to lay its foundation **within it**, or to explain it **from itself**; impossible to investigate and extract from it its origin and very beginning, in such a way that its being (*Seyn*) and essence (*Wesen*) would without contradiction reveal themselves as an absolutely autonomous being (*Seyn*) and essence (*Wesen*); indeed, as the absolutely unique being that is everything in everything and apart from which nothing exists.

Yet to demonstrate the opposite is equally impossible, namely that nature is a **product** and **not God**; that it is **not** creator and creature at the same time, and that in truth it is not the only being. Any conclusion drawn from the unfathomable character of nature that there is a cause outside it that must have originally produced it, was, is, and will remain wrong, a philosophically unjustifiable conclusion.[80]

---

78 The **living** mechanism that develops from the inside is called **organism**. On the concept of mechanism in its broader sense, see Kant, *Critique of Practical Reason*, 173. [Kant, *Critique of Practical Reason*, 79–80.]
79 [Without Goodness there cannot be Majesty.]
80 [Kant, *Critique of Pure Reason*, B 631–42.]

186 ON THE DIVINE THINGS AND THEIR REVELATION

Among the numerous efforts made to overcome this or that impossibility in philosophy, the two opposite parties of the naturalists and the theists have always referred to one and the same principle, the **principle of the unconditioned**, one way or another. And every time with and without good reason.

That every becoming necessarily presupposes a being (Seyn) or an **existing thing** which has not become yet; that every being subject to change and therefore to time presupposes something eternal not subject to change, and that anything conditioned presupposes an unconditioned **absolute:** this is a truth that all philosophers unanimously recognize as a presupposition of reason or as a positive revelation through it; they only disagree over the question whether this absolute is a **ground** or a **cause.** Naturalism asserts that it is a ground and **not** a cause, whereas theism claims it is a **cause** and **not** a **ground.**[81]

The presupposition of an absolute or unconditioned before any conditioned and the cognition that the latter cannot be [106] without the former are as necessary for the rational consciousness and a cognition essentially innate to it as are *pari passu* for the human understanding a presupposition and a cognition absolutely **inconceivable** for it.

The presupposition of the unconditioned is an inconceivable presupposition because, while it apodictically claims a relationship of all that is conditioned to a single unconditioned, it does not in any way reveal the real interconnection between the two. To conceive this interconnection, one would have to get to the bottom of how the conditioned has risen from the unconditioned that reason immediately presupposes; in other words, how from the absolute one, unchangeable and eternal, has risen the non-one, the changeable, transitory, and temporal: it could have risen out of that unconditioned either once and for all, or continuously, from eternity to eternity, not as a product but as something which in truth is **one-and-the-same** with that unconditioned.

We cannot do either the one or the other: the **being of becoming** or **temporality** is and remains inconceivable to human understanding, as does the **becoming of becoming** or the **coming into being** of temporality. This led a few philosophers audaciously to deny all temporality, change, and modification, all coming into being and away, as if they were nothing in **true actuality.** For them, the appearance of finite things, of the actual, material, and **real-objective** world is a mere deceit of a faculty of representation (no one knows

---

81 About the essential difference between ground (*Grund*) and cause (*Ursache*), see *David Hume*, 93 [see JWA 3, 226], and the supplement VII of *Concerning the Doctrine of Spinoza*, second edition.

ON THE DIVINE THINGS AND THEIR REVELATION
187

which and of what kind) that is thus necessarily given to a dualistic game.[82] This way out [107] does not however do the job: it does not help because it exceeds its purpose. In order to explain nature, the existence of a universe determined in all its parts by the law of causation and by **temporality**, it fundamentally abolishes and annihilates nature and the universe, together with the understanding that refers to them, resting entirely on the principle of causality. By coming to the insight that nature is the **mother of all things**, a being endlessly **producing** the infinite in infinite ways, one would then indeed think in truth she is not; that the unconditioned alone, the immutably eternal called God, rather is. This God that alone is; obtained by destroying the temporal, which means destroying all finite existence and efficacy; who can only be caught sight of by disregarding the **law of generation**; this God, since He has **in truth** not created anything, no nature, no world outside Himself, nothing at all, and would therefore be, in absolutely no way a **cause**, but rather only infinite ground and abyss (a totality, an All-one) – this God, I say, even if it were an agent, would nonetheless be incapable of anything except the production within Him of an empty time, a mere and totally unproductive alteration – which alteration would then portray itself as a creation, not **out of** nothing, but **of** nothing, as shown earlier.[83]

Transformation and time condition each other as do cause and effect. Cause without effect is a non-thought; equally so, cause and effect without time. Annihilating time while pretending to uphold effectiveness, an infinite **production**, is sheer absurdity. On the contrary, where nothing is brought forth,

82 This assertion can be found, *in nuce*, in early Antiquity as well as in the third chapter of the first book of *Metaphysics* where Aristotle states that: "however true it may be that everything comes into being and perishes from one or many, then follows the question: why does it happen and what is its cause? Matter does not cause its own modification, e.g., wood and bronze are not the cause of their own modification, neither wood becomes a bed on its own, nor bronze becomes a statue, but there is an external cause for their modification. And to seek this is to seek a different principle that I call the principle of motion. Those who from the beginning had followed this way and accepted only **one** matter, made things easier. Among them a few, almost overwhelmed by this investigation, stated **that this one is unmovable**. They did not deny just the coming to life and the death of the whole nature (which is the old and common opinion), **but they deny also any other modification**; this is their characteristic" (according to Fülleborn, *Beyträge*, B. I., 159–60). [Aristotle, *Metaphysics*, A, 3, 984a18–984b1.]

83 This doctrine may seem absurd in its final result; one understands, however, that it could have emerged and have won many supporters **even among the most perceptive thinkers**. See supplement C. [Spinoza, *Ethics*, II, prop. 44, corollary II.]

188   ON THE DIVINE THINGS AND THEIR REVELATION

nothing would unfold, nothing would continually rise up to be; nor also would there be time. And [108] with full reason is therefore said that time – for itself and considered as a particular being – is a non-thing. Yet temporal being exists; with equal certainty a world, a nature, and **what** we call will and understanding, resolution and execution, self-satisfaction and remorse, deserved reward and deserved punishment, human reason and human conscience exist.

Said the ancients (and the moderns confirm it): from nature **comes the rising-to-be, the proliferating, and the passing-away**[84] – but whence nature?

Unperturbed, the naturalist answers: you are thoughtlessly asking where that which is first comes from, the uncreated creator of all, the origin – you are asking where God comes from. He is, and together with Him and through Him there is a creation that we unanimously call the universe, for that is the **creator** of the universe, **God.** The existence of the universe necessarily appears to us as a miracle, as **something impossible**, because the human understanding conceives **possible** only what can or might **become, have an origin.** The universe is however necessarily as eternal as the creator. And since even the most profound **theist** would not deny it, namely, that God necessarily created from eternity, no less than the naturalist is he thereby tormented by the question of how the finite could have been generated from the infinite; the non-one from the one; what is temporal and changeable from what is eternal and unchangeable, or how the former can proceed uninterruptedly from the latter. No matter which of the two views one chooses – either to assume with the naturalist that the unconditioned or the absolute presupposed by reason is only the substratum of the conditioned in the way the **One** is to the **All**, or to agree with the theist that this unconditioned or absolute is a free and self-conscious cause analogous to a rational will; that it is a supreme intelligence that operates for a purpose – in either case it remains equally impossible to explain the existence of the universe from a First conceived as an **origin.**

Because of the balance in which naturalism and theism stand before science, the latter must in true fairness declare itself completely neutral as regards both [109]. Science does not refrain from doing what is right as soon as the understanding, to which the former belongs as its property and creature, reaches self-cognition and renounces the vain hope of gradually rising together with science – **the echo of an echo** – to omniscience,[85] and so, by means of cognition,

84 [Aristotle, *Metaphysics*, A, 3, 983b 8–18.]
85 [Cerutti argues that this is the only reference to Hegel that we find in the text. Cerutti, "Notes et Commentaires," 214.]

ON THE DIVINE THINGS AND THEIR REVELATION 189

of becoming equal to the creator of all things and, in truth, even **subjugating** him to itself.

But it is only with the highest reluctance that the understanding can give up its vain hope of bringing science to perfection, of rising with it and through it **above** reason, and thus to gain the highest respect for itself. And even after it has given it up, this same vain desire is always newly revived in it, involuntarily. For the Pauline words, "the flesh craves what is contrary to the spirit, and the spirit what is contrary to the flesh: they are in conflict with each other" can also be said of the understanding and reason in the human being.[86] In the case of the flesh and the spirit, the flesh is **revealed**, and nobody can deny that it is or that it has power; the spirit however remains **hidden**, and that it is and that it makes itself known as the more powerful can be denied. So, too, for the understanding and reason in their domain of reflection, in their case with regard to what the understanding **proves** to be true and what reason instead merely **reveals** as the superior truth. The mediated faculty of cognition rises above the unmediated; the conditioned knowledge above the unconditioned; lifeless echo above the living voice that announces the spirit; **understanding above reason,** just as appetites and passions rise above conscience, overpower it, and appear as alone to have true power.

This original antagonism, grounded in the sensory and rational nature of the human being and therefore never to be wholly eradicated, is the single reason why there can be diametrically opposed philosophical systems, and why, from earliest times to the present, there have been so many of them and so different. For the same reason, the differences can all be reduced to one major one: the systems were either **theistic** or **anti-theistic**; or, as Kant would rather say it, some have tended to **Platonism** while others to **Epicureanism**[87] [110].

One becomes either a naturalist or a theist depending on whether one subjugates reason to the understanding or the understanding to reason; or, which is the same, depending on whether one accepts or denies, besides the existence **in nature** of necessity, the existence of freedom **above it.**

Reason affirms the existence of freedom and yet does not deny the existence of necessity and its boundless power **in the entire field of nature devoid of reason.** On the other hand, the understanding utterly denies the existence of freedom, because it starts from the law of causality regarded as the highest of laws and the uppermost principles (namely, the **universal law**, according to

86 [Ga. 5:17.]
87 [Kant, *Critique of Pure Reason*, B 499.]

ON THE DIVINE THINGS AND THEIR REVELATION

which any effect must have a cause just as any cause must necessarily have an effect). The law of causality however devolves into the following proposition: **nothing is unconditioned, there is no supreme, uppermost, first being, nor is there a starting point, an absolute beginning.**

Nevertheless, the understanding cannot directly dispose of the idea of the unconditioned that reason imposes on it as the necessary presupposition for every conditioned; it cannot do it lest it loses the idea of causality with it. Cause, conceived as a mere concept of the understanding, is meaningless, fraught with contradiction; it can receive its content, truth, and meaning only from reason, from the **feeling** that I am, I act, I create and produce. Human understanding rests entirely on this **feeling**, thus it rests on **reason**; the former is based on the latter and presupposes it necessarily as something higher.

The understanding allegedly saves itself from this confusion by **disputing** the objective validity of the idea of the unconditioned and **imputing** only a subjective validity to it. Everything in the human faculty of cognition is entirely turned upside down by this artificial transformation of the unconditioned that makes something **real** into a mere **ideal**. Reason is handed over to the understanding and the philosophy of the absolute nothing begins. For if nothing is truly unconditional, nothing is then everywhere; then, together with being also truth ceases to be.

All this gets hidden from the understanding because a second transformation immediately follows upon the first. To wit: the subjective turns into the objective. An illusion, a ghost of the unconditioned takes the place of the true unconditioned [111], so that, just as before the true was deceivingly turned into a poetic fiction, now the poetic fiction, deceivingly again, is turned into the true.

This illusion, this ghost, this **idol** that the understanding creates for itself after having denied the superior authority of reason, lowering it under its supervision and rule to a mere faculty of fiction-making; this idol, which the understanding is now eager to raise above itself in the place of reason, invoking and deifying it, is called **totality**; in truth, it is only an ever-expanding **universal** that comes to be in the understanding through concept and word, nowhere to be found outside it – neither as one, nor as many, nor as all.[88]

Further, in the understanding the universal first comes to be after the individual, the concept after perception.[89] However, as soon as the concept is formed, it rises above perception and considers what it encompasses within

---

88   [Remark is present only in the second edition.] See volume 2, 77–84 [see JWA 3, 227].

89   To deny it is to confuse the undetermined with the universal. This happened and still happens here and there to very perceptive thinkers. The mere fact of not

itself – the infinity of different individuals – as having derived from itself, and considers itself and its son, the word, as both the ground and the cause of being.

It is easy to explain this illusion, to show how it grows and takes hold!

First comes the excitement of the senses. A cloudy flow of multifarious sensations inundates the mind, boiling and thundering. Then, gradually, out of this fluid element, something solid emerges; we make distinctions, we judge, conceive, count, and give names. An understanding is born; a world is born.

But just as this world came to be through **conceptual construction**, by division and connection, separation and arrangement, so it also eventually vanishes in the **ideal** of an ultimate concept that swallows up and destroys all multiplicity. All that remains is thought as thought, only the nothing as nothing facing it. And so falls the human being, with his understanding [112] and because of it, back into chaos, into shapelessness; with only one visible difference: the earlier chaos was a full one; the present chaos is empty.

The empty chaos is shapeless, the **absolutely indetermined** (Plato and the Pythagoreans named it the Infinite)[90]; it is the unconditioned, the absolute of the **understanding**; it is that phantasm that the understanding raises above the absolute of reason and in which it imagines recognizing the being of all beings, the only true objective **All and One**.

Were the philosophizing understanding, as it climbs to ever wider concepts, really capable at the end to attain its sought-after **ideal concept**, the same that swallows up and destroys all multiplicity, then, with the **end** of things it would have also found their beginning.

We say: **with the end also the beginning**. For the understanding, once it would have climbed **by way of abstraction** from the determinate to the absolutely indeterminate, it could comfortably climb down (turning back) from the absolutely indeterminate to the determinate **by way of reflection**. At its bidding, all things would resurrect, coming out of non-thing. Just as it was able to **annihilate** them, it could also with necessity recreate them all. The identity of being and non-being would be brought to light.

---

differentiating differs in every way from that of integrating under a precisely determining characteristic feature. The conscious indifference under one concept is different also from the unconscious mixing in a cloudy representation. This difference is similar to the one Spinoza speaks of **between the fact of being certain and the fact of simply not doubting**. [Spinoza, *Ethics*, II, prop. 49, schol.]

90 [Plato, *Philebus*, 25c. Aristotle, *Metaphysics*, A, 5, 986a 15–21.]

I am who I am. This sovereign proclamation grounds everything. Its echo in the human soul is the revelation of God in it: "**made in His image, a likeness of Him, of the One who is in Himself.**" By creating the human being God theomorphized him (*theomorphisirt*); necessarily then the human being anthropomorphizes (*anthropomorphisirt*). What makes the human being a human being, i.e., an **image of God**, is **reason**.[91] Reason begins with the "I am." **In the beginning was the Word.** Where this inner **word – expressing the** [113] **self-likeness** (*das sich selbst Gleiche aussprechende*) – resounds, there reason is, there the person is, there freedom is. Reason without personality is a non-thing, the same non-thing as that **fundamental matter** or that **original ground** which is all and not one, or one and none, or perfection of imperfection, the absolutely indeterminate. And this is called **God** by those who do not want to know anything of the true God, and yet hesitate to deny Him with their lips.[92]

I am who I am, who I was, and who I will be. Past, present, and future are indissolubly united in the feeling of the autonomous being, being in itself. This is the **consciousness of the spirit**, this is "**the seal impressed on us by the Eternal.**"

"Nature gave even to animals some notions of mathematics and physics with unequalled perfection. But to go back thousands of years to see **Jamshid** in the sacred hall of the royal castle imparting order and justice to the people of Iran, or, in recent times, to listen to [114] **Livy**, to learn from **Leonidas** how to die and from **William Tell** how to liberate people: this, you human!, only a human can do!"[93]

---

91 [Footnote is present in the second edition.] See the remark at 236 of this third volume [JWA 3, 28].

92 "**Without the world, there is no God**: this is the formula that expresses most simply and clearly what naturalism is. But all religions have always reversed that proposition and taught: **without God, there is no world**. Faith in God is given to us before any intuition of the world; **with our I is already posited an original-I**. Deep inside our mind we see the original image of life, and we see it reverberating through the veiled countenance of Nature, and we are astonished, we love and worship: and that is religion; it is not a chemical process of identity whereby we throw both ourselves and nature in a mix that makes up a chaotic mass, while giving up our life, that of nature and God added to it." See *Jenaische Allgemeine Lit. Zeitung*, 1807, no. 131.

93 See Joh. Müller's *Vorrede* zu Herder's *Die Vorwelt*. [Jamshid is one of the first

ON THE DIVINE THINGS AND THEIR REVELATION

"It is not what you see (even the animal observes),
It is not what you hear (even the animal perceives),
It is not what you learn (even the raven learns),
It is what you understand and conceive; it is the power
That in you works, the inner prophetess;
Who from the past world makes herself the future world;
The one who orders, untangling the skein, weaves with the yarn of nature
The beautiful tapestry within and without you;
That is what you, **yourself,** are; and the divinity is like you.

"Divinity"? Yes! Imagine
The chaos of all beings without sense or spirit,
Without a being that pervades everything, which
Is its own rule and that of everything; imagine
The great madness of this most sensible
Nature, and throw yourself insanely into
The desolate chaos that doesn't know itself:
Then **you** would be a **Self,** even if nothing else is.
Return to yourself! In your innermost
Consciousness lives a talking proof
Of the supreme **consciousness of the whole.** – Be an animal,
Lose **yourself,** but will you then be surprised, you fool,
That you have lost the deity in losing yourself?

"The essence of harmony" – An empty word,
With no listener. Listen to it, you, deep
In your heart, in the deepest silence,
In union with the choirs of the worlds,
[115] Your heart names it: It, the **highest Self,** sense
and spirit, the being of all beings, God."94

Persian kings. According to the *Vendidad,* he received the order to bring the law to
human beings and build the enclosure for the elect. Livy was a Roman historian
who lived between 59 BCE and 17 CE; he is the author of the famous *Ab urbe
condita* (From the Founding of the City), that covers the history of Rome from the
legendary arrival of Aeneas to emperor Augustus. Leonidas was the king of Sparta
who famously fought Xerxes' troops at the Thermopylae. William Tell is a folk hero
of Switzerland who rebelled against the brutal rule of Albrecht Gessler.]

94 See J.G. Herder, *Zerstörte Blätter,* VI, 78.

ON THE DIVINE THINGS AND THEIR REVELATION

If a childish manner of representation, not one sublime like this, but one that therefore anthropomorphizes, so that God appears trapped in a bodily shape like the human being; a God with hands and feet, in need of eyes to see, ears to hear, and a sensitive and reflective understanding to know and to will – then reason justly rises up against such a foolish manner of representation.

But reason should be even more outraged, if, by divinizing nature, you teach about a God who creates eyes but does not see, devises ears but does not hear, produces the understanding and has neither perception nor knowledge, nor will; who is nothing.[95] Do say it: there is no God! But do not say and do not teach: darkness is light, a rational being is a non-divine being, the coral that produces islands in the sea is more similar to God than the human being who thinks, strives for virtue and holiness, and reveals love, wisdom, the beautiful and the good. Do not say either: the original and universal being appears in the human being **transfigured and undiminished**,[96] for only in appearance and deceptively would **such an anthropomorphism** be better than the old fetishism, the worship of plants, animals, lingam, and Moloch.[97]

What there is to honour in the human being if not the fact that it is able to think what is higher than its reason, more magnificent than the universe: the **spirit** that alone is absolutely autonomous and the source of all truth, and without which no truth is possible?

Therefore, we profess an anthropomorphism that is inseparably tied to the conviction that the human being carries in itself the image of God and maintains that apart from this anthropomorphism – which has always been called theism – there is only atheism or **fetishism.**

To eradicate the idolatrous worship of nature among his people, one of the greatest legislators [116] and heroes of antiquity, **Moses**, kept his people in the desert for forty years. As a consequence, after centuries, the Jewish people made a **Christian people** possible.[98]

---

95 [Ps. 94:9.]

96 [Schelling's *Über das Verhältnis der bildenden Künste zu der Natur*, in Schelling, *Sämtliche Werke*, 7:304, 319 and 321.]

97 [A lingam is a votary object that refers to Shiva and symbolizes generative power. Moloch was a Canaanite deity associated with the practice of child sacrifice: "You shall not give any of your children to devote them by fire to Moloch, and so profane the name of your God" (Leviticus 18:21).]

98 "It is impossible to say, says Herder, what treasures of cognition and morality accrue to the human race from the concept of the unity of God. The human race turned away from superstition, from idolatry, from the vices and horrors of divinely privileged disorder, and became accustomed to see in everything unity of

ON THE DIVINE THINGS AND THEIR REVELATION

These days, two men very different from one another and yet equally remarkable, J.K. Lavater and J.G. Hamann, remembered these words of St John's: "Whosoever denieth the Son, the same hath not the Father."[99] Everyone declared them fanatics, **visionaries devoted to the idolatry of a human being,** filled with ignorance, superstition, and intolerance [117].

Is it really ignorance and fanaticism to confess that one believes in God not because of the nature that hides God, but because of the supernatural in the human being, which alone is what reveals and proves Him?[100]

Nature hides God because everywhere it reveals only fate, an unbreakable chain of mere effective (*wirkend*) causes with neither beginning nor end: it excludes with the same necessity both providence and chance. Independent activity, a free original beginning, is absolutely impossible, whether in it or originating from it. Nature operates without will and refers to neither the good nor the beautiful; nor does it create but devotes itself, aimlessly and unconsciously, out of its dark abyss, only to a perpetual transformation of itself, contributing with the same restless zeal to both decline and growth, life and

---

aim, and therefore gradually the natural laws of wisdom, love and goodness; became accustomed to find unity in multiplicity, order in disorder, light in darkness. From the concept of one creator the world came to be considered as a united whole (κόσμος), as did its reflection, the mind of men, which learned wisdom, order, and beauty. Every doctrine or poetry of the earth which has contributed to that has resulted in the most useful things. The Hebrew poetry excelled in this respect. It has been the oldest dam against idolatry, of which we have any knowledge. It poured the first beautiful beam of the light of unity and order into the chaos of creation – and by its loftiness and truth, its simplicity and wisdom, it gradually became the leader of the world." J.G. Herder, *Geist der Ebräischen Poesie*, I ed., first part, 51–2, in *Sämmtliche Werke*, part I, 59, 60.

It has often been remarked that a man like Christ could have been born only among the Jewish people, and no philosophical historian can deny it.

Regarding Christianity as historical event, its development out of Judaism, its spirit, its influence as religion over humankind, and finally the relation of this religion to philosophy, as well as their reciprocal influence on each other, one can find a highly instructive treatise in volume VII of Tennemann's *Geschichte der Philosophie* (Haupt 5. Abschnitt 1).

Joh. Müller in the sixth chapter of the ninth book of his universal history also says outstanding things about this topic.

99   [Jn. 2:23.]

100   [Footnote is present in the second edition.] Here and in the immediately following paragraph, the reader can compare what we say with what has been said in the *Vorrede* to the third volume [JWA 3, 140–53] concerning the scandal caused by the author of the mentioned review [JWA 3, 28ff] of the text about the divine things.

196 ON THE DIVINE THINGS AND THEIR REVELATION

death – unable to produce what comes only from God and presupposes freedom: virtue and immortality.

The human being reveals God insofar as he rises above nature through spirit, and thanks to this spirit, sets himself against nature as an independent and undefeatable power: he fights, overpowers, and dominates it.

The human being vividly believes in this power that lives in him and is superior to nature as much as he believes in God: he feels Him and experiences Him. If he does not believe in this power in him, then he does not believe in God either, and sees, and everywhere does he experience only nature, necessity, and fate.

If nature alone existed, it would be the **almighty** and nowhere would there be a holy will. Then a **Tiberius** and **Nero, Ezzelino** and **Borgia** would be possible, but not **Socrates** or **Christ**.

Truly, therefore, did the **Saint** testify of himself when he said that the one who recognizes him, also recognizes the Father; and that the one who [118] believes in him, does not believe in him, but **in the one he has come from.**[101]

Christianity, **conceived in this purity**, is the only religion. Apart from it there is only atheism and idolatry.

When the fourth son of the mother of the Maccabees, after having endured without flinching, like his brothers, the most terrible martyrdom, cheerfully dies pronouncing these words: **it is beautiful to lose all hope in human beings and entrust oneself only to God,**[102] every human heart repeats after him these sublime words and testifies that there exists only one God and one God-given spirit in the human breast, invincible against sin and death.

Job, proving his virtue and justifying the promise made to him by the Creator, sat on his heap of ashes as if it were God's glory and pride. God, together with His heavenly army, looked on as he endured his misfortune. – He won and his victory is a triumph beyond the stars. The author of that story – whether it is history or poetic fiction – was a seer of God.[102]

And now he, "the purest among the mighty, the mightiest among the pure, who with his pierced hand toppled empires, made the stream of centuries overflow, and continues to command the times!"[104] – Who could ever acknowledge

101   [Jn. 5:23.]
102   [2 Macc. 7:13.]
103   See Herder von *Geist der Ebräischen Poesie*, vol. 1, 143 erste Ausg. *Sämmtlichen Werke*, part I, 140.
104   Friedrich Richter, *Ueber den Gott in der Geschichte und im Leben*, in *Jean Paul's Sämmtliche Werke*, vol. 7.3 (Berlin: Reimer, 1827).

ON THE DIVINE THINGS AND THEIR REVELATION

that he was and at the same time say: there is no God, there is no providence, no love that rules over dark fate, over blind chance?

Nonetheless – "Go I straight forward, He is not there; turn I back, I do not find any trace of Him!"[105] Christ himself on the cross let out this piercing cry: "My God, my God, why hast thou forsaken me?"[106] But he expired with the words: "Into thy hands I commend [119] my spirit!"[107] Thus spoke the mightiest among the pure, the purest among the mighty. This fight and this victory is Christianity. And the author of this work professes his faith in this Christianity and with this profession of faith brings his work to an end.

105   [Job 23:8.]
106   [Mt. 27:46.]
107   [Lk. 23:46.]

Supplement A
To page 165

[120] As regards the system of absolute identity, Spinoza was not simply its forerunner: he was its founder and the first to teach it. The true great philosophical act of this discreet and profound thinker, an act that has not yet been recognized or praised as it deserves, consists in the fact that he for the first time made a **pure distinction** (*Trennung*) without **separation** (*Scheidung*) between thinking being and extended being. Since his second definition reads as follows, *at corpus non terminatur cogitatione, nec cogitatio corpore*,[1] he creatively grounded his new system that – de facto and in truth – is the same as the more recent system of object-subjectivity, or the system of the absolute identity between being and consciousness.

Spinoza posited this double proposition as a self-evident and foundational truth, a proposition that does not need any proof: thinking being can no more be derived from extended being as a consequence, a modification, or an effect than, conversely, extended being can from thinking being. That is: neither matter can generate spirit, nor spirit matter. Both, he concluded, are necessarily and from eternity united in the one and indivisible substance: they are consubstantial and relate to each other like being and consciousness.

Spirit and body do not determine each other, they do not rule over or subjugate one another; they both, in the strictest sense, constitute together one and the same being: the spirit is nothing other and nothing more than the soul of a body, it is "the immediate concept of a single thing really present, and it

---

1 [Spinoza, *Ethics*, I, Def. 2.]

SUPPLEMENT A   199

is nothing beyond that. It is therefore impossible that perfection, excellence, and power of the soul are different than perfection, excellence, and power of the body, etc."[2] [121].

Accordingly, in no way can Spinoza's extended being be considered a matter to which thinking being gives shape, as is the case in Plato, for whom the soul is **cause** and everywhere the first principle.[3] For Spinoza, extended being is **everything that is, exists, and operates objectively** (according to his lexicon, **formally**); it is, strictly speaking, the **real**. Thinking being, by contrast, is the being that produces representations only in conformity with the real. Therefore, although he clearly distinguishes the former from the latter, *essentia objectiva* from *essentia formalis*,[4] spiritual being from corporeal being, his doctrine, in fact, is wholly materialistic. This is because thinking being, notwithstanding its independence vis-à-vis extended being, does not have any other object of representation and thinking other than that extended being.[5]

In order that this system of absolute objectivity be transformed into a system of absolute subjectivity, extended being had first to be deprived of substantiality. Malebranche, Leibniz, and Berkeley tried to demonstrate the non-substantiality of extended being. Necessarily, thinking being remained the only substantial being, but only until an even more perceptive thinker stepped in and demonstrated in relation to thinking being what his predecessors had demonstrated exclusively with regard to extended being, namely that thinking being, as a substantial being, could only pass as appearance.[6] The *cogito*, conceived as a merely transferred predicate, could not pronounce its *ergo* anymore: it had lost its *sum* and, with it, it had lost reality in general.

And so was through our Kant, totally against his intentions, a second Spinozism established that I have elsewhere called **transfigured** Spinozism.[7] On

---

2 "Objectum ideae humanam mentem constituentis est corpus sive certus extensionis modus actu existens et nihil aliud." *Ethica*, Pars II, Prop 13.

3 [Plato, *Laws*, X, 892a–c.]

4 [Spinoza, *Treatise on the Emendation of the Intellect*, in *Opera Posthuma*, 366–7.]

5 Mens se ipsam non cognoscit, nisi quatenus corporis affectionum ideas percipit: ["The mind does not know itself, except insofar as it perceives the ideas of the affections of the body." Translation is mine.] *Ethica*, Pars II, Prop 23.

6 [Kant, *Critique of Pure Reason*, B 399–432.]

7 In the *Letter to Fichte* (1799). To put it briefly, it is indicated there (2–4) how speculative materialism, by developing its own metaphysics, must by itself turn into idealism; how these two main routes of philosophy – the effort to explain everything either exclusively on the basis of a matter that defines itself, or solely on the basis of an intelligence that determines itself – are not mutually exclusive, but rather slowly

this view, one could also [122] have distinguished the old system from the new by referring to the one with the name of material-**idealism**, and to the other with that of ideal-**materialism**.[8] Yet the ingenious author of the new system of identity himself showed that in that system it is the same whether one starts from the object or from the subject because, assuming that one philosophizes correctly, one will arrive either way at the same conclusion and at the **whole truth**. In his own way, this is precisely what Spinoza had already done, and nowhere does the great man appear more profound, more sublime, and more amiable than where he reveals, from the bottom of his consciousness, what certainty is and how the soul can participate in it.[9] Here he not only evokes Plato, who professed the innateness of ideas and their objective validity, but he also agrees with him in extraordinary way; and here one finds as *norma veritatis* – under similar or different names – what modern Spinozism calls **intellectual intuition of the absolute**, an expression that in my opinion is not exactly meaningless or reprehensible.[10] We really need a specific term to designate the mode of consciousness in which the true, the good and the beautiful in themselves present themselves to us, revealing themselves as something overabundant, first and supreme, that cannot be represented in any appearance; **by means of** this mode of consciousness, the **ideas, the highest pronouncements** of reason, go over to the understanding as **immediate** cognitions that are not first mediated through the senses; so that, not only does the full feeling of truth and certainty that accompanies sense intuitions undeniably attaches itself [123] to these cognitions, but also, through them, does the entire human mind come first to participate, in manner indescribable, in the most perfect certainty of the true.

---

    draw near each other until they fully touch and lead toward the same goal. I showed that, at bottom, very little was missing for the transformation later undertaken from materialism to idealism to have already been accomplished by Spinoza, because his **substance**, which is the very same ground of both extended being and thinking being, this **one** matter of two completely different beings, means ultimately nothing but the same absolute identity of object and subject, being and consciousness, body and spirit.

8 [Schelling's *Fernere Darstellungen aus dem System der Philosophie*, in Schelling, *Sämtliche Werke*, 4:361 and 368–72.]

9 See *De intellectus emendatione, et de via, qua optime in veram rerum cognitionem dirigitur. opp. posth.*, 357–92. In *Ethica* the different passages that deal with the three kinds of cognition, self-validating truth, and perfect certainty.

10 Yet not according to the judgment of the acute Fries. See *Neue Kritik der Vernunft*, I part, 194, § 53.

SUPPLEMENT A

In the *Critique of Judgment*, Kant says (introduction, xviii): "the concept of nature can well **represent** its objects in intuition, but not as things in themselves; the concept of freedom can instead **represent** its **object** as thing in itself, but not in intuition."[11] My question is why an objective **representation** without **sensible** intuition is not allowed to be called **intellectual** intuition; alternatively, whether it is even possible to think of an objective representation without something analogous to intuition – i.e., without **perception**.

No doubt if the true, the good, and the beautiful in themselves are merely ideas invented out of necessity, if they are concepts of the understanding improperly extended and lacking objective validity, mere **categories of despair**, then an intellectual intuition that validates them is absurd and superfluous because, in all truth, they must not be validated but only explained and made comprehensible as heuristic **fictions**.

In line with an authentic Platonism, I attribute to the reason of all created beings both receptivity and spontaneity, as faculties of perceiving and apprehending, finding and holding, that together constitute the original source of rational truth.[12] In any finite or sense-perceiving being (any finite being is, in fact, necessarily a sense-perceiving being) reason is nothing but the sense of the suprasensible. The corporeal sense is absolutely positive and does only one thing: it reveals; the same goes for the spiritual sense, reason. That is why the understanding philosophizes only by remaining suspended between sense perception and suprasensible perception and by relating to each in equal measure. Ignoring this twofold relationship, some have fanatically blasphemed against the understanding by trusting the suprasensible alone, as if the understanding were applicable only to the totality of the sense perception, to the world of experience. Others, by likewise failing to recognize the twofold relationship and by trusting the sense perception alone, rose up against reason and, with much apparent credibility, interpreted its immediate revelations as mere fictions. Both positions are to be rejected [124]. Nevertheless, it is hardly possible to avoid the second mistake if one rejects intellectual intuition only because it cannot actually be translated into a sense-intuition, a material intuition, i.e., because reason communicates with the understanding only by means of **invisible visions** – the contemplation of presentiment – which we call **feelings** in the most noble sense.

11 [Reference to the *Critique of Judgement*, in Kant, *Gesammelte Schriften*, 5:175.]
12 See *Republic*, VII, X, VI.

ON THE DIVINE THINGS AND THEIR REVELATION

One of the most respectable thinkers of the Middle Age, *Hugh of Saint Victor*, denied that human reason could conceive anything of God and professed only a **faith** which is midway between opinion and knowledge.[13] In fact, he claimed that God cannot be thought according to His being, not even via analogy: God is higher than everything we know, beyond bodies and spirit, and the human being can think only what is **relative**. Faith is therefore the only ground of conviction regarding God's being, since the latter cannot be perceived like external things or the soul itself. But he also adds that one cannot think of a more reliable ground of conviction than **that of believing what reason cannot understand:** "How can all the saints and the righteous, in their desire for eternal life, disregard this present life so unanimously, **if they did not have a presentiment of the truth of eternal life that surpasses our comprehension**"? Excellent idea, Tennemann notes, but it approaches mysticism.[14]

And which superior and profound thought, be it intellectual or moral, would not approach mysticism?

The beginning of our cognition is mystical, absolutely mysterious, as is the incomprehensible presupposition of an original being which contains in itself and produces outside itself all the true, the good, and the beautiful. "It is only by presupposing this hidden principle that we are capable of the concept of truth." We call **reason** the **faculty** that makes this presupposition.

But given that, "once it rises, in the process of reflection, over all sense-intuition, only the concept of nothing remains as its own pure product at the end of a process of abstraction," how does reason arrive at this **presupposition** with which the concept of truth first appears to reason itself [125]?

The answer is: that is precisely the reason why it arrives there!

"Since it is impossible for reason to consider the pure nothing that alone remains at the end of the process of abstraction as the ground and the beginning of both everything and itself, as the substratum of being, the alpha and omega, then reason – out of necessity – posits the opposite of nothing in the place of nothing, the **One that is and acts unconditionally, the Absolute, God.**"

---

13 [Theologian born toward the end of 11th century (1096). He received his education in Hamersleben, at the monastery of Sankt Pankratius. In 1116 he joined the Augustinian Abbey of Saint-Victor. There he taught until his death (1141). Beyond his famous *Didascalion*, a treatise on different learning methods, he is remembered for his highly organized system of theology (*De sacramentis christianae fidei*). One of his pivotal theses refers to the primacy of faith over theology and philosophy. This primacy is not detrimental to the rationality of faith, because that which is revealed to faith alone is above discursive knowledge and yet wholly rational.]

14 See *Geschichte der Philosophie*, Part VIII, 206–12.

SUPPLEMENT A

Or one says: "The source of such a presupposition is an unfathomable **desire** that goes beyond all subjective and objective nature, beyond all concepts, intuitions, and feelings, and with which our nature, **in the highest sense of the term**, holds onto **what is highest**, something simply **incomparable**. Thanks to this desire, reason before itself, **ideally**, the Absolute; reason **searches** for it, **sets** it like an object, but reason never identifies it as an actual being, something that exists outside of it, independent of its representation."

But how are a desire, a search, and an aspiration possible without even an obscure representation of the **object** that one desires, searches for, and aspires to? The painful feeling of hunger, Plato says, can never produce the pleasurable representation of satiety or what brings it about, food. The need as such does not reveal what remedies it: only experience discovers it. But experience itself becomes possible only through a soul **originally** endowed with providence, capable of **divine** prophesies.[15]

If the presupposition of the absolute – the concept of absolute as we defined it earlier – is just a necessary lie with which reason deceives itself, then reason is **a liar from the beginning** since it begins with that presupposition; **indeed, it is totally one and the same with it.**

But if reason is not lying, then it does not draw the concept of the Absolute from itself; rather, it itself **comes** from it and through it: the concept is **given** to reason, and reason itself is also given with it. Just as reason trusts unconditionally the reality of that concept, so it trusts itself. The **way** by which this **reality is attested in reason** is not revealed to the **understanding** [126]; only **the confidence of reason** reflects itself in the understanding, and an undefeatable feeling takes the place of intuition.

If one tries to turn that feeling, these **invisible visions**, the contemplation of presentiment, into visible representations, or to turn the first-hand certainty that we – for lack of a better expression – call **faith** into a second-hand certainty, the unconditional conviction into a conditional one, then in the first case there appears fanaticism, while in the second case there appears empty formalism, an impossible philosophy **of pure logic.**

This is the way in which I believe the expressions of the author of the excellent essay on the *Ideal-Object of Rational Desire* – from which we have earlier extracted a few passages for our considerations – must be interpreted when he claims: "the human understanding that searches for the absolute holds – from the speculative and practical point of view – **firstly and immediately**

---

15 See the *Philebus* the profound analysis and the unmatched exposition of this important truth.

nothing but a purely rational desire which is identical to reason itself, and spurns any different ground."[16] Certainly, this thinker – whose spirit is as rich as it is perceptive – did not simply want to repeat in different words Kant's anti-platonic doctrine of the idea of the absolute!

With regard to the Kantian doctrine of the absolute and of ideas in general, another excellent thinker aptly points out: "Kant's speculative reason is nothing but the simple faculty of inference, the faculty of reflection ... In Kant the **immediate knowledge of reason** is always presupposed **in the dark**, never with **clarity**. Consequently, his practical reason and its faith, which he conceived also only as a fact, remained something very obscure as soon as one asked how one arrives at them. Even in this case, he **immediately** saw only what pertains to the faculty of reflection."

This same rigorous thinker adds: "The distinction according to which **any knowledge of ours is either intuition or** [127] **concept**, is correct only to the extent that we consider it when it becomes an immediate object of internal perception. We become **conscious** of our cognition only in the form of intuitions or through concepts. Only when we do not consider this simple condition of **again becoming conscious** of the cognition in us, but rather consider its **immediate presence in our mind**, is that distinction incomplete: alongside clear **representations** of intuitions and concepts are obscure representations, **and among them one finds, above all, the immediate, inexpressible knowledge of reason**."[17]

When the light breaks through the darkness, it may appear that the former merely developed out of the latter, and the reflection that does not defer to a higher wisdom will inevitably think this way.

Look, First of all Chaos came into being ...
From Chaos were born Erebos and black Night.
From Night, again, were born Aether and Day, the goddess of light,
She conceived and bore both of them after mingling with Erebos.[18]

This ancient doctrine is still the doctrine of the highly regarded wise men. Believing in a providence appears to them as a childish thing, because they can conceive the creative freedom only as **blind chance** and reason only as a **necessity** that intuits itself and is transparent to itself.

16 *Neues Museum der Phil. u. Lit.*, I, folder 2, 37.
17 See Fries, *Neue Kritik der Vernuft*, I, 204–6.
18 Hesiod, *Theogony*, 114–25. (Translation by Voß.)

SUPPLEMENT A

Let us remember the chained cave dwellers in Book VII of Plato's *Republic*: they laugh at those who, after the intuition of higher things, come back **blinded by the light**; they are watchful not to injure their eyes and not to lose the **clarity of knowledge** which they enjoy at present. The one who would undertake to unchain them and to lead them outside, to the light that destroys the intuition of the **actual**, should be seized and killed [128].

We are firmly convinced of the following:

Those "immediate, inexpressible cognitions proper to **reason** that enter the **understanding** only in the form of **obscure representations**" are, **in themselves, the light of the supreme knowledge,** of which Spinoza, in agreement with Plato, states that **it reveals both itself and the darkness.**[19]

Says Plato: "In the knowable world, the most extreme is the idea of the good, which can hardly be seen. Where it is seen, it must be regarded as the cause of everything right and beautiful; as what in the visible world generates both the light and the sun, source of light, and in the intelligible world again as the source that offers truth and meaning. And those who want to behave wisely in public or in private must have seen it" (*Republic*, L. VII, vol. VII, 133, ed. Bipont. In the translation by Stolberg, in the third part of Plato's selected dialogues, 305).

---

19 [Spinoza, *Ethics*, II, Prop. 43, schol.]

Supplement B
To page 182

[129] Plato states: "some people, famous for their great insight, maintain that everything that exists, existed, and will exist has its origin in either **nature, art**, or **chance**. They claim that the greatest and most beautiful things come from nature and chance, while the least relevant come from art which, taking from the nature's hands the first and foremost works, processes them in different ways to mold and fabricate any objects of minor relevance that, for this reason, are called **artificial**. Fire, water, earth, air – they say – exist because of **nature** and **chance**, they are not products of **art** … From the mixing of conflicting forces **that chance had to bring about according to the laws of necessity** there sprang everything we see: the sky with its stars, animals and plants, together with the changing of seasons; all without the intervention of an intellect, without God, without art; everything has occurred – they claim – only because of **nature** and **chance**. Subsequently, from these two first and original principles flowed art, which is an invention of the mortals and is itself mortal. It cannot produce true beings through imitation, but just shadowy images which hardly bear bits of truth. In cases where art produces something more substantial, it has received help from nature and acts according to its forces. Examples are medicine, agriculture, and gymnastic. In some sense also politics, but this receives less from nature and all from art, which is why the entire law-giving lacks true ground.

"The gods – those men distinctly claim – are products of art as much as the laws, and they are not the same in every place, but they vary from people to

SUPPLEMENT B

people, depending on their respective law-givers reaching agreement on it [130] …

Thus, what is morally good is also different whether defined by nature or law; as regards the just, nature has absolutely no conception, but the human beings call just what laws – in different and often variable ways – require defining as such, without nature having any say" (*Laws*, L X., 74–6, ed. Bipont, vol. 9).[1]

Against this system that destroys any morality, Plato proves that we must necessarily admit as the absolutely first principle, from which everything else originated, not a blind causality, like those wise men claim, but a causality that follows representations, a rational **will**, and a **teleologically oriented intelligence**; therefore, that art is older than nature.

If his proofs are found deficient by the standards of strict criticism, his claims hold at least equal weight against the opposing ones. The mind chooses between naturalism and theism with the same freedom involved in choosing between morality and well-being. Faith in God is not a science, but a virtue.

1 [Plato, *Laws*, 888e–90a.]

Supplement C
To page 187

[131] In general, we define rational cognition as one based on grounds. We thus know on the basis of grounds, when the axiom, according to which the whole is necessarily equal to the sum of its parts taken together, finds its implementation for us in a particular case.

Where this axiom does not apply, nor is cognition based upon grounds possible. For in no case can such a cognition be, or ever be, other than the reciprocal cognition of the parts from the whole that together they constitute, and of this whole from its parts, inasmuch as these necessarily belong to it and, **within it, to each other**. I prove by indicating the place or location that a particular part necessarily occupies in a particular whole. What does not belong to a whole as one of its parts can be neither demonstrated nor deduced. If something is found **included**, we **affirm it**, if it is **excluded**, we **negate it**.

The failure to notice that by **grounds** we mean nothing but the sum total, the totality of determinations of an object, has led to countless mistakes in philosophy.

Now, not only are all the parts, or determinations, or predicates, taken together, the **same** as the whole that unites them in itself, are one and the same thing with it or with the object. Rather, for this very reason, they also necessarily show themselves to exist together with it, so that neither can the whole **objectively** exist before the parts, nor the parts, **as parts of this whole**, before the whole. In other words, the interpolation of time between ground and consequence, between subject and predicate, is absolutely impossible.

SUPPLEMENT C

With the interpolation of time, the concepts of ground and consequence turn into those of **cause** and **effect** [132]. But we only know how the **effect** emerges from the **cause** and how they are necessarily connected when, in the process of reflection, we leave aside the time which separates the one from the other, when we transform the cause into ground (subject), effect into mere consequence (predicate), and let them fall together (cause and effect). In this manner we explain, for instance, some or even all the consequences of the actions of a human being on the basis of the permanent constitution of his mind, his unchanging human character. Where it is not possible to proceed this way, where we cannot eradicate time in thought, we do not acquire any insight, but rather, like animals, we acquire through experience only the **expectation of similar cases.**

This truth, which has long since been expounded by David Hume, led our Kant by his own admission to his system of subjectivity.[1] But that system, Kantian criticism or **transcendental idealism**, instead of exposing the confusion and the mixing of the concept of ground with the concept of cause as a mistake, has instead justified them and systematically led to the affirmation – discussed in our work – **that in reality nothing happens.**

Long before the publication of the *Critique of Pure Reason*, and without David Hume, was the author of these considerations confronted, along his own way, by this objection against the reality of the concept of cause, only under slightly different form. He first presented it in the *Letters Concerning the Doctrine of Spinoza* (16 and 17 in the first edition, 27 in the second), and then discussed it in more detail in the dialogue *On Idealism and Realism*.[2] I refer to this discussion, where the confusion and the mixing of essentially different concepts, those of ground and cause, are denounced; I only add the following.

To be sure, the concept of ground, of the **All and the One**, is the supreme concept of the **understanding.** But the supreme concept of **reason**, one which is one and the same with it, is the concept of **cause** [133], of what exists in itself and produces exclusively by itself; that creates while remaining uncreated; in a word, of what is absolutely unconditioned.

The understanding denies the cause, which is higher than the ground and wholly different from it, because, according to Kant's correct remark (preface

---

1 [Kant, *Gesammelte Schriften*, 4:260.]

2 *David Hume on Faith, or Idealism and Realism*, 93–109. [JWA 2, 1:49–56.] See supplement VII in the second edition of the *Letters Concerning the Doctrine of Spinoza*, 414ff. [JWA 1, 1:255–7.]

to the *Critique of Pure Reason*, B 20), it cannot conceive the unconditioned other than as a contradiction. Reason, on the other hand, affirms the cause, which is higher than the ground and wholly different from it, because reason lives, moves, and exists only in it.[3]

Plato taught that one unable to distinguish the **Unity** in various ways generated by the understanding through multiplicity and diversity, **the non-one** generated by means of concept and word, from the **One** who, revealing itself immediately in reason, in the **consciousness of the spirit**, in the **soul**, is the **One itself** (*to en auto*); such a one, taught Plato, necessarily places the word always before the being, the image and its deceptive appearance before the model, so that he no longer sees the true and essential which is equal only to itself. This is the one who pretends, and even convinces himself, that he be able, like a magician, to do everything with **words**. In truth, however, with the **ground** of discourse he loses the discourse itself, for what he brings forth is only empty sound, deceit, and lies.[4]

When Plato claimed that real individual beings presuppose species as their cause and that these, in turn, presuppose genera, this was not in him the consequence of a logical fallacy, as has often been claimed and Kant believed.[5] His species and his genera are clearly not merely logical or nominal beings, they are not mere concepts derived from pre-existing actualities, drawing all their truth from these actualities and nothing without them. – Plato's genera, the **ideas**, actually and truly exist for him **before** the species and the individual things. It is only the former that make the latter possible in the truest and strictest sense, just as the thought of a first creator, and the model Plato produced in accordance with this thought, come before the innumerable reproductions of the model. Such reproductions [conform to] the intention and the rule revealed in the model, to such an extent that this later **multiplicity** [134] only became possible because of that earlier **One**; it emerged from it. But **the One**, from which the multiplicity derives, is not **multiplied** because of this multiplicity; it remains eternally the same **One**, absolutely unmultipliable.

Nothing ever emerges **as** multiplicity or **from** multiplicity or **plurality**; from one comes always only one. We do not invent watches, boats, looms, or languages. We invent, rather, **one** watch or **that** watch, **one** ship or **that** ship, **one** language or **this** language.

3   [Acts 17:28.]
4   See Plato, *Sophist*, and the conclusion of *Cratylus* and *Theaetetus*.
5   [Kant, *Critique of Pure Reason*, B370 and B596.]

SUPPLEMENT C

211

We do not say, nor would we ever be able to say, of any single or particular thing of this type – any watch, any boat, any language – that it is **the** Watch, **the** Boat, **the** Language. So to speak is allowed only of the one cause – whether one calls it species, genera, law, thinking, or soul – from which multiplicity and diversity did emerge and keep emerging.

What is one according to being cannot be dispersed into what is **non-one** according to being; cannot be dispersed into a lifeless multiplicity, and there, and out of it, produce something that would be the true one and, as such, would stand on its own. A one [thus dispersed into the non-one] can only move the parts of the latter; can compel and connect them, so that a being appears that makes the creative spirit known to a similar spirit. The unshaped then acquires a shape indeed, but one only external to it, foreign to it and imposed on it – no inner shape that would exist for its own sake, that would externally only manifest the internal, a shape capable of loving and maintaining itself. Of course, each of these shapes shows a **soul**, but this soul is external to them. They announce an **intention**, therefore a **spirit**, although none dwells in them. Their **cause**, their **spirit**, knew about them before they existed; but they, once come to be, know nothing about themselves. Their creator loved its purpose in them, its intention, and they emerged from this love. But they do not love themselves, they do not tend to preservation, but, with each of their parts, they continually decline toward the non-one, and strive to dissolve again into it.

Thus, a thinking being's self-produced thought can proceed from it, the thinking being, and prove itself a plastic force in the shapeless [135], in what is non-thinking, lifeless, essentially **non-one**; it can produce actual things in and through it, the **copies** of the image originally immanent in it. Nevertheless, the thinking being cannot **animate** these copies, since it is itself nothing but a created being, created by a higher being. Only God, the supreme being, can call into existence a being that **exists for itself.** God is the spirit, and there is no spirit that would not have **immediately** sprung out of Him. Thus, it would be impossible to be a spirit without knowing anything about **Him**, who is the **genus** of His species, the absolute One, the only to exist in Himself most perfectly – who is the cause, the beginning **purely and simply, and in the highest sense possible.**

Plato, as a dualist, has always opposed the sophists, who are consistent antidualists. He shows that to those who claim that **only the One exists**, a closer look would reveal that even this One dissolves, and at the end they are left with nowhere a being, and absolutely no truth. Upon recognizing that, the sophist becomes a strict anti-dualist or an adherent of unitotality. He has "separated everything from everything, and therefore abolished any difference."[6] He is left with mere "names of names, shadows of words":[7] the One and the non-one, all and nothing.[8]

Plato openly admits that it is impossible to refute the determined sophist because what is true, good, and beautiful in itself, which the sophist rejects, can only be shown, not demonstrated.[9] But they can be shown only to those who turn voluntarily, **with their entire being,** towards the only side where all this can be seen.[10] For its part, the nothingness of the sensory world reveals itself only to the one who somehow has sought to grasp **what exists** in it. The sophist, who turns completely and only toward that other side, claims with good reason that nothing exists, that there is only an eternal becoming, and that in it there is nothing fundamentally true or false, nor anything just, good, and beautiful, or unjust, repulsive, and evil.[11]

Only the one who has beholden the other side, beyond what comes to life and dies, finds what is true, good, and beautiful in itself [136] also on this side; recognizes that the universe exists thanks to the good that, higher than all things, produces not only the cognition of the true, but also the true itself – in the same way that the sun gives not only light and visibility to the visible, but gives it also its life – recognizes this universe as a creation, the work of a God.[12]

And so is the Platonic doctrine just as far from idealism as from materialism. It affirms the actuality of the sensible world, its objectivity, the actuality of the supreme cause, the truth of the ideas of the good and the beautiful, and separates the supernatural from the natural, what comes to life from what is immutable, the universe from its creator: it is a resolutely dualistic and **theistic** doctrine.

6   [Plato, *Sophist*, 251c–2b.]
7   [Ibid., 234b–c.]
8   See *Sophist*, the conclusion of *Cratylus* and *Theaetetus*.
9   [Plato, *Sophist*, 218c–d, 260c, and 261a.]
10   *Republic* L, VII.
11   [Plato, *Sophist*, 257d–8b.]
12   See *Republic* L, VI, vol. VII, 116 and 119.

Glossary

Absicht	Intention, purpose
Achtung	Respect
Ahndung	Presentiment
Alleinheit	Unitotality
Alleinig	Unique
Anbetung	Worship
Anbilden	Fiction
Art	Species
Anschauung	Intuition
Auswendigen	Externalists
Begierde	Appetite
Begriff	Concept
Beschränkung	Delimitation
Bestimmung	Determination, vocation
Bewußtseyn	Consciousness
Beziehung	Relationship
Bild	Image
Böse	Evil
Dasein	Existence
Dichten	Fiction-making
Dichtung	Fiction, poetry
Eigenschaft	Property
Einbildungskraft	Imagination

Einsicht	Insight
Empfindung	Sensation
Endlichkeit	Finitude
Erkenntnis	Cognition
Erkenntnissvermögen	Faculty of cognition
Erscheinung	Appearance
Factum	Fact
Fähigkeit	Capacity
Form	Form
Fürwahrhalten	Holding-to-be-true
Gattung	Genus (pl. genera)
Gedächtnis	Memory
Gefühl	Feeling
Geist	Spirit
Gemüth	Mind
Gerechtig(ch)keit	Justice
Geschaftigkeit	Industry
Gesetzt	Law
Gesinnung	Disposition
Gestalt	Shape
Gewissen	Conscience
Gewissheit	Certainty
Glaube	Faith
Grund	Ground
Güte	Goodness
Hervorbringen	To produce
Himmel	Heaven
Hirngespinst	Delusion
Inbegriff	Sum total
Inhalt	Content
Instinkt	Instinct
Inwendigen	Internalists
Kraft	Power/force
Leidenschaft	Passion
Lust	Desire
Mensch	Human being
Menschheit	Humankind
Merkmal	Characteristic feature

GLOSSARY

Neigung	Inclination
Nichtige/Nichtigkeit	Nothingness
Nichts	Nothing
Personlichkeit	Personality
Pflicht	Duty
Recht	Right
Scharfsinn	Acumen
Scharfsinnig	Perceptive
Schranke	Limitation
Schwärmerey	Fanaticism, enthusiasm
Seele	Soul
Seiend	Existing
Selbständig	Autonomous
Selbständigkeit	Autonomy
Selbstheit	Personal identity
Selbstsein	Selfhood
Sinn	Sense
Sinnlich	Sense … [in a few cases, translated with "sensory"]
Sinnlichkeit	Sense perception
Sittlich	Moral
T(h)at	Deed [in some cases, it has been translated with "action"; when so, I wrote the German between brackets]
Tiefsinnig	Profound
Trennung	Separation
Trieb	Drive
Tugend	Virtue
Uebel	Ill
Uebersinnlich	Suprasensible
Überzeugung	Conviction
Unabhängig	Independent
Unding	Non-thing
Unvernünftig	Unreasonable
Urkraft	Primal power
Ursache	Cause
Ursprung	Origin
Veränderungskraft	Transformative power

Verbindung	Connection
Verhältnins	Relation
Vermögen	Faculty or power
Vernunft	Reason
Vernunftlos	Deprived of reason
Verstand	Understanding
Vorsatz	Resolution
Vorsehung	Providence
Vorstellung	Representation
Wahn	Illusion
Wahrnehmung	Perception
Weisheit	Wisdom
Weltordnung	World-order
Wesen (noun used for creature)	Being(s) [when used as "essence" the German appears in brackets]
Wirken	To operate [or "activity" when used as noun]
Wirklich	Actual
Wirklichkeit	Actuality
Wirksamkeit	Effectiveness
Wirkung	Effect
Wissen	Knowing, knowledge
Wissenschaft	Science
Zesammenhang	Interconnection
Zuversicht	Confidence, trust
Zweck	Purpose, goal

Bibliography

PRIMARY SOURCES

Aristotle. *Metaphysica*. Edited by W.D. Ross and J.A. Smith. Oxford: Clarendon Press, 1928.

Claudius, Matthias. *Asmus omnia sua secum portans, oder Sämmtliche Werke des Wandsbecker Boten*. Vols. 4 and 6. Hamburg: F. Perthes, 1783 and 1797.

– *Werke. Asmus omnia sua secum portans; oder, Sämtliche Werke des Wandsbecker Boten*. Edited by Urban Roedl. Stuttgart: Cotta, 1960.

Descartes, René. *Méditations Métaphysiques*. In *Œuvres de Descartes*, vol. 7. Paris: Vrin, 1904.

Eckhart, Meister. *Deutsche Predigten und Traktate*. 3rd edition. Munich: Hanser, 1969.

– *Lectura Eckhardi: Predigten Meister Eckharts von Fachgelehrten gelesen und gedeutet*. Edited by Georg Steer and Loris Sturlese. Stuttgart and Berlin: Kohlhammer, 1998.

Epictetus. *Discourses and Selected Writings*. Edited by Robert Dobbin. London: Penguin, 2008.

– *Discourses of Epictetus*. Edited by George Long. New York: Appleton, 1904.

Fichte, Johann Gottlieb. *Introductions to the Wissenschaftslehre and Other Writings, 1797–1800*. Edited by Daniel Breazeale. Indianapolis: Hackett Publishing, 1994.

– "On the Basis of Our Belief in a Divine Governance of the World." In *Introductions to the Wissenschaftslehre and Other Writings, 1797–1800*, edited by Daniel Breazeale, 141–54. Indianapolis: Hackett Publishing, 1994.

Fries, Jakob Friedrich. *Aus Seinem Handschriftlichen Nachlasse*. Edited by Ernst Ludwig Theodor Henke. Leipzig: F.A. Brockhaus, 1867.

218   BIBLIOGRAPHY

– *Von deutscher Philosophie, Art und Kunst. Ein Votum für Friedrich Heinrich Jacobi gegen F. W. J. Schelling.* Heidelberg: Mohr und Zimmer, 1812.

Goethe, Johann Wolfgang von. *Briefe, Tagebücher und Gespräche.* Edited by Hendrik Birus et al. In *Sämtliche Werke*, Abt. 1, vol. 6. Berlin: Suhrkamp, 1993.

Hamann, Johann Georg. *Schriften über Philosophie, Philologie, Kritik, 1758–1763.* In *Sämtliche Werke.* Vienna: Thomas Morus Presse im Verlag Herder, 1950.

Humboldt, Wilhelm von. *Briefe von Wilhelm von Humboldt an Friedrich Heinrich Jacobi.* Halle: M. Niemeyer, 1892.

Jacobi, Friedrich Heinrich. *Allwill. Textkritisch herausgegeben, eingeleitet und kommentiert.* Edited by Jan Ulbe Terpstra. Groningen: Noordhoff Uitgevers, 1957.

– *Aus F.H. Jacobi's Nachlass: ungedruckte Briefe von und an Jacobi und Andere: nebst ungedruckten Gedichten von Goethe und Lenz.* Edited by Rudolf Zoeppritz. Leipzig: W. Engelmann, 1869.

– *Die Bibliothek. Ein Katalog.* Edited by Konrad Wiedemann with Peter-Paul Schneider. Stuttgart-Bad Cannstatt: frommann-holzboog, 1989.

– *Briefwechsel.* Edited by Walter Jaeschke and Birgit Sandkaulen. Stuttgart-Bad Cannstatt: frommann-holzboog, 1981–.

– *Des choses divines et de leur révélation.* Edited by Patrick Cerutti. Paris: J. Vrin, 2008.

– *Concerning the Doctrine of Spinoza in Letters to Herr Moses Mendelssohn* (1785). In Jacobi, *The Main Philosophical Writings*, 173–252.

– *Concerning the Doctrine of Spinoza in Letters to Moses Mendelssohn* (1789). In Jacobi, *The Main Philosophical Writings*, 339–78.

– *David Hume on Faith, or Idealism and Realism, a Dialogue* (1787). In Jacobi, *The Main Philosophical Writings*, 253–338.

– *Die Denkbücher.* Edited by Sophia Victoria Krebs. Stuttgart-Bad Cannstatt: frommann-holzboog, 2000.

– *Edward Allwill's Collection of Letters* (1792). In Jacobi, *The Main Philosophical Writings*, 379–496.

– *Jacobi to Fichte.* In Jacobi, *The Main Philosophical Writings*, 497–536.

– *Lettera a Fichte: (1799, 1816).* Edited by Ariberto Acerbi. Naples: La scuola di Pitagora, 2017.

– *The Main Philosophical Writings and the Novel* Allwill. Edited by George di Giovanni. Montreal and Kingston: McGill-Queen's University Press, 1994.

– *Œuvres philosophiques.* Paris: Éditions Aubier-Montaigne, 1946.

– *Preface and also Introduction to the Author's Collected Philosophical Works* (1815). In Jacobi, *The Main Philosophical Writings*, 537–90.

– *Werke. Gesamtausgabe.* [JWA] Edited by Klaus Hammacher and Walter Jaeschke. Vols. 1–7. Hamburg and Stuttgart-Bad Cannstatt: Felix Meiner and frommann-holzboog, 1998–.

BIBLIOGRAPHY

Jacobi, Friedrich Heinrich, and Friedrich Bouterwek. *Briefe an Friedr. Bouterwek: aus den Jahren 1800 bis 1819*. Edited by W. Mejer. Göttingen: Deuerlich, 1868.

Jacobi, Friedrich Heinrich, and Friedrich Wilhelm Joseph Schelling. *Streit um die Göttlichen Dinge*. Edited by Wilhelm Weischedel. Darmstadt: Wiss.Buchges, 1967.

Jacobi, Johann Georg, ed. *Taschenbuch für das jahr 1802*. Hamburg: F. Perthes, 1802.

Kant, Immanuel. *Critique of Practical Reason*. Edited by Mary Gregor. Cambridge: Cambridge University Press, 2015.

– *Critique of Pure Reason*. Edited by Allen W. Wood and Paul Guyer. Cambridge: Cambridge University Press, 1998.

– *Gesammelte Schriften*. Edited by Königlich (Deutsche) Preußische Akademie der Wissenschaften (from volume 24, by the Akademie der Wissenschaften zu Göttingen). Berlin: George Reimer/Walter de Gruyter, 1900–.

– "Inquiry Concerning the Distinctness of the Principles of Natural Theology and Morality (1764)." In *Theoretical Philosophy, 1755–1770*, edited by David Walford, 243–75. Cambridge: Cambridge University Press, 1992.

– "The Only Possible Argument in Support of a Demonstration of the Existence of God." In *Theoretical Philosophy, 1755–1770*, edited by David Walford, 107–201. Cambridge: Cambridge University Press, 1992.

Köppen, Friedrich. *Schellings Lehre oder das Ganze der Philosophie des absoluten Nichts. Nebst 3 Briefen verwandten Inhalts von Friedr. Heinr. Jacobi*. Hamburg: Perthes, 1803.

Lichtenberg, Georg Christoph. *Schriften und Briefe*. Edited by Franz H. Mautner. Frankfurt am Main: Insel-Verl, 1983.

– *Vermischte Schriften*. Edited by Ludwig Christian Lichtenberg and Friedrich Christian Kries. Göttingen: Verlag der D. Buchhandlung, 1800–06.

Marcus Aurelius Antoninus. *The Meditations*. Edited by G.M.A. Grube, New York: Bobbs-Merrill, 1963.

Musil, Robert. *The Man without Qualities*. London: Seker and Warburg, 1979.

New English Bible. The New Testament. Oxford: Oxford University Press, 1970.

Plato. *Complete Works*. Edited by John M. Cooper. Indianapolis: Hackett Publishing, 1997.

Paul, Jean. *Sämtliche Briefe*. Edited by Eduard Berend. Berlin: Akademie Verlag, 1952.

Perthes, Clemens Theodor. *Friedrich Perthes' Leben: nach dessen schriftlichen und mündlichen Mitteilungen*. Gotha: F.A. Perthes, 1896.

Pseudo-Longinus. *On the Sublime*. Edited by Donald Andrew Russell. Oxford: Clarendon, 1970.

Reinhold, Karl Leonhard. *Beyträge zur leichtern Uebersicht des Zustandes der Philosophie beym Anfange des 19. Jahrhunderts*, Heft 1–3 (1801). In *Gesammelte Schriften*, vol. 7, 1. Edited by M. Bondeli. Basel and Berlin: Schwabe Verlag, 2020.

BIBLIOGRAPHY

Religionsphilosophie und speculative Theologie. Der Streit um die Göttlichen Dinge (1799–1812), Quellenband. Edited by Walter Jaeschke. Hamburg: F. Meiner, 1993.

Schelling, Friedrich Wilhelm Joseph. *Aus Schellings Leben in Briefen,* vol.1, *1775–1803.* Edited by G.L. Plitt. Leipzig: S. Hirzel, 1869.

– *Historisch-kritische Ausgabe, im Auftrag der Schelling-Kommission der Bayerischen Akademie der Wissenschaften.* Edited by H.M. Baumgartner, W.G. Jacobs, and H. Krings. Stuttgart: frommann-holzboog, 1976–.

– *Monument de l'écrit sur les choses divines, etc. de M. Friedrich Heinrich Jacobi et de l'accusation qui y est faite d'athéisme mensonger et expressément trompeur.* Edited by Patrick Cerutti. Paris: Vrin, 2012.

– *Sämtliche Werke.* Edited by K.F.A. Schelling. Stuttgart: Cotta, 1856–61.

Schlegel, Friedrich von. *Kritische Friedrich-Schlegel-Ausgabe.* Vols. 1–35. Edited by Ernst Behler et al. Munich: Schöningh, 1958–2002.

– "Recension (1812)." In *F.H. Jacobi, Des choses divines et de leur révélation,* edited by Patrick Cerutti, 157–71. Paris: J. Vrin, 2008.

SECONDARY SOURCES

Acerbi, Ariberto. "Commento." In *Lettera a Fichte: (1799, 1816).* Edited by Ariberto Acerbi, 249–328. Naples: La scuola di Pitagora, 2017.

– "Osservazioni sulla lettura Jacobiana di Platone." In *Una filosofia del non-sapere: Studi su Friedrich Heinrich Jacobi,* edited by Guido Frilli, Federica Pitillo, e Pierluigi Valenza, 49–61. Pisa and Rome: Serra, 2020.

Albert, Hans. *Traktat über kritische Vernunft.* Tübingen: Mohr, 1975.

Agamben, Giorgio. *L'irrealizzabile. Per una politica dell'ontologia.* Turin: Einaudi, 2022.

Arendt, Dieter, ed. *Nihilismus. Die Anfänge von Jacobi bis Nietzsche.* Cologne: Hegner, 1970.

Baum, Günter. "Friedrich Heinrich Jacobi und die Philosophie Spinozas." In *Spinoza im Deutschland des achtzehnten Jahrhunderts: Zur Erinnerung an Hans–Christian Lucas,* edited by Eva Schürmann, Norbert Waszek, and Frank Weinrich, 251–63. Stuttgart-Bad Cannstatt: frommann-holzboog, 2002.

– *Vernunft und Erkenntnis: die Philosophie F.H. Jacobis.* Bonn: Bouvier, 1969.

Berger, Benjamin. *The Schelling-Eschenmayer Controversy, 1801: Nature and Identity.* Edinburgh: Edinburgh University Press, 2020.

Bollnow, Otto Friedrich. *Die Lebensphilosophie F.H. Jacobis.* Stuttgart: Kohlhammer, 1933.

Bowie, Andrew. "Rethinking the History of the Subject." In *Demonstrative Subjectivities,* edited by Simon Critchley and Peter Dews, 105–26. Albany: State University of New York Press, 1996.

BIBLIOGRAPHY

Bowman, Brady. "Die Wirklichkeit des wahren Gewissheit und Glauben bei Jacobi und Kant." In *Jacobi und Kant*, edited by Walter Jaeschke and Birgit Sandkaulen, 27–46. Hamburg: Meiner, 2021.

– "Notiones Communes und Common Sense. Zu den Spinozanischen Voraussetzungen von Jacobis Rezeption der Philosophie Thomas Rieds." In *Friedrich Heinrich Jacobi. Ein Wendepunkt der geistigen Bildung der Zeit*, edited by Walter Jaeschke and Birgit Sandkaulen, 159–76. Hamburg: Meiner Verlag, 2004.

Brüggen, Michael. "La critique de Jacobi par Hegel dans 'Foi et Savoir.'" *Archives de Philosophie* 30 (1967): 187–98.

– "Jacobi, Schelling und Hegel." In *Friedrich Heinrich Jacobi: ein Wendepunkt der geistigen Bildung der Zeit*, edited by Walter Jaeschke and Birgit Sandkaulen, 209–32. Hamburg: Meiner, 2004.

Buchheim, Thomas. "Die Idee des Existierenden und der Raum. Vernunfthintergründe einer Welt äußerer Dinge nach Schellings Darstellung des Naturprocesses von 1843/44." *Kant-Studien*, no. 1 (2015): 36–66.

Buée, Jean-Michel. *Savoir immédiat et savoir absolu. La lecture de Jacobi par Hegel*. Paris: Classiques Garnier, 2012.

Busch, Wilhelm. *Die Erkenntnistheorie des Friedrich Heinrich Jacobi*. Karlsruhe: J.J. Reiff, 1892.

Butler, Gerald J. "Fielding's Panzaic Voice: Enlightenment as Critique of the Mythical." In *La Grande-Bretagne et l'Europe des Lumières*, edited by Serge Soupel, 189–206. Paris: Presses Sorbonne Nouvelle, 2018.

Calker, Friedrich. *Urgesetzlehre des Wahren, Guten und Schönen*. Berlin: Dümmler, 1820.

Cassirer, Ernst. *Das Erkenntnisproblem in der Philosophie und Wissenschaft der neueren Zeit*. Vol. 3. Berlin: Verlag B. Cassirer, 1920.

– *Hölderlin e l'idealismo tedesco*. Edited by Andrea Mecacci. Rome: Donzelli, 2000.

Cerutti, Patrick. Présentation to *Des choses divines et de leur révélation*, by Friedrich Heinrich Jacobi, 7–25. Paris: J. Vrin, 2008.

Chiereghin, Franco. "Ipocrisia e Dialettica." *Verifiche*, no. 4 (1980): 343–76.

– *Sul Principio*. Padua: CUSL, 2000.

Cottier, Marie-Martin, "Foi et surnaturel chez F.H. Jacobi." *Reveu Thomiste* 62 (1954): 337–73.

Cousin, Victor. *Fragments philosophiques pour servir à l'histoire de la philosophie*. Vol. 5. Paris: Didier, 1866.

Crawford, Alexander W. *The Philosophy of F.H. Jacobi*. New York and London: The Macmillan Company, 1905.

Danz, Christian. "Wir 'halten mit Lessing selbst die Ausbildung geoffenbarter Wahrheiten in Vernunftwahrheiten für schlechterdings nothwendig.' Bemerkungen zur Lessingrezeption in Schellings Freiheitsschrift." In *Gott, Natur, Kunst und Geschichte: Schelling zwischen Identitätsphilosophie und Freiheitsschrift*, edited by Christian Danz and Jörg Jantzen, 127–52. Göttingen: V&R Unipress, 2011.

Danz, Christian, and Stolzenberg, Jürgen, eds. *System und Systemkritik um 1800.* Hamburg: Meiner, 2011.

De Vos, Ludovicus. "Hegel und Jacobi (ab1807). Jacobi-Kritik in Fortsetzung Jacobischer Motive?" In *Hegel und die Geschichte der Philosophie*, edited by Dietmar H. Heidemann and Christian Krijnen, 218–37. Darmstadt: Wissenschaftliche Buchgesellschaft, 2007.

di Giovanni, George. "1799: The Year of Reinhold's Conversion to Jacobi." In *Die Philosophie Karl Leonhard Reinholds*, edited by Martin Bondeli and Wolfgang Schrader, 259–82. Amsterdam and New York: Rodopi, 2003.

– *Freedom and Religion in Kant and His Immediate Successors: The Vocation of Humankind, 1774–1800.* Cambridge: Cambridge University Press, 2005.

– "Hegel, Jacobi, and Crypto-Catholicism, or, Hegel in Dialogue with the Enlightenment." In *Hegel on the Modern World.* Edited by Ardis Collins. Albany: State University of New York Press, 1995.

– "Hume, Jacobi, and Common Sense: An Episode in the Reception of Hume in Germany at the Time of Kant." *Kant-Studien* 88 (1997): 44–58.

– *The Unfinished Philosophy of Friedrich Heinrich Jacobi.* In *The Main Philosophical Writings and the Novel* Allwill, by Friedrich Heinrich Jacobi, edited by George Di Giovanni, 3–167. Montreal and Kingston: McGill-Queen's University Press, 1994.

Dilthey, Wilhelm, ed. *Aus Schleiermacher's Leben. In Briefen.* Vol. 2. Berlin: G. Reimer, 1858.

Dini, Tristana, and Salvatore Principe, eds. *Jacobi in discussione.* Milan: Franco Angeli, 2012.

Doran, Robert. *The Theory of the Sublime from Longinus to Kant.* Cambridge: Cambridge University Press, 2015.

Essen, Georg, and Christian Danz, eds. *Philosophisch-theologische Streitsachen. Pantheismusstreit – Atheismusstreit – Theismusstreit.* Darmstadt: Wissenschaftliche Buchgesellschaft, 2012.

Feldmeier, Majk. "Der Mensch, ein 'krummes Holz'? Zur anthropologischen Fundierung von Religion bei Jacobi und Kant." In *Jacobi und Kant*, edited by Birgit Sandkaulen and Walter Jaeschke, 157–74. Hamburg: Meiner, 2021.

Fetzer, Dirk. *Jacobis Philosophie des Unbedigten.* Paderborn: Schöningh, 2007.

Flasch, Kurt. "Predigt 52: Beati pauperes spiritu." In *Lectura Eckhardi: Predigten Meister Eckharts von Fachgelehrten gelesen und gedeutet*, edited by Georg Steer and Loris Sturlese, 163–99. Stuttgart and Berlin: Kohlhammer, 1998.

Ford, Lewis. "The Controversy between Schelling and Jacobi." *Journal of the History of*

BIBLIOGRAPHY

Philosophy 3, no. 1 (April 1965): 75–89.

Frank, Arthur. *Friedrich Heinrich Jacobis Lehre vom Glauben. Eine Darstellung ihrer Entstehung, Wandlung und Vollendung.* Halle: Kaemmerer, 1910.

Franks, Paul. "All or Nothing: Systematicity and Nihilism in Jacobi, Reinhold, and Maimon." In *The Cambridge Companion to German Idealism*, edited by Karl Ameriks, 95–116. Cambridge: Cambridge University Press, 2000.

– *All or Nothing: Systematicity, Transcendental Arguments, and Skepticism in German Idealism.* Cambridge, MA: Harvard University Press, 2005.

Frilli, Guido, Federica Pitillo, and Pierluigi Valenza, eds. *Una filosofia del non-sapere: Studi su Friedrich Heinrich Jacobi.* Pisa and Rome: Serra, 2020.

Goldenbaum, Ursula. "Der Pantheismusstreit als Angriff auf die Berliner Aufklärung und Judenemanzipation." In *Aufklärung: Interdisziplinäres Jahrbuch zur Erforschung des 18. Jahrhunderts und seiner Wirkungsgeschichte*, edited by Robert Theis, 199–226. Hamburg: Meiner, 2009.

Goretzki, Catia. "Jacobis Denken im Spannungsfeld des Kantischen Theismus-Begriffs." In *Jacobi und Kant*, edited by Birgit Sandkaulen and Walter Jaeschke, 125–40. Hamburg: Meiner, 2021.

Halbig, Christoph. "The Philosopher as Polyphemus? Philosophy and Common Sense in Hegel and Jacobi." In *Internationales Jahrbuch des Deutschen Idealismus*, edited by Jürgen Stolzenberg and Karl Ameriks, 261–82. Berlin: De Gruyter, 2005.

Hammacher, Klaus. "Ein bemerkenswerter Einfluss französischen Denkens: Friedrich Heinrich Jacobis (1743–1819) Auseinandersetzung mit Voltaire und Rousseau." *Revue internationale de philosophie* 32, nos. 124–5 (2/3) (1978): 327–47.

– "Biographie als Problemgeschichte." In *Transzendenz und Existenz. idealistische Grundlagen und moderne Perspektiven des transzendentalen Gedankens. Wolfgang Janke Zum 70. Geburtstage*, edited by Klaus Hammacher and Manfred Baum, 101–20. Amsterdam: Rodopoi, 2004.

– ed. *Fichte und Jacobi (Fichte-Studien*, Volume 14). Amsterdam and Atlanta: Rodopoi, 1998.

– "Jacobis Schrift 'Von den göttlichen Dingen.'" In *Religionsphilosophie und Spekulative Theologie. Der Streit um die göttlichen Dinge (1799–1812)*, edited by Walter Jaeschke, 129–41. Hamburg: Meiner, 1994.

– "Der persönliche Gott im Dialog? J.G. Hamanns Auseinandersetzung mit F.H. Jacobis Spinozabriefen." In *Johannes Georg Hamann. Acta des Internationalen Hamann-Colloquium in Lüneburg 1976*, edited by Bernhard Gajek, 194–210. Frankfurt am Main: Vittorio Klostermann, 1979.

– "'Die Vernuft hat also nicht nur Vorstellungen, sondern wirkliche Dinge zu Gegen-stände.' Zur nachkantische Leibniz-Rezeption, vornehmlich bei F.H. Jacobi." In *Beiträge zur Wirkungs- und Rezeptionsgeschichte von Gottfried Wilhelm Leibniz (Studia Leibnitiana,* Supplementa 26), edited by A.F. Heinekamp, 213–24. Wiesbaden and Stuttgart: Steiner Verlag, 1986.

– "Über Friedrich Heinrich Jacobis Beziehungen zu Lessing im Zusammenhang mit dem Streit um Spinoza." In *Lessing und der Kreis seiner Freunde,* edited by Günter Schulz, 51–74. Heidelberg: L. Schneider, 1985.

Harms, Friedrich. *Über Die Lehre von Friedrich Heinrich Jacobi.* Berlin: Akad. Wiss., 1876.

Heidemann, Dietmar H. *Hegel und die Geschichte der Philosophie.* Darmstadt: Wiss-Buchges, 2007.

Henke, Ernst Ludwig Theodor. *Jakob Friedrich Fries aus seinem handschriftlichen Nachlaß dargestellt.* Berlin: VerlÖffentliches Leben, 1937.

Henrich, Dieter. "Der Ursprung der Doppelphilosophie. Friedrich Heinrich Jacobis Bedeutung für das nachkantische Denken." In *Friedrich Heinrich Jacobi. Präsident der Akademie, Philosoph, Theoretiker der Sprache,* edited by D. Henrich, 13–27. Munich: Verlag der Bayerischen Akademie der Wissenschaften, 1993.

Herms, Eilert. "Selbsterkenntnis und Metaphysik in den philosophischen Hauptschriften Jacobis." *Archiv für Geschichte der Philosophie* 58 (1976): 121–63.

Höhn, Gerhard. "F.H. Jacobi et G.W. Hegel ou la naissance du nihilisme et la renaissance du 'Logos.'" *Revue de Métaphysique et de Morale* 75, no. 2 (1970): 129–50.

Iacovacci, Alberto. *Idealismo e Nichilismo. La Lettera di Jacobi a Fichte.* Padua: CEDAM, 1992.

Ike, Frank. *Das Gefühl in seiner Funktion für die menschliche Erkenntnis bei Jacobi, Fichte und Schelling.* Berlin: Wiss. Verl., 1998.

Ivaldo, Marco. *Filosofia delle cose divine: Saggio su Jacobi.* Brescia: Morcelliana, 1996.

– *Introduzione a Jacobi.* Rome and Bari: Laterza, 2003.

– "Jacobi, Kant (e Aristotele) sulla Virtù." In *Jacobi in discussione,* edited by Tristana Dini and Salvatore Principe, 47–64. Milan: FrancoAngeli, 2012.

– "Sul Teismo: Jacobi versus Schelling." In *Una filosofia del non-sapere. Studi su Friedrich Heinrich Jacobi,* edited by Guido Frilli, Federica Pitillo, and Pierluigi Valenza, 139–50. Pisa and Rome: Serra, 2020.

Jacobs, Wilhelm G. "Von der Offenbarung göttlicher Dinge oder von dem Interesse der Vernunft an der Faktizität." In *Religionsphilosophie und Spekulative Philosophie. Der Streit um die göttlichen Dinge (1799–1812),* edited by Walter Jaeschke, 142–54. Hamburg: Meiner, 1994.

Jaeschke, Walter. "Editorischer Bericht." In F.H. Jacobi, *Werke. Gesamtausgabe,* 3, 173–90. Hamburg: Meiner, 2000.

– "Kommentar." In F.H. Jacobi, *Werke. Gesamtausgabe,* 3, 191–246. Hamburg: Meiner,

BIBLIOGRAPHY

2000.

– *Reason in Religion: The Foundations of Hegel's Philosophy of Religion.* Berkeley: University of California Press, 1990.

– ed. *Religionsphilosophie und spekulative Theologie: Der Streit um die göttlichen Dinge.* Hamburg: Felix Meiner Verlag, 1994.

– ed. *Religionsphilosophie und spekulative Theologie. Quellenbd.* Hamburg: Meiner, 1994.

– ed. *Transzendentalphilosophie und Spekulation. Quellenbd.* Hamburg: Meiner Verlag, 1993.

Jaeschke, Walter, and Irmgard-Maria Piske. "Editorischer Bericht." In F.H. Jacobi, *Werke. Gesamtausgabe,* 2, 441–94. Hamburg: Meiner, 2004.

Jaeschke, Walter, and Birgit Sandkaulen, eds. *Friedrich Heinrich Jacobi: ein Wendepunkt der geistigen Bildung der Zeit.* Hamburg: Meiner, 2004.

Jonkers, Peter. "Jacobi und die kahlen Reste der Metaphysik." In *Metaphysik und Metaphysikkritik in der klassischen deutschen Philosophie,* edited by Myriam Gerhard, Annette Sell, and Lu de Vos, 61–81. Hamburg: Meiner Verlag, 2012.

– "Leben bei Hegel und Jacobi: Ein Vergleich." In *Das Lebendenken. Zweiter Teil,* edited by Andreas Arndt, Paul Cruysberghs, Andrzej Przylebski, 110–15. Berlin: Akedemie Verlag, 2007.

Kahlefeld, Susanna. *Dialektik und Sprung in Jacobis Philosophie.* Würzburh: Königshausen and Neumann, 2000.

Kinder, Ernst. *Natürlicher Glaube und Offenbarungsglaube. Eine Untersuchung im Anschluß an die Glaubensphilosophie Fr.H. Jacobi.* Munich: Keiser, 1935.

Koch, Oliver. *Individualität als Fundamentalgefühl: Zur Metaphysik der Person bei Jacobi und Jean Paul.* Hamburg: Meiner, 2013.

Körner, Josef, ed. *Briefe von und an Friedrich und Dorothea Schlegel.* Berlin: Kindle, 1926.

Kranefuss, Annelen. *Matthias Claudius. Eine Biographie.* Hamburg: Hoffmann und Campe Verlag, 2011.

Krieck, Ernst. "F.H. Jacobi als Geshichtsphilosoph." *Monatshefte der Comenius-Gesellschaft für Kultur und Geistesleben* 9, no. 5 (1917): 118–26.

Lauth, Reinhard. "Fichtes Verhältnis zu Jacobi unter besonderer Berücksichtigung der Rolle Friedrich Schlegels in dieser Sache." In *Friedrich Heinrich Jacobi. Philosoph und Literat der Goethezeit. Beiträge einer Tagung in Düsseldorf (16.-19. 10. 1969) aus Anlaß seines 150. Todestages und Berichte,* edited by K. Hammacher, 165–97. Frankfurt: Vittorio Klostermann, 1971.

– "Friedrich Heinrich Jacobis Allwill und Fedor Michajlovi Dostoevskijs Dämonen." *Russian Literature,* no. 2 (1973): 51–64.

– "Nouvelles recherches sur Jacobi – II." *Archives de Philosophie* 34, no. 3 (1971): 495–502.

Lévy-Bruhl, Lucien. *La philosophie de Jacobi.* Paris: Alcan, 1894.

Livieri, Paolo. *Metafisica dell'Esistenza. La rivelazione della realtà in F.H. Jacobi*. Padua: Padua University Press, 2023.

– "On the Necessity of Origin in F.H. Jacobi's Last Work." In *Una filosofia del non-sapere. Studi su Friedrich Heinrich Jacobi*, edited by P. Valenza, G. Frilli, and F. Pitillo, 151–63. Rome: Serra, 2020.

Löhnert, Paul. *Sitz und Stimme in Gottes Unterhaus. Christentum und Aufklärung im Werk Georg Christoph Lichtenbergs*. Pfaffenweiler: Centaurus-Verlagsgesellschaft, 1991.

Lorenz, Hilmar. "Sur la portée historique du fidéisme de Jacobi." In *Années 1781–1801, Kant "Critique de la raison pure": Vingt ans de réception*, edited by Claude Piché, 111–18. Paris: Vrin, 2002.

Mengaldo, Elisabetta. *Zwischen Naturlehre und Rhetorik: kleine Formen des Wissens in Lichtenbergs "Sudelbüchern."* Göttingen: Wallstein Verlag, 2021.

Mues, Albert. "Editionspraxis in dürftiger Zeit am Beispiel der F.H. Jacobi-Werkeausgabe Band 3." *Fichte-Studien* 25 (2005): 155–85.

Nuzzo, Angelica. "Nachklänge der Fichte-Rezeption Jacobis in der Schrift von den göttlichen Dingen und ihrer Offenbarung (1811)." *Fichte-Studien* 14 (1998): 121–37.

Olivetti, Marco M. "Der Einfluß Hamanns auf die Religionsphilosophie Jacobis." In *Friedrich Heinrich Jacobi. Philosoph und Literat der Goethezeit. Beiträge einer Tagung in Düsseldorf (16.-19. 10. 1969) aus Anlaß seines 150. Todestages und Berichte*, edited by Klaus Hammacher, 85–112. Frankfurt: Vittorio Klostermann, 1971.

– *L'esito teologico della filosofia del linguaggio di Jacobi*. Padua: CEDAM, 1970.

– "Vernunft, Verstehen und Sprache in Verhältnis Hamanns zu Jacobi." In *Johannes Georg Hamann. Acta des Internationalen Hamann-Colloquium in Lüneburg 1976*, edited by Bernhard Gajek, 169–93. Frankfurt: Vittorio Klostermann, 1979.

Ortlieb, Cornelia. *Friedrich Heinrich Jacobi und die Philosophie als Schreibart*. Munich: Wilhelm Fink, 2010.

Pinkard, Terry. *German Philosophy 1760–1860: The Legacy of Idealism*. Cambridge: Cambridge University Press, 2002.

Pistilli, Emanuela. *Tra dogmatismo e scetticismo: fonti e genesi della filosofia di F.H. Jacobi*. Pisa and Rome: Serra, 2008.

Pluder, Valentin, *Die Vermittlung von Idealismus und Realismus in der klassischen deutschen Philosophie: eine Studie zu Jacobi, Kant, Fichte, Schelling und Hegel*. Stuttgart-Bad Cannstatt: Frommann-Holzboog, 2013.

Promies, Wolfgang. *Georg Christoph Lichtenberg in Selbstzeugnissen und Bilddokumenten*. Reinbek bei Hamburg: Rowohlt, 1964.

Reinhold, Karl Leonhard, ed. *Beyträge Zur leichtern Übersicht des Zustandes der Philosophie beym Anfange des 19. Jahrhunderts*. Vol. 3. Hamburg: Perthes, 1801.

Requadt, Paul. *Lichtenberg*. Stuttgart: Kohlhammer, 1964.

BIBLIOGRAPHY

Roedl, Urban. *Matthias Claudius. Sein Weg und seine Welt*. Berlin: Kurt Wolff Verlag, 1934.

Rohs, Peter. "Was ist das Problem bei Kants Annhame einer Affektion durch Dinge an sich?" In *Jacobi und Kant*, edited by Birgit Sandkaulen and Walter Jaeschke, 67–85. Hamburg: Meiner, 2021.

Roth, Friedrich von, ed. *Friedrich Heinrich Jacobi's auserlesener Briefwechsel*. Vols. 1 and 2. Bern: H. Lang, 1970.

Sandkaulen, Birgit. *Ausgang vom Unbedingten Über den Anfang in der Philosophie Schellings*. Göttingen: Vandenhoeck & Ruprecht, 1990.

– "Dass, was oder wer? Jacobi im Diskurs über Personen." In *Jacobis Philosophie: über den Widerspruch zwischen System und Freiheit*, edited by Birgit Sandkaulen, 95–118. Hamburg: Meiner, 2019.

– "Fürwahrhalten ohne Gründe. Eine Provokation philosophischen Denkens." In *Jacobis Philosophie: über den Widerspruch zwischen System und Freiheit*, edited by Birgit Sandkaulen, 33–53. Hamburg: Meiner, 2019.

– *Grund und Ursache. Die Vernunftkritik Jacobis*. Munich: Fink, 2000.

– "'Ich bin und es sind Dinge außer mir': Jacobis Realismus und die Überwindung des Bewusstseinsparadigmas." In *Bewusstsein/Consciousness*, edited by Sally Sedgwick and Dina Emundts, 169–96. Berlin: De Gruyter, 2016.

– "Ichheit und Person. Zur Aporie der Wissenschaftslehre in der Debatte zwischen Fichte und Jacobi." In *Jacobis Philosophie. Über den Widerspruch zwischen System und Freiheit*, edited by Birgit Sandkaulen, 201–24. Hamburg: Meiner, 2019.

– *Jacobis Philosophie: über den Widerspruch zwischen System und Freiheit*. Hamburg: Meiner, 2019.

– "Das 'leidige Ding an Sich.' Kant – Jacobi – Fichte." In *Jacobis Philosophie*, edited by Birgit Sandkaulen, 169–97. Hamburg: Meiner, 2019.

– "Letzte oder erste Fragen? Zum Bedürfnis nach Metaphysik in einer Skizze zu Kant und Jacobi." In *Das Neue Bedürfnis Nach Metaphysik / The New Desire for Metaphysics*, edited by Markus Gabriel, Wolfram Hogrebe, and Andreas Speer, 49–58. Berlin and Boston: De Gruyter, 2015.

– "'Oder hat Vernunft den Menschen?' Zur Vernunft des Gefühls bei Jacobi." *Zeitschrift für philosophische Forschung* 49, no. 3 (1995): 416–29.

– ed. *System und Systemkritik: Beiträge zu einem Grundproblem der klassischen deutschen Philosophie*. Würzburg: Königshausen & Neumann, 2006.

– "System und Systemkritik. Überlegungen zur gegenwärtigen Bedeutung eines fundamentalen Problemzusammenhangs." In *System und Systemkritik: Beiträge zu einem Grundproblem der klassischen deutschen Philosophie*, edited by Birgit Sandkaulen, 11–34. Würzburg: Königshausen & Neumann, 2006.

– "System und Zeitlichkeit. Jacobi im Streit mit Hegel und Schelling." In *Jacobis Philos-*

ophie. Über den Widerspruch zwischen System und Freiheit, edited by Birgit Sandkaulen, 271–87. Hamburg: Meiner, 2019.

– "Wie 'geistreich' darf Geist Sein? Zu Den Figuren von Geist und Seele im Denken Jacobis." In *Jacobis Philosophie. Über den Widerspruch zwischen System und Freiheit*, edited by Birgit Sandakaulen, 55–76. Hamburg: Meiner, 2019.

– "Zur Vernunft des Gefühls bei Jacobi." *Fichte-Studien* 11 (1997): 351–65.

Sandkaulen, Birgit, and Walter Jaeschke, eds. *Jacobi und Kant*. Hamburg: Meiner Verlag, 2021.

Sautermeister, Gert. *Georg Christoph Lichtenberg*. Munich: Beck, 1993.

Sayre, Kenneth M. *Plato's Late Ontology*. Revised edition. Las Vegas: Parmenides Publishing, 2005.

Schick, Stefan. "Möglich, Wirklich oder Notwendig? Kant, Jacobi und Hegel über synthetische Urteile a priori." In *Jacobi und Kant*, edited by Birgit Sandkaulen and Walter Jaeschke, 87–103. Hamburg: Meiner Verlag, 2021.

– *Vermittelte Unmittelbarkeit: Jacobis "Salto mortale" als Konzept zur Aufhebung des Gegensatzes von Glaube und Spekulation in der intellektuellen Anschauung der Vernunft.* Würzburg: Königshausen & Neumann, 2006.

Snow, Dale E. "F.H. Jacobi and the Development of German Idealism." *Journal of the History of Philosophy* 25, no. 3 (1987): 397–415.

Société d'études kantiennes de langue française, ed. *Années 1781–1801, Kant "Critique de la raison pure": vingt ans de réception*. Paris: J. Vrin, 2002.

Sommer, Konstanze. *Zwischen Metaphysik und Metaphysikkritik: Heidegger, Schelling und Jacobi*. Hamburg: Meiner, 2015.

Stolzenberg, Jürgen. "Was ist Freiheit? Jacobis Kritik der Moralphilosophie Kants." In *Wendepunkt der geistigen Bildung der Zeit*, edited by Walter Jaeschke and Birgit Sandkaulen, 19–36. Hamburg: Meiner, 2004.

Strauss, Leo. *Philosophie und Gesetz – frühe Schriften*. Stuttgart: J.B. Metzler, 1997.

Summerer, Stefan. *Wirkliche Sittlichkeit und ästhetische Illusion: die Fichterezeption in den Fragmenten und Aufzeichnungen Friedrich Schlegels und Hardenbergs*. Bonn: Bouvier, 1974.

Tilliette, Xavier, ed. *Schelling im Spiegel seiner Zeitgenossen. 1*. Milan: Mursia, 1974.

Valenza, Pierluigi. "Naturalismo e teismo. Un bilancio Jacobiano sull'idealismo tedesco." In *Una filosofia del non-sapere. Studi su Friedrich Heinrich Jacobi*, edited by P. Valenza, G. Frilli, and F. Pitillo, 125–37. Rome and Pisa: Serra, 2020.

Verra, Valerio. *F.H. Jacobi. Dall'Illuminismo all'Idealismo*. Turin: Edizioni di Filosofia, 1963.

– "Jacobis Kritik am deutschen Idealismus." *Hegel-Studien* 5 (1969): 201–23.

Verrecchia, Anacleto. *Georg Christoph Lichtenberg. Der Ketzer des deutschen Geistes.*

BIBLIOGRAPHY

Vienna: Böhlau, 1988.

Weischedel, Wilhelm. *Jacobi und Schelling: eine philosophisch-theologische Kontroverse.* Darmstadt: WisssBuchges, 1969.

– ed. *Streit um die göttlichen Dinge: die Auseinandersetzung zwischen Jacobi und Schelling.* Darmstadt: Wissenschaftliche Buchgesellschaft, 1967.

Wenz, Gunther. *Von den göttlichen Dingen und ihrer Offenbarung: zum Streit Jacobis mit Schelling 1811/12.* Munich: Verlag der Bayerischen Akademie der Wissenschaften, 2011.

White, Nicholas. *Plato on Knowledge and Reality.* Indianapolis: Hackett Publishing, 1976.

Wieland, Wolfgang. "Friedrich Henrich Jacobi." In *Die Religion in Geschichte und Gegenwart,* edited by Kurt Galling, 508–9. Tübingen: Mohr, 1959.

Zubke, Friedhelm. *Georg Christoph Lichtenberg: der Zweifel als Lebensprinzip.* Cologne: Böhlau Verlag, 1990.

Index

Abelard, P., 139

absolute, 2, 3–4; activity, 27; autonomous being, 175n63, 194; beginning, 58, 190; God 69, 71, 202, 211; identity, 13, 162, 175, 198, 199n7; individuality, 92, 172; knowledge, 169; nothing, 83, 179, 190; productivity, 180; reality 167; unconditioned, 39, 74, 186, 188

Acerbi, A., 80, 87, 211

actuality, 14, 18–19, 27–8, 61, 69, 112, 119, 125, 136–7, 157, 186, 212

Agamben, G., 82

agent, 20, 40–7, 51, 66, 68–74, 91, 187

Albert, H., 87

analytical approach, 8–9, 32, 38, 48, 53, 75, 85

Anaxagoras, 87, 92, 175–6, 176n66

annihilation, 4, 13, 28, 52, 57, 74, 81, 119, 120, 183–4

anthropomorphism, 192, 194

Aristotle, 38, 54–5, 59, 60–3, 72, 83, 88, 108n4, 166, 175, 176–9, 187–91

Asmus. *See* Claudius, M.

atheism (atheist), 178n71, 194, 196

authority, 23, 39, 41, 44, 47, 52, 63–4, 73, 143, 157–8, 170, 190

autonomy, 20, 27–8, 40, 46–50, 55, 59–60, 63–73, 85, 96, 123, 162, 169, 178

Bardili, C.G., 14

Baum, G., 75, 80–4

Berger, B., 91

Berkeley, G., 199

Blossius, Caius, 142

body, 30, 40, 89, 113–14, 140, 156, 183, 198–9

Bollnow, O.F., 81

Borgia, 196

Bouterwek, F., 14–15, 76, 78–9, 165–8, 172n59, 178n71

Bowman, B., 82, 85

Brüggen, M., 78–9

Buchheim, T., 91

Buée, J.-M., 74

Busch, W., 86

Butler, G.J., 77

Calker, F., 85

Capella, M., 165

Cassirer, E., 75, 86

Cato, 111

cause, 29–30, 43, 64, 81, 84, 105n6, 119, 122n16, 125–6, 160–2, 175–7, 181–2, 185–8, 190–1, 195n100, 199, 205, 209–12

certainty, 3, 30–1, 34, 41, 51, 53, 82, 86, 111n8, 122, 146, 148–9, 170, 173n61, 175, 188, 200, 203

Cerutti, P., 76, 78, 95, 105n5, 108n3, 133n9, 141n13, 148n21, 150n23, 182n77, 188n85

chance, 125, 131, 153, 176, 182, 195, 197, 204, 206

Chiereghin, F., 88

chimera, 171, 178n71

Christianity, 6–7, 57, 75–6, 87–9, 91, 103, 194, 196–7; Christ, 62, 65–6, 102, 135–8

Cicero, M.T., 110n7, 142n15, 149n22, 150, 156n31, 165n47

Claudius, M., 6, 10–11, 61–7, 76, 78, 85, 90, 103–4, 106, 127–9, 135, 153

Confucius, 62, 65, 134

consciousness, 14, 23–4, 27, 29–30, 34, 46, 48–9, 54, 85, 89, 111–12, 118–19, 122n16, 131–2, 138, 144, 149, 152–3, 163, 173n61, 177, 182–6, 192–3, 198, 200, 210; self-consciousness, 31, 39–40, 49, 60, 123–5, 138, 161

Copernicus, N., 163–5

Crawford, A.W., 81

creation, 41, 61, 71, 74, 108, 112–13, 119n15, 121, 130, 138, 152, 162, 177, 184, 187–8, 194n98, 212

creator, 156, 170, 175, 177, 181, 184–5, 188–9, 194n98, 196, 210–12

Danz, C., 75, 91

di Giovanni, G., VII, 74–5, 80, 83, 90–1, 97

dialectic 3–4, 24–5, 28, 39, 41, 48, 50–1, 57, 61, 73–4, 86

divine being, 11, 33, 136, 194

divinity, 40, 47, 73, 135–7, 139, 193

Doran, R., 80

drive, 55, 62–3, 71, 108–9, 117, 137, 149, 151n26, 152, 156, 183

dualism, 8, 67, 89, 162, 182

Duclos, 101

duty, 44, 148, 150, 152, 157

Eckhart, M., 87

egoism, 24, 26, 42

Enlightenment, 3–4, 9, 54, 96, 124

enthusiasm, 80, 102, 136, 139, 156

Epictetus, 103, 115, 133, 138, 150

Epicureanism, 173, 189

Esau, 163

Eschenmayer, A.K.A. v., 14, 91

eternity, 43, 47, 88, 109, 121, 151, 180–1, 186, 188, 198

Euclid, 164n45

evil, 135, 150, 152, 179, 182, 212

existence, 5, 7, 11, 13, 19, 21, 28–31, 35–50, 68–73, 80, 92, 96, 111, 113, 121, 135, 143–4, 151, 167n53, 175, 180–1; absolute positing, 83;

finite, 8, 18, 131, 139, 148, 187; of freedom, 189; of God, 52–4, 85, 108, 125, 157, 160–4, 170, 211; human, 4, 66, 109–10, 112, 120, 122, 139, 152, 159; of a universe, 170, 187–8

explanation, 17–19, 21, 26, 30, 39, 64, 72, 129, 136, 145, 172–3, 179

externalist, 11, 102, 157–8

Ezzelino, 196

faith, 30, 72, 90, 97, 103, 111, 122n16, 135, 138, 140–1, 147n18, 148, 158, 164, 172–4, 177, 179n72, 203–4; in God, 52, 110, 115, 153, 156, 158, 160, 171, 178n71, 192, 197, 202, 207; pure rational, 16, 160

feeling, 50–3, 64, 103, 111, 114, 126, 138–9, 149–50, 169, 173n61, 190, 192, 201, 203; of truth, 23, 90, 136, 200

Feldmeier, M., 84

Fenelon, F., 47

Fichte, J.G., 3, 11, 18, 46, 67, 102, 105

Flasch, K., 87

freedom, 8, 13, 16, 26, 27, 38, 40–8, 63–74, 80, 84, 87, 89–91, 102, 123n17, 131–2, 141, 152–3, 159, 160–3, 168, 170, 172, 179, 181–92, 196, 201, 204, 207

Fries, J.F., 6, 14–15, 76, 78, 86, 91, 165, 169n54, 173n61, 175n63, 200n10, 204n17

Fülleborn, G.G., 176n66, 187n82

Glaube, 5, 10, 13, 19, 50; *GlaubesWahn*, 178n71; *Vernunftglaube*, 161

Goethe, J.W., 75, 79, 124

good, 43–4, 50–1, 56, 58, 62, 72, 89, 92, 109, 128, 131–42, 150–5, 157, 163, 169, 172, 175–7, 179, 182–4, 195, 201–2, 205, 207, 212; goodness, 112, 149–51, 185, 194n98

Goretzki, C., 93

Hain, 129

Halbig, C., 74

Hamann, J.G., 32, 81–2, 140n12, 152n27, 153n30, 195

Hammacher, K., 77–8, 86, 92, 95

Harms, F., 81

heart, 34, 38, 48, 50–1, 54, 63, 66, 88–9, 100, 108, 109, 110n6, 114, 126, 132–7, 140–3, 148–9, 153, 193, 196

Hegel, G.W.F., 3–4, 13, 74, 76, 188n85

Henke, E.L.T., 78

INDEX

Henrich, D., 92
Herder, J.G., 88, 92, 162, 192n93, 193n94, 194n98, 196n103
Hesiod, 204n18
Höhn, G., 76
Homer, 140
Hugh of Saint Victor, 202
human being, 10, 16, 27, 38, 63–6, 70, 73, 89, 91, 93, 96, 97, 101, 103, 108–15, 118, 120–4, 130–6, 139, 142, 144–5, 147, 149–55, 157–62, 168–71, 173, 175, 178–9, 182–4, 191–6, 202, 207, 209
Hume, D., 23, 30, 81, 97, 209

Iacovacci, A., 89
ideal(ism, -ist), 61, 66–8, 71, 73, 102, 122n16, 135, 140, 151–2, 155, 158, 163–6, 170, 199n7, 200, 212; ideality, 44, 147; religious, 103, 106; transcendental, 173, 182n77, 209
identity, 13, 21, 27, 40, 42, 44, 46, 53, 56–7, 68, 71, 181–2, 191; principle of, 18, 67; system of, 12–13, 39, 69, 79, 101, 122, 162, 165–6, 175, 198, 200
illusion, 4, 20, 115, 120–1, 136, 139, 145, 156, 168–9, 179n72, 190–1
imagination, 4, 118, 120–1, 122n16, 129, 137–8, 146, 151–2, 167n53
immortality of the soul, 16, 40–5, 62, 73, 113, 129–30, 134, 159, 163, 168, 170, 172, 196
individual, 17, 28, 35, 64, 69, 73–4, 112, 141, 148, 191; individual being, 123, 152, 180, 210; individuality, 19–20, 42, 48, 68, 71, 119, 145
infinite, 8, 17, 42, 47, 50, 56–7, 87, 110, 113, 123n17, 132, 152, 167n53, 180, 185, 187–9; Platonic, 56–7, 112, 121, 191
intention, 127–8, 131, 145, 149–50, 153, 158, 166, 177, 180, 182n77, 183, 199, 210–11
internalist, 11, 61, 66, 102, 157–8
intuition, 18, 25, 39, 80, 83, 85, 113, 117, 140, 142, 147n18, 149, 167, 173n61, 178n71, 192n92, 203–5; immediate, 130; intellectual, 200–1; sense intuition, 173n61, 174n62, 200, 202
Ivaldo, M., 79, 81, 85, 87–91, 95

Jacobs, W.G., 77, 91
Jaeschke, W., 75–9, 86, 95, 106n7, 147n19, 162n40
Jamshid, 192

Jean Paul. see Richter, J.P.F.
Jeremiah, 140
Job, 112, 113n9, 196, 197n105

Kant I., 3–4, 11–18, 24–6, 32–53, 60–2, 68, 71–2, 75, 79–83, 85, 88, 92, 96, 115n13, 118n14, 145, 147n17, 151n25, 159–79, 185–9, 199–204, 209–11
Klopstock, F.G., 6
Köppen, F., 14, 67, 71, 79

Lauth, R., 85, 87
Lavater, J.K., 195
Leibniz, G.W., 26–7, 199
Leonidas, 192
Lessing, G.E., 10, 14, 91
Lévy-Bruhl, L., 81
Lichtenberg, G.C., 9–12, 50–2
living being, 19–22, 27–9, 109–10, 113–14, 141, 182–3
Livy, 192
love, 16–17, 50–3, 74, 88, 91, 100, 103, 109, 113, 125, 129, 131–3, 137, 139, 141–2, 149, 151n26, 156, 183, 192n92, 194n98; of God, 123n17, 194, 197, 211

Malebranche, N., 199
Marcus Aurelius, 111n8, 115
Martini, 157n32, 164n47, 172n59
materialism, 26, 163, 165–6, 174, 199n7, 200, 212; religious, 66, 137–8
measure, 65–6, 71–2, 88, 92, 112–13, 130, 134, 147, 152, 201
mediation, 11, 22–8, 30–1, 48–50, 68, 70; immanent (internal), 17–18
Mendelssohn, M., 10, 78, 82
Mengaldo, E., 24
Messenger of Wandsbeck. See Claudius, M.
metaphysics, 6, 9, 12, 16, 33–53, 60, 68, 70–2, 163–4, 199n7
mind, 8–12, 15–21, 28, 30, 46, 50, 67, 69, 88–90, 100, 108, 118, 123n17, 137–8, 145, 147, 149, 151n26, 154, 159, 160, 168–72, 178n71, 181, 184, 191–5, 199–200, 194, 207, 209
mission, 8, 32, 157, 159
modern, 3–4, 17–18, 26, 28, 30–1, 45, 50, 52, 54, 71, 74, 123n17, 140, 145, 176, 188, 200
morality, 43, 132, 136, 140, 179, 194n98, 207
Moses, 194

Mues, A., 76, 97, 104, 107
Müller, J. v., 50–1, 100, 192n93, 194n98
mysticism, 16, 48, 57, 87, 157n32, 178n71, 202

Nathan, 128
naturalism (naturalist), 7–9, 13, 54, 61, 66–7, 71, 73, 92, 162, 173, 177–81, 186, 188–9, 192n92, 207
nature, philosophy of, 101, 162, 172
Nero, 196
Nicetas, 164n47
Niethammer, F.I., 161n37, 162n39
nihilism, 11, 42, 52, 56, 74, 138
non-thing (*Unding*), 57, 108–9, 112–13, 117–18, 121, 142, 153, 180, 182, 188, 191–2
noumenon, 25, 85
Nuzzo A., 75,

Olivetti, M.M., 83
organism, 20, 23, 25, 27, 29–30, 45, 185n78
Osterod, 157n32

Pascal, B., 9, 50–1, 63, 100, 151n26, 164
perception, 23–4, 32, 132, 139, 142, 163, 190, 194, 201, 204; principle of, 27–8; faculty of, 4
personality, 40, 54, 60, 74, 102, 123, 123n17, 125, 161, 192
Perthes, F., 4, 76, 78, 80, 104
Philolaus, 164
Pistilli, E., 83
Pitt, W., 127
Plato, 48, 56–7, 87, 90, 103, 112, 123n17, 137n10, 141, 146n16, 148n20, 150, 166–7, 174–7, 191, 199–200, 203, 205–7, 210–12; Platonism, 60, 72, 86, 121, 173, 189, 201, 204
Plutarch, 165
presentiment, 108, 173n61, 201–3
Protarchus, 146n16
providence, 16, 114–15, 123n17, 177, 182–3, 195, 197, 203–4
Pseudo-Longinus, 15–16, 80
Pythagoras, 111, 159

Rakau, 157n32
Raphael, 155
realism, 6, 23, 25, 54, 73, 81, 83, 158, 209; religious, 11, 106
Reimarus, H.S., 6

Reinhold, K.L., 14, 91, 105
religion, 6, 9–10, 19, 32–4, 46, 50, 52, 55, 65, 112, 132–3, 137, 145, 154, 157n32, 158–61, 178n71, 192n92, 194n98, 196; philosophy of, VII, 9, 65
representation, 23–6, 30–4, 38, 51, 53, 82, 111, 117, 133–7, 142, 145, 151n26, 162, 167–8, 170, 172, 176, 186, 190n89, 194, 199, 201, 203–7
revelation: immediate, 32, 53, 114, 201; external, 10–11, 153, 157n32
Richter, J.P.F., 6, 9, 75, 79–80, 145, 196n104
Roedl, U., 78,
Roth, F., 75–7, 80, 141n13

Salat, J., 15
Sandkaulen, B., VIII, 79–86, 91–2
Schelling, F.W.J., 3, 8, 11–15, 39, 67–71, 76, 78–80, 85, 91–2, 101n1, 105n6, 162n40–1, 173n61, 179n74, 180n76, 182n77, 194n96, 200n8
Schick, S., 75, 90
Schlegel, F., 14–15, 79, 96, 123n17, 147n18, 179n72,
Schleiermacher, F., 123n17, 146n16, 148n21
Schulze, G.E., 14, 179
sensation, 48, 54, 96, 109, 111, 114–15, 118–19, 122, 132, 139, 143, 149, 156, 162, 191
sense perception, 57, 116–25, 123, 123n17, 125, 151–2, 167, 167n53, 172–3, 172n59, 175, 201
sensory, 109, 115, 120, 131, 169, 183, 212
Shakespeare, W., 167n53
Simplicius, 133
skepticism, 10, 23, 86, 161
Socini, F., 157n32
Socrates, 62, 66, 90, 111, 134, 146n16, 196
Spinoza, B., 3–5, 10, 17–19, 27–31, 64, 67, 71, 78, 82, 158, 166, 177, 187n83, 190n89, 198–200, 205
subjective, 10–12, 19, 23, 25, 29, 31, 40–6, 55, 62, 66, 73, 81, 171–2, 190, 203

Tamar, 163
Tennemann, W.G., 176n66, 194n98, 202
theism, 3, 5–14, 22, 40, 54, 56, 58, 63, 65, 67, 72–5, 92–3, 173, 177–81, 186, 188, 194, 196, 207
Tiberius Gracchus, 142, 196
Timoleon, 111
totality, 13, 71, 121, 162, 165–6, 175, 181, 187, 190, 201, 208, 212

INDEX

transcendental, 13, 41, 48, 667, 173n61; idealism, 3–5, 7–8, 14, 24–6, 29, 42, 61, 78, 85, 173, 209

unitotality. *See* totality
unity, 5, 20, 25, 27, 53–4, 59, 67, 69, 96, 113, 121, 158–9, 166, 194n98, 210

Valenza ,P., 88, 92
Verra, V., 76
Vico, G., 164

Weiller, K., 105n6
Weischedel, W., 78, 91

Wenz, G., 79, 86
whole, the, 7–8, 18–19, 21, 68–71, 123n17, 184, 193, 195, 208
Wieland, W., 78, 86
William Tell, 192
Wolff, C., 164n45

Xerxes, 192n93

Zerah, 163